Courtesans and Tantric Consorts

Advance Praise for ***Courtesans and Tantric Consorts***

"This book is a tour de force, marshalling a broad range of materials—textual, ritual, and iconographical—to tackle a complex issue in the forefront of Buddhist studies today, that of sexuality and gender. Drawing on sources primarily in the Indian Mahayana and Tibetan traditions, Young deftly connects the Tantric consort cycle to that of the more ancient Buddhist courtesan convert. In the process, she raises compelling questions about the human condition as envisioned in Buddhism. Given the physical, cultural, and spiritual nature of gender and sexuality, the categories of male and female are ones of great instability, with dynamic relations emerging at the great distance of these two gendered extremes and with unusual visions about gender populating the rich continuum between them. This book is not to be missed and is a significant contribution to our understanding of the Indo-Tibetan culture of Buddism."

—Ellison Findly, Professor of Religion and Asian Studies,
Trinity College, Hartford

"Young's book examines the place of women in the Indian and Tibetan Buddhist traditions through the lens of two important classes of women: consorts and courtesans. By considering both the textual and the art historical data, this interdisciplinary study offers us many new insights concerning both women and women's relationships to men. An erudite book that, while taking into account all of the most recent scholarship in the field, goes beyond it to offer us fresh new insights . . . A major contribution to the literature on women in Buddhism."

—José Ignacio Cabezón, XIVth Dalai Lama Professor of Tibetan Buddhism
and Cultural Studies at the University of California, Santa Barbara

This is a groundbreaking investigation into several aspects of gender in Buddhism that have not been sufficiently taken into consideration before. Evenhanded and thorough, and written in clear and accessible language, Young analyzes textual sources as well as Buddhist art from a refreshingly new point of view. The book is highly recommended for all those who love and appreciate Buddhism without idealizing it, scholars as well as practitioners. A pioneering work!

—Dr. Adelheid Herrmann-Pfandt, Lecturer in Religious Studies,
Philipps-University, Marburg, Germany

Courtesans and Tantric Consorts

Sexualities in Buddhist Narrative, Iconography, and Ritual

Serinity Young

ROUTLEDGE
NEW YORK AND LONDON

Published in 2004 by
Routledge
711 Third Avenue
New York, NY 10007
www.routledge-ny.com

Published in Great Britain by
Routledge
2 Park Square, Milton Park,
Abingdon, Oxon OX14 4RN
www.routledge.co.uk

Routledge in an imprint of the Taylor & Francis Group, an informa business

Library of Congress Cataloging-in-Publication Data

Young, Serinity.
Courtesans and tantric consorts : sexualities in buddhist narrative, iconography and ritual/ Serinity Young.
p. cm.
Includes bibliographical references and index.
ISBN 0-415-91482-5 (hdb. : alk. paper) — ISBN 0-415-91483-3 (pbk. : alk. paper) 1. Women in the Tripiòtaka. 2. Gautama Buddha. 3. Gautama Buddha—Relations with women. 4. Women in Buddhism—India. 5. Buddhist art and symbolism. I. Title: Sexualities in buddhist narrative, iconography and ritual. II. Title.

BQ1133.W6Y68 2001
294.3'082—dc22

2003022472

For Tim

CONTENTS

ILLUSTRATIONS

FIGURES

PLATES

ACKNOWLEDGMENTS

I am grateful to several granting organizations for supporting the early research that developed into this book, beginning with a Research Assistance Grant from the American Academy of Religion that enabled me to pursue research in the Tibetan communities of India in the spring of 1995. At the Central Institute of Higher Tibetan Studies in Sarnath I am particularly grateful to Samdong Rinpoche for facilitating my research. I am indebted also to the Venerable Rashmi of the Thai Monastery in Sarnath for his enthusiasm, warm hospitality, introductions to learned Theravāda monks, and for arranging my visits to the major Buddhist Indian pilgrimage sites.

In 1997, with the support of the Asian Arts Council, I was able to interview Tibetan scholars and advanced practitioners in Kathmandu. This grant also enabled me to visit major pilgrimage sites in Tibet. Dr. Walter Spinks also granted me a partial fellowship for his Fourteenth Annual Ajanta Site Seminar that enriched my understanding of early Buddhist iconography and archaeology.

The American Institute of Bangladesh Studies (AIBS) provided me with access to important Buddhist sites and museum collections in Bangladesh and provided much needed time for reflection and writing. Special thanks to director Dr. Rahman Shelly and the entire staff at AIBS who were so kind. Special thanks go to Sarwa who facilitated field trips and dealt with innumerable problems with humor and patience. This grant also enabled me to make brief trips to sites in Thailand, Cambodia, and Burma.

A first draft of this book was written at the New York Public Library through a generous fellowship at the Center for Scholars and Writers in 2000–2001. Special thanks go to Dorothy and Lewis Cullman for creating such a sparkling, joyful, and productive community. Its director, Peter Gay, was unstinting with his time and taught me a great deal about writing history. John Lundquist, Chief Librarian of the Oriental Division, provided invaluable assistance with multiple language sources and shared my enthusiasm for things Tibetan. Librarian Sunita Vaze was equally generous when it came to locating obscure texts or shedding light on obscure Sanskrit phrases. Lee Robinson of the Arts and Architecture Collection was particularly helpful in locating iconographic sources.

A South Asian Regional Research Fulbright enabled me to visit major Buddhist archaeological sites in Pakistan, India, Sri Lanka, and Nepal in the summer and fall of 2001. Dr. Arundhati Banerjee of the Archaeological Survey of India in New Delhi was an unfailing guide to my specific interests and kindly arranged introductions for me with local curators. Also in India, Dr. Mary Storm provided warm hospitality and stimulating conversations about South Asian iconography as well as practical advice on getting to some of the more inaccessible sites. In Kathmandu, Dr. Ramesh Dhungal of Tribuvan University shared his knowledge and arranged for me to meet additional scholars and see rare collections. He and his family made me feel very much at home.

In 2000 I became a research scholar in the Anthropology Division of the American Museum of Natural History (AMNH) in New York City, and it has proved to be a supportive and stimulating environment. Special thanks to Laurel Kendall, Curator of Asian Ethnology, who has always supported my research; to Laila Williamson, who shared her knowledge of things Tibetan; and to Stan Freed, who generously shared his Indian field experience with me. All three also read parts of this work and offered pertinent advice. The librarians at AMNH have been generous with their time and expertise, and Ingrid Lennon was always enthusiastic in tracking down my many interlibrary loan requests.

I was most fortunate in Vidya Dehejia's return to Columbia University, where she allowed me to audit her class "The Development of Buddhist Art in India, Pakistan, and Afghanistan." With her guidance I was able to sharpen my perspective on the vast geographical and temporal range of early Buddhist archaeology and iconography.

I have presented portions of this text, in various incarnations, at the Center for Scholars and Writers of the New York Public Library, at several meetings of the American Academy of Religion, Hofstra University, the Eleventh Berkshire Conference on the History of Women, the New England Conference of the Association for Asian Studies, the Hagiography Society of New York, the Society for the Anthropology of Religion, and the National Women's Studies Association. Additionally, two academic conferences, the annual God and Sexuality conference at Bard College and the Eros and Religious Experience conference at New York University in 2002, provided stimulating environments for discussion and debate. My heartfelt thanks go out to the many scholars at these meetings who took the time to discuss my work. Any errors, though, are my responsibility.

I am once again indebted to the Schoff Publication Grant of the University Seminars at Columbia University for their help in publishing this work and to the University Seminar on Buddhist Studies for many beneficial discussions.

I also benefited from the support of friends and colleagues who willingly discussed aspects of this work in its various stages: Rawn Harding and Natalie Maxwell Hauptman, who both read the entire manuscript, Carol Anderson, Carol Dysinger, Tina Eisenbeis, Tim Harwood, Adelheid Hermann-Pfandt, Mary Hughes, Jeffrey Kripal, Rob Linrothe (who brought the cover image of Tārā to my attention), Ralph Martin, Jo Ann McNamara, Francis Tiso, James Waller, and Homer Williams.

Damian Treffs proved to be an indefatigable editor with an eye toward the subleties of argument. This is a better book because of him.

ABBREVIATIONS

AN	*Aṅguttara-Nikāya*
AS	*Abiniṣkramaṇasūtra*
BC	*Buddhacarita*
CS	*Caraka Samhitā*
EOR	*The Encyclopedia of Religion*, ed. Mircea Eliade
EOW	*The Encyclopedia of Women and Religion*, ed. Serinity Young
JIABS	*Journal of the International Association for Buddhist Studies*
LV	*Lalitavistara*
Mgur 'bum	*Mi la mgur 'bum* (*The Hundred Thousand Songs of Milarepa*)
Mi la	*Mi la ras pa'i rnam thar* (Milarepa's biography)
MSV	*Vinaya of the Mūlasarvāstivādin*
MV	*Mahāvastu*
NK	*Nidānakathā*
Padma	*Padma bka' thang shel brag ma*
SS	*Suśruta Saṁhitā*
TPS	*Tibetan Painted Scrolls*, Giuseppe Tucci

NOTE ON TRANSLITERATION

In order to produce a reader-friendly text, I have dropped silent Tibetan letters when discussing key terms and persons, though full spellings using the Wylie transliteration system appear in parentheses the first time a name or term is used.

INTRODUCTION

Buddhist biographies, iconography, and rituals provide vivid, compelling, and somewhat contradictory views of how Buddhists lived and what they believed. In focusing on beliefs and practices that surround gender and sexuality I have uncovered an ongoing, complex, and even contentious discourse on what it meant—and what it continues to mean—to be gendered, sexual, and Buddhist. This discourse began in fifth century B.C.E. India and continues to be debated today in Asia and the West. Throughout its long history, wherever Buddhism flourished, the meaning of gender and the place of sexuality was argued, portrayed, and enacted in biographies, works of art, and rituals.

Monastic Buddhism was and is a religion that exalts celibacy and one that has always been dominated by men. This is reflected in biographies and other texts that made some very negative statements about women, and which explicitly connected women, not men, to sexuality, relegating men to some not-female/not-sexual hinterland. Yet, sexual women, such as wives and courtesans, made frequent and meaningful appearances in the biographies of the Buddha (566–486 B.C.E.), while early Buddhist iconography is prolific in its depictions of positive images of women and female divinities that emphasize their beauty and their auspicious powers of fertility. Simply put, the iconography seemed to be expressively exalting women while the texts often condemned them. As I pondered this incongruity a third dimension of Buddhist life, ritual activity, became relevant. Early Indian Buddhists had rituals for securing fertility and abundance for themselves, their domestic animals, and their fields that were focused on curvaceous nude and seminude female images.

Buddhism never had a central authority that dictated belief and practice. This just never developed, and within a few years of the Buddha's demise Buddhism split into different schools, though these managed to coexist rather well. Due to the success of its missionary activities, quite soon Buddhism spread across South Asia, and no longer had a common language. At the same time it was remarkably accommodating to local customs. As early as the time of Emperor Aśoka (third century B.C.E.), the plentitude of Buddhist cultural environments was conducive to multiple viewpoints in both lay and monastic life. The monastics, however, did have detailed rule books, the *vinayas*, to guide them. Guidelines for the laity are more elusive. With this in mind I have chosen to focus, in the first part of this study, on lay aspects of the Buddha's life as presented in his biographies, both textual and iconographic. The Buddha had been a husband, a father, and a son before he became a spiritual seeker, and although he rejected these roles, the relationships endured after his enlightenment. This has particular relevance for Buddhists, especially lay Buddhists, because the Buddha is the primary model for those who would follow his teachings. What the Buddha did set the standard to be imitated. Concentrating on his familial relationships, I compare their textual presentation with their iconographic presentation. My first question was, Are these relationships significantly represented in the iconography? They are, though often different tones are sounded by the texts and the iconography. Thus, another question arises: Whose voices are we hearing in these texts and images, and what do they tell us about Buddhist attitudes toward sexuality and gender? For instance, what did it mean for a Buddhist to be sexually active as a wife or husband, and to become a parent? Not surprisingly, simple answers do not follow.

A good example of the complexities surrounding these issues can be found in portrayals of the Buddha's mother, Queen Māyā, who is a significant indicator of attitudes toward women and motherhood. Having died shortly after giving birth, she is a minor figure in the texts, but iconographically she is ubiquitous. The most frequent images of her focus on the Buddha's conception and birth, presenting her as a beautiful, voluptuous, and seminude woman, and asserting the auspicious powers of fecundity and prosperity possessed by women. Yet, the Buddha's conception is depicted as a miraculous, nonsexual event, and his birth is sometimes, but not always, also depicted as miraculous as when he is shown being born from his mother's side, not her birth canal. This disparity between the semidivine fertility of women grounded in the natural world and the supernatural representation of these natural events reflects inconsistencies in the biographical texts, not all of which emphasize a miraculous birth and conception. Such disparity is also indicative of contending points of view about sexuality and about what it means to be parents.

The biographies of other important Buddhists and certain rituals show that the Buddhist position on sexuality and parenthood was somewhat conflicted. On the one hand, sexuality and procreation should be avoided, while on the other hand parents are to be honored. Buddhism acknowledged that children have obligations to parents, as parents do to children. Looked at in terms of gender, the Buddhist position on parents gets downright contradictory. Despite an abundance of negative ideas about women and the dominance of men in the tradition, mothers are symbolically and ritually privileged over fathers. As Buddhism spread through time and space, however, new voices accent the old stories and practices in surprising ways.

A very different kind of woman also appears in the Buddha's biographies: courtesans, who are a lightning rod for discussions about sexuality, women, and the body. Courtesans personified ideas about the negative power of desire, women's voracious sexual appetites, and the impermanence of the body. They also made great converts. If these women could turn their backs on sexuality, anyone can. But the courtesans in these texts are far from being one-dimensional stock characters: they present a wide range of female characterizations in that some are heroic (nonsexual) while others are the lowest possible criminals (sexual).

I have pursued these early themes about gender and sexuality into the tantric forms of Buddhism that became influential in India around the sixth century C.E. and later flourished in Tibetan Buddhism. Tantra seemingly presented new religious understandings of sexuality through the introduction of tantric consorts, most of whom were female, although a few were male. Tantric consorts, both human and divine, become an important element in Indo-Tibetan biographical literature, iconography, and ritual. I argue, however, that the tantric emphasis on sexuality was not entirely new, but rather a continuation of the highly sexualized female imagery found at the earliest Buddhist archaeological sites. Tantric consorts are examined through the iconography and biographies of the tantric masters of India and Tibet, such as Padmasambhava (eight century C.E.) and Milarepa (1040–1123), and great women practitioners such as Yeshe Tsogyel, Mandāravā (both eighth century C.E.) and Machig Lapdron (1055–1153), among others.

As with any historical world religion, Buddhism functioned in various patriarchal societies where it played out the tensions between religious innovation and social constraint at the same time it created new religious opportunities for both women and men. Buddhist texts, iconography, and rituals reveal these tensions and their accommodations in word, form, and action. Since the producers of these cultural items were men, the women who are written about, painted, and sculpted are for the most part objects of the male imagination, or at least imaginative interpretations of core legends. This had both positive and negative sides. For instance, male authors sometimes used female characters to explore what it means to be gendered beings searching for enlightenment. In other cases they tell a sad story of not only accepting the low social status of women, but blaming women for it, reifying such beliefs in rituals, and by physically excluding women from certain sacred areas.

The texts are often rather blunt in their presentation of gender and sexuality, in part because none of the individuals being studied here are typical; they are all extraordinary, and in this they pushed against social boundaries—which allows us to know where those boundaries were—and they uninhibitedly declaim their beliefs. All are visionaries, women and men devoted to ideas about spiritual perfection that reveal the tense yet porous boundaries between the social and the sacred.

Underlying all these opinions and representations about sexuality and gender is the belief that sexual characteristics—the biological basis of gender—are not stable, enabling women to change into men and men into women. This is shown in Buddhist medical texts and in discussions of sex changes through rebirth and in the afterlife. In support of these beliefs, rituals were created to ensure or deter sex changes. Often interspersed in these discussions is an ongoing debate as to whether or not women are capable of achieving enlightenment. Generally, the answer is no. This point is emphatically made in discussions of male-only heavens such as Amitābha's western paradise, Sukhāvatī, where rebirth assures enlightenment. The texts affirm that women must want to become men to be reborn there and the rich iconography of this heaven shows no female forms. Instead, the paintings often depict men being reborn in lotuses—because there are no wombs, there are no women—they are not needed.

Like most of us, South Asians were quite capable of living within contradictions and one of the most interesting contradictions revolves around the nature of sex distinctions. When men declare a male-only space they also declare a belief in female and male as a pair of binary opposites in which the presence of one is the absence of the other, as for example in the mutually excluding terms left and right. These are solid and absolute boundaries. This script is, however, challenged by a second model of female and male as a polarity, as part of the human continuum in which sex distinctions can and do change. The idea here is that women and men are alike. Both views are expressed in medical discussions about conception, which before conception present sexual difference as binary opposites generated by karma, yet after conception present sexual difference as a polarity whose outcome is dependant on whether the female or the male has a stronger influence on the forming embryo. Indeed, if they are too well balanced hermaphrodites are believed to result. Nonetheless, in practice both models conflate sex (biology) and gender (culture), and they both presume that the male body is the normative body, the body one should aspire to.

These and other examples show that many forms of Buddhism wholeheartedly embraced the concept of women and men as binary opposites and thus incorporated the social denigration of women, some even going so far as to literally and symbolically co-opt female reproductive powers for the creation of male-only spiritual lineages and male-only realms. I found such positions go hand-in-hand with a fractured sense of masculinity, a masculinity that was defined primarily as not-female, but highly vulnerable to women through seduction and pollution. Masculinity was thought to be weakened by sexual activity, by contact with menstruating women, or simply by the presence of a woman. The belief that one's sex can change, that literally genitals can fall off and be replaced with their opposite, requires constant male vigilance and creates male anxieties about such loss. However, viewing the male form as normative and believing that woman were unable to achieve enlightenment remained debatable and had to be continually restated in the face of alternative views, such as heavens populated with women and men, a view suggestive of female and male as a human continuum.

Fundamentally, I am looking at what biography, iconography, and ritual reveal about gender and sexuality. I do this across a broad range of time, space, and materials. For instance, I provide a cultural context for the biographies through iconography and explorations of related literatures, such as philosophical and medical texts that theorize about the meanings of gender and sexuality, as well as the earthier views of folk tales. In the course of my research I have uncovered a colorful mosaic of beliefs that inform Buddhist views about gender and sexuality. Portrayals of virtuous women and men, and nonvirtuous ones such as courtesans and tantric consorts, as well as attitudes toward sexuality, marriage, and parenthood, and beliefs about other realms such as heavens, hells, and mythic lands of women, all reveal a highly problematic universe stimulated by sexuality and gender difference.

PART I
Life of the Buddha

CHAPTER 1

REJECTION AND RECONCILIATION

REJECTION: THE PRINCE IN THE WOMEN'S QUARTERS

As a young man the Buddha is said to have lived a carefree, luxurious life in which he was purposely protected from the harsher realities of human existence. His father, King Śuddhodana, conspired in this deception due to a dream the Buddha's mother, Queen Māyā, had at the time of his conception. She dreamed a white elephant approached her, struck her side with its trunk, and then entered her womb.[1] When sages were consulted about the dream, they predicted it meant Queen Māyā was pregnant with a son who would become a *cakravartin*, either a great king or a great ascetic. Hearing that, the Buddha's father was determined to shape his son's future toward kingship and away from asceticism by focusing him on life's pleasures, which he did by removing all unpleasant sights from the palace compound. Inevitably, cracks began to appear in Śuddhodana's fortifications, and what followed next is crucial to understanding the one-pointedness of the Buddha's spiritual quest. When he was thirty years old he rode out of the palace and was radically changed by four visions created by the gods. On four consecutive days the Buddha mounted his chariot and left through one of the four palace gates. Each day, during his ride, he had a different vision. For the first time in his life he saw an old man, followed by a sick man, and on the third day, a dead man. These three visions introduced him to the existence of suffering and to the transitory nature of the human condition. His fourth and final vision, that of a male ascetic, became the solution to the existential problem of suffering and impermanence posed by the first three visions. He would become an ascetic and seek a way to liberate himself from the repetitive cycle of birth, death, and rebirth.

This well-known story is fraught with meaning for Buddhists, beginning with its emphasis on the number four: four days, four gates representing the four cardinal points, and four visions. Four is a number signifying wholeness in South Asia,[2] and in this instance it signifies the Buddha's sudden, but complete, grasp of all existence: all beings experience the suffering of becoming sick, growing old, and dying, only to once again be reborn and go through the same process, endlessly caught on the Wheel of Becoming.

The story is meant to express the Buddha's shock, the shock of a thirty-year-old man for whom this was news, and to awaken those who hear the story into realizing that they too, like the Buddha, live as if such suffering does not exist. The biographies stress that the Buddha was a handsome and coddled prince, a young man of overly refined sensitivities, to make his realization more palpable, so that we can comprehend how these four encounters changed his life. The story tries to make us understand that if we, too, truly looked reality in the face, as the Buddha did in these visions, we would recoil from the pleasures of life and ask, as he did, Is this all there is, or is there something beyond what we now know, a way out of the inevitable suffering of growing old, being ill, and dying? In this way, as the Buddha begins his search, the story invites us to join him.

The story also anticipates its audience's reluctance to abandon worldly life and it gets around this by lingering over just what the Buddha is giving up, particularly his sexual involvement with women. The *Lalitavistara*, hereinafter the *LV*, refers to this period of the Buddha's life as when "the Bodhisattva resided in the women's quarters" (*bodhisatvasya-antaṃpura-madhyagatasya*), sometimes translated as the harem.[3] Further, it lists the enjoyment of women as one of the activities of a bodhisattva.[4] A bodhisattva is someone who has made the vow to become a buddha, and is the term used for the Buddha before his enlightenment. The *Buddhacarita*, hereinafter the *BC*, also refers to the *antaṃpura*, which includes courtesans (*vāramukya*), and refers to the Buddha as a captive of women who are skilled in sexual pleasure.[5] He also has wives, who will be discussed at length in chapter 5. The ensuing drama of the Buddha's abandonment of worldly life is decorated with long passages describing the harem women that emphasize three stages in his relationship to them: (1) the appropriateness of the young prince's involvement with beautiful, sexually available women; (2) his turning away from such pleasures, which heightens the seductive ploys of the women as they attempt to hold on to him; and (3) his disgust with the (female) body and complete rejection of women.

The Buddha's four visions changed his relationship with the world, and the biographies personify the world through the harem women: like them, it is as beautiful and seductive as it is illusory and transitory. The biographies ascribe familiar and gender-specific qualities to the Buddha: a lone, heroic man struggling against almost insurmountable forces, such as chaos and illusion, which are personified by women.[6] In these early sections of the biographies a Buddhist gender dynamic is established: men cut through to ultimate reality and women try to impede their progress; women are the opposition.[7] Women are not participants on the same human journey, but are obstacles to it.[8] The Buddha's biographies identify women with materiality (*saṃsāra*) and sexuality, in contrast to men who are identified with spirituality (*dharma*). Portraying the Buddha's resistance to these, the most beautiful and seductive of women, may originally have been meant to inspire men to imitate the Buddha and turn away from more average women, but it carried within it the seeds of a wholesale rejection of women.[9] Representations of this rejection in texts and iconography when combined with the prevailing social reality, eventually led Buddhists to question women's ability to achieve enlightenment. What began as a symbolic use of women to represent the worldly life and sexuality actually perpetuated the prevailing negative views about women, such as their polluted status.[10] Marina Warner has made the point that "a symbolized female presence both gives and takes value and meaning in relation to actual women."[11] In other words, a constant exchange takes places between images, both textual and iconographic, and reality. As we shall see below, this happens time and again as Buddhism spreads into different cultural areas, including its current encounter with feminism in the West.

There are, however, other moments in the *LV* when women are portrayed positively. For example, at one point the Buddha is reclining in the women's quarters listening to the women as they play musical instruments, but through these instruments he hears divine beings make long speeches exhorting him to leave home. The Buddha, now set on his course to abandon worldly life, preaches to the women, who make a strong wish for his enlightenment.[12] This wish demonstrates positive, if traditional, female characteristics, such as the ability to support and sustain male practitioners, and contrasts with their ability to ensnare men. Significantly, these women are the first beings the Buddha instructs and makes ready for enlightenment. Actually, the *LV* is a rather woman-friendly text, especially when compared to the *BC*, which is much more unrelenting in its negative representations of women and does not mention either their wish or their future enlightenment. This may in part be due to the fact that although both texts were composed sometime between the first century B.C.E. and the first century C.E., the *LV* is the work of anonymous compilers of oral stories about the Buddha, while the *BC* is the work of a single author, the monk Aśvaghoṣa. Additional comparisons between these two texts will be made below.

A careful reading of both texts, though, reveals that it is actually men who are behind the women's efforts to keep the Buddha involved in worldly life. In the *BC*, when he asks his father's permission to leave home, King Śuddhodana orders guards to prevent this and also orders the women of the harem to use their sexuality to distract the Buddha.[13] His friend Udāyin takes the Buddha to a pleasure grove filled with harem women, whom he has instructed in the art of seduction. The women act out page after page of sexual ensnarement, such as stumbling against the Buddha, whispering in his ear, letting their garments slip, and so on.[14] Aśvaghoṣa places a greater emphasis on the harem women and gives them more space than does the *LV*. Maurice Winternitz explains the inclusion of these passages as follows:

> The presentation of love scenes is one of the indispensible elements of an ornate court poem. The poet [Aśvaghoṣa] fulfills this requirement by describing the blandishments of the beautiful women, by which they seek to tempt the prince (IV, 24–53); and in the highly-coloured description of the night scene in the harem, which is the cause of the prince's flight from the palace, the poet reveals his knowledge of the science of love.[15]

A short time later, though, the sexual attractiveness of the women is swept away when the gods cause the women to fall asleep in awkward positions. Long, dramatic passages now describe the ugliness of the women as they "lay in immodest attitudes, snoring, and stretched their limbs, all distorted and tossing their arms about."[16] Others looked like corpses and oozed saliva. Seeing them in this way, the Buddha concludes: "Such is the real nature of woman in the world of the living, impure and loathsome; yet man, deceived by dress and ornaments, succumbs to passion for women."[17]

The *LV* has similar, if briefer passages on the sleeping women. The gods appear and ask the Buddha: "How can you be joyful in the midst of this cemetery in which you live?" The Buddha then looked around the women's quarters and answers: "I do, in truth, dwell in the middle of a cemetery!"[18]

The Buddha is seeing women, and the world, with different eyes. Significantly, this scene introduces cemeteries into the imagery associated with women, which is the beginning of enduring Buddhist associations between women, death, and desire.[19] The Buddha is seeing their inevitable fate, which is death; for him, they are already in a cemetery.

Men are not associated with death and decay in the way women are, in spite of the fact that the Buddha's realization about death and decay occurs through his three visions of men, not women, in varying stages of decline. These three visions of an old man, a sick man, and a dead man form the core of his doctrine about the human condition, for both women and men, but aside from these three visions, its realization in the world is portrayed exclusively through women, as will be shown in chapter 7.[20] The fourth vision of a male ascetic is the solution to impermanence, which is to become a monk or a nun, and its realization remains male in that monks play prominent roles in his full-length biographies and in Buddhist iconography, while nuns do not.

Returning to the sleeping women in the *LV*, the Buddha makes a long speech about their unfortunate spiritual state using thirty-two similes to analyze the women. In addition to being a mnemonic device—all the early Buddhist texts were originally oral—as just mentioned, in South Asia the number four signifies wholeness and completeness, and thirty-two adds thoroughness. Thirty-two is a delightful combination of fours: four times eight equals thirty-two, with eight doubling the meaning of four by being the sum of two times four, so thirty-two is a number signifying the most thorough and most complete. Here thirty-two is used to suggest that these similes capture the essence of the women, that the thirty-two similes completely delineate their nature. We shall meet this number again, especially in the thirty-two physical marks of a Buddha. Here each simile begins with the phrase "these childish ones" (Skt: *te bālā*). For instance: "These childish ones are full of desire like idiots clutching pretty vases full of vomit. . . . These childish ones jump with excitement like dogs in the midst of bones. These childish ones throw themselves like moths into the burning flames."[21]

This builds to the Buddha's speech against the human body:

"The body, born from the field of karma,
issuing from the water of desire, is characterized by decay.
Disfigured by tears and sweat, by saliva, urine, and blood,
filled with filth from the belly,
with marrow, blood, and liquids from the brain,
always letting impurities flow—
bodies are the abode of impure teachings and ugly stenches.

"Covered with leathery skin
punctured by pores, teeth, and hair;
weakened by the accumulation
of excrement, pus, fat, and saliva;
held together like a machine by sinews and nerves;
made beautiful by the flesh
but subject to the pains of disease;
always tormented by hunger and thirst—

"This body with its many apertures
is the abode of old age and *death*.
Having seen this, what wise man
would not look upon his own body as an enemy?"[22]

It is important to note that this speech against the body evolves out of disgust for women's bodies,[23] a theme that will be continued in other contexts, such as around the bodies of courtesans. Even though the text says, "[r]eflecting on his own body, he [the Buddha] saw clearly its afflictions and cut off all inclination toward it,"[24] the point is personified through women's bodies, equating women with the human body, in addition to death and desire. In its emphasis on asceticism, Buddhism, along with other ancient Indian ascetic movements, used narrative to revise the general understanding of body.[25] The purpose of these passages, and iconographic representations of them, is to encourage men to be repelled rather than sexually aroused when they look at women. This creates at least two problems within the tradition. First, it emphasizes that Buddhist teachings are directed toward men and not women, thereby excluding women as recipients of the text while using them as a rhetorical device. Second, it makes all contact with women problematic, especially for monks, the carriers of the tradition, thereby limiting women's access to Buddhist teachings and cruelly curtailing the role of nuns in the monastic hierarchy.

Appropriately, it is the nameless women of the harem who provoke the final stage of the Buddha's spiritual crisis.[26] The harem women are a nameless collectivity, partly because they are meant to represent all women, but in reality they represent only one aspect of women—the sexual seductress. The harem women are not individuals, they are the ocean in which men's spiritual hopes may flounder.

This rejection of women equates them with all that early Buddhism rejects: sexuality, the body, and death. All three are connected to women through the pan-Indian emphasis on women's fecundity as the source of this world; but for Buddhists it means that through sexuality one gets a body that leads inevitably to sickness, old age, and death.[27] The Buddha's biographies use women's bodies to represent that which opposes salvation. In this process, the symbolic use of women also lends support to the Buddhist rejection of actual women as full participants in the Buddhist path. As we shall see in the chapters that follow, however, this view is grounded in the textual tradition that often markedly contrasts with the symbolic uses of women's bodies in Buddhist iconography.

Significantly, when men are used symbolically in text or iconography the situation is quite different. Of course, the male presence of the Buddha is ubiquitous in his biographical texts and in iconography, but Warner has made a subtle point about the distinction between symbolic uses of the female and male forms when she writes: "The female form tends to be perceived as generic and universal, with symbolic overtones; the male as individual, even when it is being used to express a generalized idea."[28] One of her examples of this contrast is Uncle Sam and the Statue of Liberty; Uncle Sam is a distinct character, a person if you will, in a way that is inconceivable for the Statue of Liberty. In the same way, images of the Buddha function both to represent the historical individual and the state of enlightenment, while the predominance of monks over nuns in both text and iconography represent historical individuals at the same time they portray the monastic path as male. This certainly contributed to the decline and eventually the total demise of the ordination lineage of Buddhist nuns. Interestingly enough, the unequal iconographic representation of female and male monastics contrasted with the widespread presence of other female forms, both of historical women, especially Queen Māyā, and of mostly anonymous female forms symbolizing the auspiciousness of female fecundity. As we shall see, the different gender ideologies expressed in the texts and the iconography have parallels to male monastic control of the text and the laity's influence on iconography. But the Buddha's story and his relationship to women does not end here.

RECONCILIATION: THE ASCETIC AND THE REQUISITE OF ENLIGHTENMENT

When the Buddha left home he also left civilization, seeking the solitude of the yet untamed forests of ancient India. Here he began to practice severe austerities believed to free the spirit from the body, such as exposing his body to the elements and barely eating enough food to stay alive. He was said to have consumed only one grain of rice, one juniper berry, and one sesame seed a day during this period. His determination attracted five male disciples, but after six years of this practice he had the appearance of a corpse and the gods who were watching over him feared he would die. Filled with concern they turned to a woman, Queen Māyā, who, having died seven days after the Buddha's birth, was residing in Trāyastriṃśa heaven (the realm of the thirty-three gods). Once she learned about her son's condition, Māyā appeared before the Buddha and reminded him of his miraculous birth and the prediction of his future buddhahood, all of which were in jeopardy because of his continued austerities. The Buddha reassured her that he would attain his goal and she returned to heaven.[29] It is at this point that the Buddha began to change his regimen, began to turn back toward the world, and, indeed, began his reconciliation with women.

Realizing that his body was too weak to achieve enlightenment, he decided to eat solid food. His five male disciples, believing he had abandoned asceticism, deserted him. But some young village women came and offered him a dish of rice and milk, which he accepted (Figure 1.1).[30] One of them, Sujātā, echoed the earlier wish of the harem women when she said: "May the Bodhisattva, having received food from me, attain perfect and fulfilled Enlightenment and become a Buddha!"[31] In accepting this food the Buddha also began to accept, indeed to internalize, women. We begin to see him reverse his earlier rejection of women. That this is an intentional point of the compilers of the *LV* is shown by the contrasting behavior of his male disciples, who

Fig. 1.1 Sujātā and friends feeding the Buddha. American Institute of Indian Studies 648–23. Mathurā (Maholi), c. second century C.E.

deserted him, and the village women, who sustained him. This, of course, is a complete inversion of his earlier abandonment of women and the years spent almost exclusively with male ascetics. Significantly, in contrast to the nameless women of the harem, not only Sujātā, but several of her female companions are named[32] and thus individualized.

After having eaten the food, the Buddha looked for something to replace the tattered robe he had worn for six years. Here the connection between women and cemeteries reasserts itself, but in a new guise. Entering a cemetery, he picked up a cloth that had been used to wrap the body of a dead woman.[33] Having equated women with cemeteries on the night he left home, the Buddha now put the shroud of a dead woman on himself.

Next he wanted to bathe, so the gods created a pond. When he finished his bath and tried to step out of the pond, the demon Māra caused the water to rise. The Buddha then requested the goddess of a nearby tree to bend down a branch of the tree so he could pull himself out, which she did.[34]

The next day Sujātā invited the Buddha to a meal in her home. Here he truly reenters the women's quarters, reenters the world, and once again he accepts food offerings from a woman. His biography describes this as a propitious event: "The Bodhisattva thought: 'Now that Sujātā has offered such food to me, there can be no doubt: after partaking of it, I will attain the perfect, supreme, and complete Enlightenment of a Buddha.'" He addresses her as "my sister," and gives her spiritual teachings. As with the harem women, this demonstrates that his teachings are very much for women as well as for men. After leaving Sujātā's house he bathes in a river where a female *nāga* (semidivine snakelike creatures) offers him "a resplendent lion throne"[35] as a sign of his imminent achievement of enlightenment when he will roar like a lion. Restored by this reconciliation with all aspects of the feminine, the Buddha approaches the Bo tree, the seat of his enlightenment.

The *LV* has presented an intriguing sequence of female characters: a woman who is dead yet lives (Māyā), living women (the village women), a dead woman (the corpse), and semidivine women (the tree goddess and the female *nāga*). All these females, in their various states of existence, living/dead, human/divine, are able to aid the Buddha in some way. In his first sustained contact with women since his initial rejection of them the Buddha established an appropriate role for lay women in Buddhism, that of being donors (*dāna*). This will develop into the doctrine that lay people who are unable to pursue monastic life can still acquire merit (*puṇya*) that will enable them to attain enlightenment in a future lifetime.

This series of reconciliations with various females enabled the Buddha to demonstrate his acceptance of the feminine on all levels of existence, and indeed his acceptance of existence itself as he prepared to transcend it. Through Queen Māyā, living among the gods, he made contact with the heavens. But his contact with the earth was the most thorough in that the village women provided contact with human beings, the tree goddess provided contact with semidivine earth beings and the vegetable world, while the female *nāga* provided contact with both the animal world, the waters, and the underworld. As will be shown in the following chapter, tree goddesses, or *yakṣīs*, and *naginīs*, can bestow abundance, they can make women, fields, and animals fertile, and can confer other forms of wealth. Images of *yakṣīs* and *naginīs* are prominently displayed at important Buddhist sites, revealing that Buddhists incorporated the auspicious powers of these pre-Buddhist deities. When these deities helped the Buddha and then worshipped him, they gave him command of their formidable powers, which he could now bestow on his followers. These deities are also connected to sovereignty, and in this they represent the fulfillment of the predictions at the Buddha's birth that he would become a *cakravartin*, a world conqueror.

Of course, Māra, demonic god of the realm of desire, must challenge the Buddha's passage beyond the control of his realm to an enlightened state. He asked the Buddha: "Through what merit will you gain deliverance?" This is a reference to the Buddhist belief that acts of generosity confer merit (*puṇya*), which, accrued over many lifetimes, leads to enlightenment. The Buddha answered:

> "I have freely made hundreds of millions of offerings. I have cut off my hands, my feet, my eyes, and my head as gifts for those who wished them; ardently desiring the deliverance of beings, I distributed houses, riches, seeds, beds, garments, gardens, and parks to all who asked."[36]

Māra was not satisfied by the Buddha's answer and he demanded a witness. The Buddha then called upon the earth to be his witness by touching it with his right hand. The earth responds first by trembling, and then the goddess of the earth, called Sthāvarā in the *LV*, "revealed the upper half of her body"[37] and spoke as witness for the Buddha.

This is a powerful and famous image, the earth itself siding with the Buddha against Māra and his legions of demons. In this context, it is interesting to note that the *BC* has a *bhutam* (a sky being), a neuter nominative,[38] act as the Buddha's witness, speaking from the sky, which not only takes away the feminine element but removes the process of witnessing from the earth to the sky. The *BC* describes many of the same events as the *LV*, but with much of the feminine element removed or played down. Another example occurs when the Buddha first accepted food. In the *BC* it is from a single woman, called Nandabalā,[39] and he does not take a meal at her house the next day as he did with Sujātā in the *LV*.

The *BC* also differs from the *LV* in not regarding the Buddha's acceptance of food from a woman as a stimulus toward his enlightenment. The Buddha's reconciliation with women is the subject of the *LV*, not the *BC*.[40] As a single author drawing on various sources for the Buddha's life, Aśvaghoṣa is revealed to have made just the sort of cuts and modifications that various scholars have suggested were done by the anonymous monk-compilers of various other canonical Buddhist texts. A telling example of this is the inclusion of the first ordination of Buddhist monks and the exclusion of the first ordination of Buddhist nuns in all the full-length biographies of the Buddha.

In all the biographies, though, Māra also has feminine forces on his side, demonic ones, in the form of his daughters. The *LV* creates strong parallels between the harem women and Māra's three daughters, Discontent, Delight, and Thirst.[41] For instance, when they try to tempt the Buddha on the night of enlightenment, like the women of the harem, they do not act of their own volition, but are instructed by their father, Māra.[42] These texts tell us not so much about women being sexual temptresses as women being under the control of men, as being part of the sexual economy of their time. In actuality these scenes are about two powerful males who want to deter the Buddha—the Buddha's father and Māra—and their sexual use of dependent women as their tools.

The *LV* describes Māra's daughters as having thirty-two kinds of feminine wiles that recall the thirty-two negative similes the Buddha used to analyze the harem women. These wiles vividly reflect the harem women's attempted seduction of the Buddha.

> What are these thirty-two? Some of the goddesses veiled half their faces; some showed off their firm round breasts; some with half-smiles flashed their pearl-like teeth; some stretched out their rounded arms while yawning; some showed their lips, which were red like the fruit of the bimba; some gazed at the Bodhisattva; with half-closed eyes, glancing at him, and then quickly looking away; some were showing their half-covered breasts; with garments which were loosely belted, or in fitted, transparent garments, they revealed the curve of their waists. Some made their anklets jingle; some were wearing garlands of flowers on their breasts; some were baring half their thighs; some were parading parrots and jays on their shoulders and their heads.[43]

Unlike the harem women, though, the daughters of Māra speak, or actually sing, to the Buddha, using the third person to describe themselves:

> "They have the bearing of a swan, swaying as they walk;
> they speak with grace the language of love,
> the language that touches the heart;
> they are beautiful and finely adorned;
> they are skilled as well in the joys of the gods!
>
> "They know the arts of music,
> singing, playing instruments, and dancing.
> They are ruled by love, they live to give pleasure."[44]

Like the women of the harem, Māra's daughters are beautiful, finely adorned, musical, and above all, skilled in the sexual arts. The text lingers over their description, enticing the reader/hearer with visions of their loveliness. Their beauty is soon subverted, though, when the Buddha makes another anti-body speech that is quite similar to his earlier speech inspired by the sleeping harem women. He concludes by saying to them: "I have given up the company of women, whose tendencies are to captivate."[45]

This rejection completely parallels that of the harem women and in this way the *LV* seems to stumble over the whole process of reconciliation leading up to this scene. The iconography, though, does not. One of the most popular images of the historical Buddha is from the night of enlightenment and it depicts the moment he called upon the earth to be his witness. It is called the *bhūmisparśa,* the earth-touching pose (Plate 1). This is the main iconographic representation of the Buddha's supreme achievement, enlightenment, and by the gesture of his right hand extending downward to touch the earth it signals the necessary female component of that achievement. This gesture, or *mudra,* comes to represent the state of enlightenment, and is incorporated into the iconography of other enlightened beings, such as the celestial Buddha Akṣobhya.

The importance of the earth and of divine feminine forces continued after Māra's daughters admitted defeat and advised their father to give up as well. At that moment the goddess of the Bo tree (*vṛkṣadevata*) spoke, also advising Māra to relent.[46]

The scene of Māra's daughters is about defining good and bad women: good women are respectful and make offerings; bad women are seductive: their thirty-two feminine wiles are comparable to the thirty-two negative similes of the harem women and strongly contrast with the thirty-two good qualities of Queen Māyā.[47] Additionally, the text contrasts good and bad female deities: the seductive daughters of Māra and the bountiful earth goddesses and tree goddesses who can bestow fertility. In these auspicious goddesses we can see an attempt to answer the needs of the laity which are discussed in the next chapter. The biographies of the Buddha began as oral texts and the earliest texts did not get written down much before the first century C.E., which is several hundred years after the development of Buddhist pilgrimage sites with their iconographic evidence of the incorporation of pre-Buddhist nature deities. The compilers of these texts were trying to make sense of what already existed, rather than trying to present a comprehensive or even consistent view of Buddhism.

In early Buddhism the maleness of the Buddha took on an exaggerated importance that culminated in debates as to whether women are capable of achieving enlightenment or if they must first reincarnate as men. Such a view is not limited to Buddhists—it was part of a pan-Indian view in which male superiority most often looked to female inferiority for validation.[48] In fact, it is all too familiar in the religions of the world as well as in other cultural constructs. Buddha's maleness, which belonged to his historical identity, was misinterpreted as essential to his salvational role.[49] In this way existing male social privileges were confirmed by the Buddha's maleness, in part because male privileges went beyond what was socially permissible for women, and in part because the greater physical accuracy of men's resemblance to the Buddha led to an identification with the Buddha that was physically impossible for women. As will be shown below, this is all about penises. In spite of this, the Buddha's life is a redefinition of masculinity, one that introduces new masculine values and reinterprets some old ones, such as the heroic masculine ideals of his early life that were based on his royal status. A slightly later formulation of the masculine ideal by the Hindu lawmaker Manu is suggestive of how far the Buddha strayed. This lists four stages in a man's life: celibate student, married householder, forest-dwelling ascetic, and wandering ascetic. In this system one abandons the householder life when he sees his son's son.[50] (In this system women were mainly a male appendage: first, a dutiful daughter, then devoted wife and loving mother.) The Buddha rejected these ideal stages of a man's life and their attendant duties when he decided to pursue the ascetic path at the age of thirty, when he chose to be celibate before seeing his son's son. He chose instead to build on the Indian myth of the virile ascetic whose abstinence is the source of his power. Indian myths abound with examples of ascetics who by withholding their semen gained tremendous power and even threatened the gods.[51] Though there were stories about female ascetics, and even though many of the early Buddhist nuns are said to have achieved enlightenment, the belief arose that men alone are capable of fully representing and/or achieving what the Buddha did.[52] The power to facilitate this ideology resided within a male, monastic hierarchy that questioned women's access to ordination, gave official voice and visibility primarily to men, controlled the texts of the tradition, and finally, so completely marginalized women's monastic participation that the ordination of nuns completely ceased throughout South and Southeast Asia.[53]

That issues of masculinity were involved in the Buddha's personal history is suggested by the fact that the Buddha's choice of celibacy seems to have led some of his opponents to challenge his virility, a point answered in a third century C.E. biographical source, the *Vinaya of the Mūlasarvāstivādin*, hereinafter the *MSV*,[54] by paralleling his seven years of asceticism with his wife having a miraculous pregnancy that lasted seven years.[55]

In conclusion, I would like to suggest that some Buddhist practitioners have remained in the Buddha's harem, focusing on his initial rejection of women which contributed to reduced roles for women in Buddhist practice and the more or less strict separation of women from male monastics. But the Buddha's reconciliation with women *before* he achieved enlightenment described the necessary inclusion of woman's auspicious powers in order to achieve enlightenment.

In what follows I unpack these and other ideas about gender expressed in the early biographies of the Buddha, beginning with the Buddhist concept of motherhood, the subject of the next chapter.

NOTES

1. This dream and its interpretation are discussed in Serinity Young, *Dreaming in the Lotus: Buddhist Dream Narrative, Imagery, and Practice* (Boston, MA: Wisdom Publications, 1999), 21–24.
2. Annemarie Schimmel, "Numbers: An Overview," in vol. 11 of *Encyclopedia of Religion*, ed. Mircea Eliade (New York: Macmillan Publishing Company, 1987), 17.
3. The *Lalitavistara* is available in a Sanskrit edition, edited by P. L. Vaidya, (Darbhanga: Mithila Institute, 1958), hereinafter *LV*, Vaidya; and an English edition is available through Gwendolyn Bays's translation of Edouard Foucaux's French translation from the Sanskrit, *The Voice of the Buddha: The Beauty of Compassion* (Oakland, CA: Dharma Press, 1983), hereinafter, Bays, *Voice*. It was composed anonymously around the beginning of the Common Era, although it contains much earlier material from the oral tradition. *LV*, Vaidya, 111.1; see also 130.13 and 19; 133.13.

4. Bays, *Voice*, 77.
5. Aśvaghoṣa, *Buddhacarita*, ed. and trans. E. H. Johnston (1936, Delhi: Motilal Banarsidass, 1984), I.4, hereinafter the *BC*. It was composed around the beginning of the Common Era and Johnston's edition contains the extant early chapters in Sanskrit, which are translated into English along with an English translation of the later chapters, which are available in Tibetan. *BC*, respectively, III.51–52 and II.32.
6. The paradigm of the solitary, male hero has been set forth by Joseph Campbell, *The Hero With a Thousand Faces* (1949. Cleveland and New York: The World Publishing Company, 1956, 1968), passim. For a general discussion of the hero see Lord Raglan, *The Hero: A Study in Tradition, Myth, and Drama, Part II*, reprinted *In Quest of the Hero*, ed. Robert A. Segal (Princeton, NJ: Princeton University Press, 1990), 87–175, and Theodor H. Gaster, "Heroes," *EOR*, vol. 6, 302–05. For the Buddhist hero see Nathan Katz, *Buddhist Images of Human Perfection* (Delhi: Motilal Banarsidass, 1982). See also Nancy Chodorow, *The Reproduction of Mothering: Psychoanalysis and the Sociology of Gender* (Berkeley, CA: University of California Press, 1978) for a gendered and psychoanalytic analysis of the male need to separate from women, especially 164–70.
7. The motif of seductive women impeding the progress of a young, virtuous male hero is well documented around the world. For instance, in ancient times, there is the story of Potiphar's wife in Genesis 39, Bellerophon and Anteia in Book Six of the *Iliad*, Phaedre in Euripedes' *Hippolytus*, and so on. South Asia, too, abounds in such examples, especially about evil queens.
8. For a discussion of the separation of men and women in social and religious activities before and after the spread of Buddhism, see Serinity Young, "Gendered Politics in Ancient Indian Asceticism," *Union Seminary Quarterly Review*, 48. 3–4 (1994), 73–92.
9. See the story of the Buddha's brother, Nanda, discussed in chapter 5 herein, for an elaborate ploy involving the rejection of women centered on degrees of women's attractiveness.
10. Clifford Geertz has spelled out some of the ways in which religious symbols expand into a society's mental and emotional life when he wrote of such symbols being both models *of* and models *for* reality in "Religion as a Cultural System," in *The Interpretation of Cultures* (New York: Basic Books, 1973), 87–125, especially 93. In the example of the Buddha, his biography functions as a model *of* the ideal behavior that leads to salvation and as a model *for* achieving salvation. Carol Christ has demonstrated the usefulness of Geertz's formulation for feminist analysis in "Why Women Need the Goddess," in Carol P. Christ and Judith Plaskow, ed., *Womanspirit Rising: A Feminist Reader in Religion* (San Francisco: Harper and Row, Publishers, 1979), 273–87; but see also Caroline Walker Bynum's critique of Geertz's formulation in Introduction to *Gender and Religion: On the Complexity of Symbols*, ed. Caroline Walker Bynum, et al. (Boston, MA: Beacon Press, 1986), 1–20. For an excellent feminist and anthropological discussion of gendered symbols see Sherry B. Ortner and Harriet Whitehead, "Introduction: Accounting for sexual meanings," in *Sexual Meanings: The Cultural Construction of Gender and Sexuality*, ed. Ortner and Whitehead (Cambridge: Cambridge University Press, 1981), 1–27. More recently Luce Irigaray has articulated some powerful ideas about the connections between patriarchy and religion, see, e.g., *Sexes and Genealogies* (New York: Columbia University Press, 1993).
11. Marina Warner, *Monuments and Maidens: The Allegory of the Female Form* (Berkeley, CA: University of California Press, 1985), xx.

12. *LV*, 133.12.
13. *BC*, II.28ff, IV.26 and V.69. In the *LV* it is the Buddha's aunt and stepmother, Mahāprajāpatī, who instructs the women by telling them to stand guard and to distract him with music, Bays, *Voice*, 304–06.
14. *BC*, IV.29ff. Udāyin also debates with the Buddha, berating him for not enjoying women, IV.62ff.
15. Maurice Winternitz, *A History of Indian Literature*, 3 vols. (1927. Delhi: Oriental Books Reprint Corporation, 1977), II.262.
16. *BC*, V.59.
17. Ibid., V.64.
18. Bays, *Voice*, 310
19. For some of the connections between women and death in world religion see Serinity Young, *An Anthology of Sacred Texts By and About Women* (New York: Crossroad, 1993), xxi and accompanying notes; Mary Storm, "Death," in *EOW*, 243–45; for India see Wendy Doniger O'Flaherty, *The Origins of Evil in Hindu Mythology* (Berkeley, CA: University of California Press, 1976), 27–35 and passim; for South Asia see Young, *Dreaming in the Lotus*, 160–62.
20. See the discussion in chapter 7 herein.
21. *LV*, 149.21ff; Bays translates *bālā* as ignorant ones, *Voice*, 312.
22. Bays, *Voice*, 314–15, emphasis added.
23. The *EOR* has two good articles on the symbolic meaning of the body under the caption of the "Human Body": Bruce Lincoln, "Myths and Symbolism" and Roger Lipsey, "The Human Figure as a Religious Sign," vol. 6, 499–511. For a stimulating discussion of the relation of women and the body in medieval Christianity see Caroline Walker Bynum, *Fragmentation and Redemption: Essays on Gender and the Human Body in Medieval Religion* (New York: Zone Books, 1992), especially 181–238; for uses of the body in a variety of Western literatures, both secular and religious, see Elaine Scarry, ed., *Literature and the Body: Essays on Populations and Persons* (Baltimore and London: The Johns Hopkins University Press,1988).
24. Bays, *Voice*, 314.
25. Indian ideas about the polluting aspects of the body predate Buddhism, but ascetic (sramanic) texts, whether Hindu or Buddhist, reject the body in contrast to brahmanic texts, which, in accepting the four stages of life (the *āśramas*), accommodate the body, pollution and all. And, of course, later Tantric Buddhism valorizes the body as the means to liberation.
26. Mieke Bal has written about the function of such namelessness or anonymity, which "eliminates them [the nameless ones] from the historic narrative as utterly forgettable." "The Rape of Narrative and the Narrative of Rape" in Scarry, *Literature and the Body*, 1.
27. For more on this point see Nancy E. Falk, "An Image of Woman in Old Buddhist Literature: The Daughters of Māra," in *Women and Religion*, ed. Judith Plaskow Goldenberg (Missoula, MT: American Academy of Religion, 1973), esp. 77–79.
28. Warner, *Monuments and Maidens*, 12.
29. Bays, *Voice*, 385.
30. Ibid., 404.
31. *LV*, 194.7–8; Bays, *Voice*, 404–405. The *BC* removes much of the feminine element from this sequence of events, but keeps a single woman offering food to the Buddha, calling her Nandabalā, XII.109.
32. Their names are: "Balā, Balguptā, Supriyā, Vijayasenā, Atimuktakamalā, Sundarī, and Kumbhakārī, Uluvillikā, Jātilikā, and Sujātā," *LV*, 194.1–2;

Bays, *Voice*, 404. This last, Sujātā, the daughter of the head villager, is named in other early sources as well, and the scene of her offering food to the Buddha is depicted at many other early sites, such as Sanchi, Amarāvatī, and Ajanta. Indeed, her food offering is commemorated on Tibetan paper currency, the fifteen *Tam* note; Wolfgang Bertsch, *A Study of Tibetan Paper Money* (Dharamsala: Library of Tibetan Works and Archives, 1997), 6 and plate VI.

33. *LV*, 194.11–13; Bays, *Voice*, 405.
34. The text calls her a *devatā*, a species of deity that will be discussed in the following chapter as a *yakṣī*. *LV*, 195.2; Bays, *Voice*, 406.
35. Bays, *Voice*, 408–12.
36. Bays, *Voice*, 480; *LV*, 232.11–16.
37. Bays, *Voice*, 482; *LV*, 233.3–8.
38. *BC*, XIII.56–58.
39. *BC*, XII.109.
40. The *BC* does, however, briefly mention the Buddha's conversion of some women in chapter XXI, e.g. the five hundred queens of King Ajātaśatru (v. 6), Nanda's mother (v.8), and several other women (v. 33). In between these verses he also converts innumerable men as well as some birds (v. 30) and snakes (v. 34).
41. Bays, *Voice*, 571; *BC*, XIII.3.
42. *LV*, 233.21–23; Bays, *Voice*, 483.
43. Bays, *Voice*, 484; *LV*, 233.25–234.5.
44. Bays, *Voice*, 486–87; *LV*, 235.19–24. As we shall see, these are also the characteristics of courtesans.
45. Bays, *Voice*, 494.
46. *LV*, 248.27–249.10; Bays, *Voice*, 509–10.
47. Bays, *Voice*, 42.
48. See, for instance, the important gender discussion in another great ascetic movement of ancient India, Jainism, in Padmanabh S. Jaini, *Gender and Salvation: Jaina Debates on the Spiritual Liberation of Women* (Berkeley, CA: University of California Press, 1991), passim. For a discussion of various ascetic views of and opportunities for women in ancient India see Young, "Gendered Politics."
49. My thinking on this issue has been enriched by Elizabeth Johnson's discussion of the role of Christology in Christianity's suppression and exclusion of women. See Elizabeth A. Johnson, *She Who Is: The Mystery of God in Feminist Theological Discourse* (New York, Crossroad, 1992), especially 151–54.
50. *The Laws of Manu*, trans. Wendy Doniger and Brian K. Smith (London: Penguin Books, 1991), 6.2.
51. Some of these stories will be discussed in chapter 6.
52. Even though the Buddha is sometimes credited with extraordinary qualities and powers, the tradition emphasizes his human (read *male*) nature, especially in the early tradition. See Katz, *Buddhist Images*.
53. For information on Buddhist nuns around the world see Karma Lekshe Tsomo, ed., *Sakyadhītā: Daughters of the Buddha*, (Ithaca, NY: Snow Lion Publications, 1988); for Sri Lanka see Tessa Bartholomeusz, *Women Under the Bo Tree* (New York: Cambridge University Press, 1994).
54. *The Gilgit Manuscript of the Saṅghabhedvastu, Being the 17th and Last Section of the Vinaya of the Mūlasarvāstivādin*, hereinafter the *MSV*, ed. Raniero Gnoli (Rome: Istituto Italiano per il Medio ed Estremo Oriente, 1977).
55. John Strong has translated this section in *The Experience of Buddhism: Sources and Interpretations* (Belmont, CA: Wadsworth Publishing Company, 1994), 9–12; *MSV* I.120.

PART II

Parents and Procreation

CHAPTER 2

MOTHERS AND SONS[1]

QUEEN MĀYĀ

Contradictory ideas about women and what it means to be female cluster around the figure of the Buddha's mother, Queen Māyā. Having died seven days after giving birth to the Buddha, in texts she is alternately the good, dead mother, so familiar in folktales from around the world,[2] and a lightning rod for male fears about female sexuality and pollution. The *Mahāvastu*, hereinafter the *MV*,[3] explains that the mothers of all buddhas, of the past and of the future, die seven days after giving birth because it is inappropriate for them ever to have sex again.[4] It adds that the Buddha is not polluted by the foul matter of the womb, but remains pure while in the womb because his body is rubbed with perfume and washed clean.[5] The *LV* tells us that while in his mother's womb the Buddha was enclosed in a jeweled casket (*ratnavyūha*) to protect him from its pollution (Plate 2).[6] In contrast to these negative textual statements about the pollution of all female bodies, including Queen Māyā's, her iconography positively represents female sexuality and celebrates its auspicious powers of fecundity. Of even further interest, although Queen Māyā is only briefly treated in the Buddha's biographies, in part because she died so soon after his birth, she is pervasive in Buddhist iconography. This suggests that her image carried additional meanings that went beyond her individuality as a particular historical character. In the same way that images of the Buddha represent both the historical Buddha and the state of enlightenment, so, too, images of Queen Māyā represent her historical individuality and the auspicious fecundity of human and divine females.

In South Asia fertile women are believed to possess part of the sacred powers of creation and are thus defined as auspicious (*maṅgalam*), which endows them with the power to confer blessings, especially of fertility, and other forms of wealth, as well as to curse. The most auspicious woman is one who has given birth to living children and whose husband is still alive, while the least auspicious is the widow, who has lost the power to bless or to bring auspiciousness to places and events such as births and weddings.[7] Auspiciousness is a state "of well-being and health or more generally of all that creates, promotes, and maintains life,"[8] while the inauspicious (*amaṅgala*) is associated with death and decay. The validation of fertile sexuality is inherent in the concept of female auspiciousness, and as we shall see, it is contrasted with male purity achieved through celibacy. Buddhists quite consciously incorporated, or at least never discarded, this ethos of female power that pervaded pan-Indian culture. In early Buddhism it was included primarily through iconography, but in the later tantric period it entered texts and rituals as well. The iconography of Queen Māyā is an important early example of this incorporation.

Conception and Birth Images

Four biographical events dominate the iconography of the historical Buddha and establish the four major Buddhist pilgrimage sites: his birth, which features Māyā, and three adult images of the Buddha at his enlightenment, first sermon, and death.[9] The earliest stone images of these events all depict the Buddha symbolically rather than anthropomorphically; respectively, the last three are represented by the Bo tree, the wheel, and the cremation. In the birth scene Māyā is posed standing, grasping a tree branch, while attendants hold an empty blanket at her right side on which the infant Buddha can be imagined rather than imaged. When stone images of the Buddha in human form began to be depicted around the first century B.C.E.,[10] the infant was sometimes, though not always (Figure 2.1), included, and was placed either floating at her right side (Figure 2.2) and being received on a blanket and/or standing by her right foot. There are even some images of the infant miraculously emerging from her side (Plate 2). These are among the earliest and most widespread female images in Buddhist art. Queen Māyā is depicted as a beautiful, young, seminude woman, with the slim-waisted and full, curvaceous figure that to this day remains the female ideal in South Asian art and literature. This image is depicted at various sites throughout Gandhara, at Bhārhut, Sanchi, Amarāvatī, Mathurā, Nāgārjunakoṇḍa, and so on, and it continued to be depicted in later periods throughout the Buddhist world. Additionally, this image is included in carvings

Fig. 2.1 Middle panel: Māyā giving birth without infant being imaged. American Institute of Indian Studies A1–95, Nāgārjunakoṇḍa, c. second century C.E.

Fig. 2.2 Māyā giving birth with infant imaged. © AAAUM (ACSAA 2822, Kushan)

Fig. 2.3 Māyā's dream. Gandhara, photograph by Mary Storm.

from all over South Asia that depict eight events in the life of the Buddha: his birth, enlightenment, first sermon, and death, plus four other events discussed later in this chapter. Consequently, these carvings encapsulate his four primary and four secondary pilgrimage sites.

A second frequent depiction of Queen Māyā represents her dream when she conceived the Buddha. Like the birth scene, it is a potent image of auspicious female sexuality: Māyā is shown asleep on her side while above her an elephant descends (Figure 2.3), symbolizing the Buddha's miraculous conception through a dream rather than through intercourse.[11] Many ancient people believed that women could conceive through dreams,[12] and some women slept in temples in order to have dreams as a cure for infertility.[13] Significantly, the image of Māyā's conception dream could also be one of the earliest stone images in Buddhist art,[14] because it allows for the Buddha to be represented by an elephant rather than in human form as an infant. Representations of this dream appear at various important sites throughout Buddhist history, such as Sanchi, Bhārut, Sarnath, Amarāvatī, Nāgārjunakoṇḍa, Ajanta, Gandhara, and sites in central, Southeast and East Asia.

Returning to the image of Māyā giving birth, it is particularly intriguing when compared to other female figures similarly posed with trees, such as the *śālabhañjikā* (woman and the *śāl* tree; Figures 2.4 and 2.5) and the *dohada* (two-hearted one, referring to a pregnant woman

Figs. 2.4 and 2.5 *Śālabhañjikā*. American Institute of Indian Studies 243.38 and A36.83, both Bharhut, c. second century B.C.E.

Fig 2.5

who thus has her own heart and that of her baby) that are also depicted at early Buddhist sites. These voluptuous female figures stand unself-consciously, often bejeweled and with uncovered breasts, under a blooming tree, one hand stretched overhead, grasping a branch, with one leg bent back at the knee, toward the tree, the foot raised to touch the trunk, or with one leg twined around the tree trunk. This pose clearly alludes to sexual encounters in that the literary tradition often described the sexual embrace as a woman encircling a man like a vine encircles a tree trunk. More significantly, it suggests folk beliefs that an auspicious woman who kicks or touches a tree with her foot can cause it to bloom. For example, *dohada* is a word that also refers to budding plants that long for the touch of a beautiful woman in order to bloom.[15] To this day one of the most frequently drawn auspicious images at the entrance to a wedding is that of a young woman holding plantain trees.[16] Similar ancient beliefs focus on female tree spirits (*yakṣīs*) who were believed capable of conferring fertility.[17] All these beliefs were incorporated into Buddhism. By incorporating such figures Buddhists hoped to endow their sacred sites with the powers of these chthonic females to protect and to confer blessings.

Yakṣīs are ambivalent deities because they can confer or withhold blessings, or even bring disasters. As vegetation deities they can grant plentiful crops and make herds fruitful; thus they are givers of wealth. Even more important, they can cure barrenness or sterility in humans—they can give children. Casting Queen Māyā in this pose directly connects her with these powers, and it incorporates these chthonic powers into Buddhism. Statues and carvings of Māyā, *yakṣīs*, and similar female images were included to empower early Buddhist sites with their auspiciousness.[18] Consequently, these images are all about womanliness: they have large, full breasts and broad curving hips that stress fertility and stimulate male desire. They are a celebration of female biology, but they also carry powerful religious meanings as bestowers of fertility and wealth in all its forms.

Relevant to the gendered meaning of images dedicated at various important Buddhist sites is the *yakṣī* iconography of the Kushan Dynasty (c. first to third century C.E.). Not only the breasts, but frequently the vulvas on female figures are clearly displayed (Figures 2.6, 2.7, and 2.10).[19] Reciprocally, male figures from the Kushan period emphasize the penis under the folds of their lower garments, even statues of the Buddha and the future Buddha Maitreya (Figure 2.8),[20] which were actually modeled on those of the *yakṣa*, male equivalents of *yakṣīs*. There is a distinct articulation of muscles and strength, an expression of male powers of fertility complimenting that of the fe-

Fig. 2.6 Voluptuous women. American Institute of Indian Studies 485–13. Mathurā (Bhutesvara), second century C.E.

male figures.[21] This articulation of the male form disappears rather quickly; indeed male forms become somewhat feminized, or at least lose any suggestion of overt masculinity,[22] while voluptuous female forms continue. Thus, the deeply entrenched pan-Indian belief in the auspicious powers of female fertility continued to be anthropomorphized by the sexualized female body, while the commitment to spiritual advancement was anthropomorphized by the nonsexualized male bodies of buddhas, bodhisattvas, and monks, as it was in early Buddhist literature. I will return to this topic in chapter 4.

South Asia is replete with stories that connect beautiful, often seductive, women with male ascetics, from the *apśaras* (divine women) Indra sends to seduce male sages to the happy family scenes of the as-

Fig. 2.7 Kushan *yakṣī*, exposed vulva. © AAAUM (ACSAA 2828)

Fig. 2.8 Future Buddha Maitreya Kushan, photograph by John C. Huntington, courtesy of the Huntington Archive.

cetic god Śiva and his beautiful wife Pārvartī. Some of these stories are explored in chapter 6, but for now it is relevant to recall this was a theme in the Buddha's life as well, and that prior to his abandonment of worldly life, he fully enjoyed life and its pleasures with his wife and harem women. As will be discussed further in chapter 4, at least one text, the *MSV*, is at pains to make the point that the Buddha did not abandon sexual activity due to impotency.

Male ascetics were believed to be highly potent because they could retain their semen, and just like the fecundity of auspicious females, it could be directed for the benefit of others. Yet in the biographies of the Buddha fertile women are represented as problematic, while any such problem is for the most part ignored by the iconography of early Buddhist sites; the texts are saying one thing about being female, and the iconography another.

A leading example of this can be seen in textual and iconographic representations of the *yakṣī*. Though statues and carvings of *yakṣī*s and of Queen Māyā are to be found at major early Buddhist sites all over India, in texts *yakṣī*s began to be portrayed as inauspicious.[23] I am arguing that the texts tarred Māyā with the same brush. Iconographically Māyā is a *yakṣī* figure, a beautiful, fertile woman who can bestow the blessings of fecundity and wealth, and whose presence empowers any site with female auspiciousness. Textually, we have seen that her female body is a dangerous source of pollution. For the most part, the ideas expressed in texts are those of male monastics who controlled the texts once they began to be written down, perhaps as early as the first century B.C.E., although material continued to be added into the fifth century C.E.[24] On the other hand, the laity, both the wealthy through individual donations and poorer people through collective donations, had a significant influence on the development, maintenance, and iconography of Buddhist pilgrimage sites.[25]

The *Mahāparinibbānasuttanta* (v.24) states that the Buddha, as he lay dying, recommended visiting places that had been important in his life.[26] These developed into Buddhist pilgrimage sites focused on *stūpas*[27] (Figure 2.9), cylindrical or rounded solid architectural structures that house the bodily relics of the Buddha or of other important Buddhist figures. *Stūpa*s are the center of devotional activities by both the lay and monastic communities through ritual circumambulation of the *stūpa*, offerings of incense, flowers and burning candles, chanting, and so on. The sides of the *stūpa*s were decorated with carvings, as were the walkway railings that often surrounded them (Figures 2.4, 2.5, 2.6, 2.9, and 2.10). Carvings and statuary depicted auspicious motifs such as garlands and lotuses, and pan-Indian divinities such as

Fig. 2.9 A stūpa at Sanchi. © AAAUM, photograph by Suresh Vasant. (ACSAA 3004)

yakṣīs and *yakṣas*, serpent beings (*nāgas*) and guardian deities, along with biographical narratives about the Buddha and other Buddhist saints, including episodes from the Buddha's past lives, the *jātakas*.[28] In brief, the Buddha's life story was used to carve out a distinctly Buddhist sacred geography, one that devotees could contemplate when they journeyed to pilgrimage sites and during their circumambulations of *stūpas*.

Vidya Dehejia has written a masterful study of the surviving visual narratives Buddhists carved in stone, especially those with densely packed scenes (Figures 2.1 and 2.12), the earliest of which she dates from the first century B.C.E.[29] Statues are also found at these sites, for instance adult images of the Buddha at his enlightenment, first sermon, and death, and those of pan-Indian divinities, such as the *yakṣīs*.

The iconographic evidence indicates that Buddhist sites celebrated the esoteric experience of enlightenment associated with celibacy as well as the exoteric experience of happiness in this life, be it a good crop, a successful caravan,[30] protection from misfortune, or a cure for barrenness. The negative views of some monks about women, which

Fig. 2.10 Sanchi *yakṣī*. © AAAUM, photograph by Suresh Vasant. (ACSAA 3016, detail of Figure 2.9)

were slowly included in oral and eventually written narratives about Buddha's life, did not lead to immediate iconographic changes. Dehejia has explained the time lag between the ideas expressed in texts and those expressed in iconography, or between ideas and actual practices,[31] a point also amply demonstrated by the research of Gregory Schopen.[32] It could take a century or even two for new ideologies of the monastic communities to influence lay ideas or to be depicted iconographically. It is clear that individuals who visited these sites had various goals, and some visitors must have been non-Buddhists. While I am taking a strong position on what these female images meant, it is impossible to deny that people, then as now, saw what they wanted in them.[33]

Monastic and lay devotion did, however, merge in the practice of commissioning iconography and then dedicating the merit (*puṇya*, a spiritual reward) accrued from such a pious act to one's deceased parents. The evidence for this comes from the inscriptions donors had carved along with the iconography, and from which Schopen argues that dedicating merit to one's parents was a major preoccupation of monastics,[34] at least those who could afford it. This is further evidence for the discrepancies between texts and iconography as the *vinaya*s (monastic rule books) proscribed against monastics handling money and required them to abandon all family life, while many texts emphasized that there is no self to endure after death.[35]

I will return to this subject of enduring relationships between Buddhists and their dead parents, especially their mothers, shortly. For now, I want to emphasize an additional disjunction between what the texts say and what the iconography shows. As mentioned above, the image of Queen Māyā giving birth sometimes shows the infant Buddha and sometimes it does not. As difficult as it is to date these images with precision, the presence or absence of the infant may be an important part of the discussion surrounding exactly when and where the Buddha was first depicted in anthropomorphic form. Central to any discussion, though, is understanding the relationship between the development of the Buddha's biographies and its iconography. Dehejia has made the point that early Buddhist texts were written down after the earliest stone iconography was created, thus the texts often had to explain the iconographic narrations of the Buddha's life that predated them. At the same time, the texts were articulating negative images of women, even of Māyā, as with the jeweled casket that protected the Buddha while in her womb. Clearly, having the Buddha born from her side in order to avoid the pollution of the birth channel undermines representations of female fertility as auspicious. Granting that prevailing beliefs attributed pollution to women's bodies and granting that heroes are often given miraculous births, not all the texts agree that this was the way Queen Māyā gave birth. For example, the birth from her side is not contained in the *Nidānakathā*, hereinafter the *NK*,[36] or the *MSV*. Images of attendants holding an empty blanket by Māyā's right side could be depicting the moments before or after the Buddha's birth, and one cannot argue that they indicate birth from her side based on textual versions of the birth because the texts came after the earliest iconography. And, though Māyā's body is depicted as brimming with fertility, her narrow waist and flat stomach contradict the idea of a full-term pregnancy. That empty blanket, which is meant to indicate the presence of the Buddha, could have given some redactors of the texts an opportunity to state that the infant exited from her side in order to shore up their negative representations of women and *yakṣīs*. By having an unnatural birth Māyā, somewhat like the Virgin Mary, gets stung twice. First, she is taken out of the natural realm and put into the realm of the miraculous, far above other women. Second, the auspiciousness of the birth is diminished by this emphasis on her polluted state. In chapter 4 I will elaborate on this argument in relation to problems with male powers of fertility in Buddhist texts and iconography.

Such negative ideas about women were quite obviously not shared by all monastics because some joined the laity in commissioning female statues imbibed with auspiciousness in order to empower Buddhist sites. For instance, at Bhārhut, one of the earliest sites to utilize stone in such work, all the statues bear inscriptions identifying their donors, and many statues of *yakṣīs* and other females were donated by monks and nuns.[37] The pan-Indian belief in the auspiciousness of female fertility was one shared by both the lay and monastic communities.

Lay interests, however, appear to be more fully represented in iconography than those of monastics for philosophical and financial reasons. Philosophically, the new and abstract ideals of Buddhism, such as enlightenment and the concept of no-self, were difficult to represent; consequently, it took several centuries for them to reach their fullest development in the plastic arts.[38] Financially, the arts were centered in the courtly and mercantile circles that were their main support and whose tastes they reflected.[39] In addition to royal support, early Buddhism flourished through the support of a new and rapidly rising merchant class who wanted material success and made generous donations when their enterprises by land and sea succeeded. Many were men who were trying to build fortunes, and they desired material success and the pleasures it could supply, and they also desired children.

Evidence for lay religious interests can be seen in the frequent depictions of Hārītī and Kubera, either as a couple or separately, from the earliest periods. Kubera is often said to be the king of the *yakṣas* and he was worshipped as a god of wealth. Hārītī especially draws our attention because she is among the first female deities to play a part in early Buddhist worship[40] and because she was so frequently depicted.[41] Hārītī is sometimes said to be a *yakṣī*, and almost always is shown with children in her lap or at her feet: the children she can protect or can confer on barren couples (Figure 2.11). The fact that her image was usually in or near monastic refectories where she was given a daily share of food is one indication of the popularity of her cult. Additionally, when a member of the laity invited the monastic community to her or his home, the host made food offerings to her.[42] This is explained in her legend that says originally she was a protective and fertility deity (being the mother of five hundred children), a *yakṣī* who became a child-devouring demon connected with miscarriage, abortion, and smallpox (a disease particularly devastating to children). She was later converted by the Buddha when he hid her youngest child in his alms bowl so that the suffering Hārītī experienced while searching for her child would awaken her sympathy with other mothers who lose their children. As a Buddhist, she became a deity who protects children (especially from smallpox) and bestows prosperity and fertility, and the Buddha ordained that she and her five hundred children should receive a share of food from every monastery,[43] which is why her shrine was usually in or near monastic refectories. Interestingly, she is rarely mentioned in texts, and does not appear in the full-length biographies of the Buddha.[44] Despite her presence in refectories and during lay food offerings to the monastic community, she seems to have been of more interest to the laity than the monastics. The seventh-century Chinese pilgrim-monk Hsüan Tsang records that in order to have children, lay people worshipped her at a *stūpa* that marked the spot where she was converted.[45] Actually, her conversion was commemorated at several widely separated sites.[46] Her cult developed in northwestern India, in the cultural pluralism of the Kushan period (first century C.E. to fourth century C.E.).[47] From there it spread with Buddhism to Borobudur, central Asia, Tibet, Nepal, China, Korea, and Japan, though in the latter three countries she was absorbed into Kuan Yin.[48] Besides being another example of a female iconographic pres-

Fig. 2.11 Hāritī. Kushan, photograph by John C. Huntington, courtesy of the Huntington Archive.

ence and textual absence, the enduring popularity of her images reflected lay interests, while the scanty textual references to her reflected a lack of interest on the part of early monastics.[49]

As already mentioned, Buddhist pilgrimage sites were focused on *stūpas*, memorial mounds containing the relics of the sainted dead. Despite certain varieties among them, such as rounded or cylindrical shapes, they are consistent in naming the central mass the egg (*aṇḍa*) or the womb (*garbha*) because it contains the seed (*dhātu*), the relic. In Sri Lanka *stūpa*s are actually called *dagoba*s, from the Sanskrit *dhātu-garbha*: *dhātu* meaning seed and relic.[50] As memorials, *stūpa*s are clearly connected to death, yet they also evoke the fertility of life and of rebirth. Even though death is deeply connected to pollution, *stūpa*s are located in preeminently pure and sacred places, places that we have seen were heavily decorated with many symbols of auspicious fertility, as were the *stūpas*. Seen in this context, *stūpas* confer a fertility desired by laity and monastics alike: rebirth into a better life whether that be enlightenment, and thus freedom from the cycle of birth, death, and rebirth, or rebirth into a life possessing the freedom and ease to pursue enlightenment, or rebirth into one of the Buddhist heavens.

Returning to Queen Māyā, placed in this context her iconography does more than just reflect this imagery of female auspiciousness and fecundity—it embraces it. The birth scene clearly and obviously represents the fertile link between women and trees and confers on her the powers of the *yakṣīs*.[51] This is further shown by several carvings of the infant Buddha being presented to the local *yakṣa* deity, for instance at Amarāvartī and Nāgārjunakoṇḍa.

Trāyastriṃśa Heaven

A third important iconographic reference to Māyā is contained in the Buddha's descent at Sāṃkāśya from Trāyastriṃśa (Pali: Tāvatisṃa) heaven, the heaven of the thirty-three gods, where he had gone to preach to her. It, too, is the focus of pilgrimage, being one of four secondary pilgrimage sites that were added to the original four sites by the end of the second century B.C.E.[52] Together, these eight events from the life of the Buddha become a major theme in Buddhist art that was represented throughout Buddhist South Asia. The descent from Trāyastriṃśa heaven (Figure 2.12) is an additional example of differences in iconographic and textual representations because it was a fairly widespread image,[53] while textual references to it are quite thin.

Fig. 2.12 Buddha's descent from Trāyastriṃśa Heaven. © The Mathura Museum (ACSAA 2822, Kushan)

The *BC* treats it briefly (xx.56–xxi.1), but gives more extensive treatment to the Buddha teaching his father (xix.1–41). Other sources are the *Divyāvadāna*[54] and the commentary on the *Dhammapada*, the *Dhammapada-Aṭṭhakathā*.[55] This last text is particularly interesting in that it states the Buddha spent the rainy season (about three months) in this heaven, teaching his mother the all-important *abhidharma* corpus. Additionally, the fourth-century Chinese pilgrim-monk Fa Hsien adds the intriguing story of the nun Utpalavarṇā, who is often depicted kneeling at the foot of the ladder as the Buddha descends.[56] She had vowed to be the first to see the Buddha when he descended, but stood little chance of doing so in the press of people who awaited him. Because of her past accumulation of merit, the Buddha transformed her into a man, and a *cakravartin* at that, a universal monarch. She was then able to walk to the front of the crowd because of her increased status, where the Buddha transformed her back into a woman, in which form she greeted him. He then predicted her future enlightenment.[57] More will be said about her in chapter 12.

The frequent depictions of the Buddha's descent from Trāyastriṃśa heaven, coupled with the many scenes of Māyā conceiving the Buddha and giving birth, when compared to the rare representations of the Buddha's father, King Śuddhodana, (and then more as king than father) emphasize the importance of motherhood. Another instance of this is found in the *MSV*, in the list of "the causal chain of events in the Buddha's life." Śuddhodana is not mentioned once, but Māyā receives several mentions, including the cleansing of her body before her conception, the conception, birth, and Buddha going to heaven to preach to her.[58] Of significance to my argument that women were represented more often in iconography than in texts, this is a list of images. The *BC* offers some proof for this rule. As we have seen and will continue to see, this is a distinctly unfriendly text toward women. It says that the twin miracles of Śrāvastī, which led to the Buddha's ascension to Trāyastriṃśa heaven, were performed for the edification of his father (xix.12–16), to whom he then preached for almost an entire chapter (xix). Later, it allots two stanzas to his preaching to his mother (xx.56 and 57).

ŚYĀMA JĀTAKA

Fathers were not completely absent from early Buddhist conceptions of filial piety, and they will be discussed further in the next chapter. For now, suffice it to say there was a rhetoric that called for the honoring of parents,[59] and ample evidence for participation in filial piety is demonstrated by innumerable inscriptions that transferred the merit accrued from donations to the donor's parents. However, filial piety was rarely represented in South Asian Buddhist art.[60] An exception is the frequently depicted *Śyāma Jātaka*[61] which tells about the Buddha's past life as Śyāma, the filial son of a Brahman couple who lived as ascetics in the forest. As they aged and grew blind they became completely dependant on their son's support, especially because they lived in such an isolated place. In all ways Śyāma treated them with respect, even serving them food before himself.

One day a king went hunting and accidentally shot and killed Śyāma, who before dying says "one arrow has killed three" (*MV*, II.213), meaning himself and his helpless parents. The king is appalled by what he has done and vows to take Śyāma's place in serving his parents. Śyāma's parents forestall this by explaining to the king that they can resurrect their son from the dead. They are able to perform this miracle through a combination of the powers they gained from their ascetic practices and from Śyāma's two main virtues: kindness to all creatures and his outstanding filial piety (II.219). In this story the Buddha is represented as the ideal filial son to both his mother and his father. As we have seen, though, in the Trāyastriṃśa heaven story, he is shown favoring his mother, and this favoritism is duplicated by later Buddhist heroes.

SONS SAVING MOTHERS

Filial piety is an important virtue throughout Asia, one that was articulated in many Buddhist texts, but in South Asia filial piety was and remains especially directed toward mothers. A telling example of this occurs in the *Amitāyus Dhyāna Sūtra*, which opens with King Ajataśatru's usurpation of his father King Bimbisāra's throne and his father's imprisonment. In an attempt to starve the former king to death, Ajataśatru orders that no one can approach his father. His mother, Vaidehī, the chief queen of Bimbisāra, breaks this order and manages to feed her husband. When Ajataśatru finds out, he wants to kill her himself, but is deterred from this by his ministers. They all but condone patricide, but draw the line at matricide, saying even the most evil men have never killed their mothers.[62] The Buddha then privately preaches the *Amitāyus Dhyāna Sūtra* to Queen Vaidehī.[63]

Interestingly, while Buddha is preaching to her, his disciples Maudgalyāyana and Pūrṇa are preaching to King Bimbisāra. These two disciples are the leading actors in the *Pūrṇāvadāna*, the legend of Pūrṇa. This is a text that dramatizes at length the obligations of children, especially sons, to their parents for having raised and nourished them, an obligation that they can repay in full by converting their parents to Buddhism. As we shall see, though, this story also favors mothers over fathers. In addition to being a short biography of Pūrṇa and his conversion to Buddhism, the *Pūrṇāvadāna* describes Maudgalyāyana's journey to Maricika heaven where he preached to his mother.[64] Nothing is said about his father.[65] This teaching about filial piety is put in the mouth of the Buddha, who specifically refers to the obligations of sons, not daughters, and to a mother's breast milk. Note also in the following that in the Sanskrit phrase "mother and father," mother always comes first, a grammatical precedence that points to the prominence of the mother in South Asia.[66] Buddha says:

> "Monks, the mother and father of a son are indeed performers of difficult tasks. They nourish and nurture the child; they raise him, *provide milk* and are his guides to the diverse beauties of this Rose-Apple Isle [India]. Were a son to serve with half his energy his mother and with the other half his father for a full hundred years; were he to present them with (all) the jewels, pearls . . . [etc.] that son would not have repaid the great service done him by his mother and father.

> "But a son who introduces to the riches of faith a mother and father without faith, who inspires them with it, trains them in it and establishes them in it; . . . the son who does these things for his mother and father does indeed repay the great service done him by his mother and father."[67]

Of course, the Buddha is the prime example of the good son for having gone to heaven to preach to his mother. Correspondingly, he also established the lack of such attention for the father, a lack duplicated by Maudgalyāyana. On a more mundane level, an additional important example of a good Buddhist son preaching to his mother is contained in the two ancient chronicles of Sri Lanka when Emperor Aśoka's son Mahinda instructs his mother in the dharma before he leaves to begin his successful conversion of Sri Lanka to Buddhism.[68]

On the one hand this teaching exalts mothers over fathers, especially dead mothers, while on the other it diminishes daughters by excluding them from this salvational role. Since repaying this debt involves preaching, the emphasis on sons suggests that preaching is not open to women, or at least is no longer open to women as it had been during the early days of Buddhism.[69] In point of fact, this text uses a discourse about mothers to exalt men, the sons who have the ability to save their mothers. The success of this discourse, with its emphasis on the mother-son relationship, is demonstrated in Chinese Buddhism, which was slowly and quite surprisingly able to redefine the Chinese emphasis on the father-son relationship to that of the mother-son relationship.[70]

Toward that end, the story of Buddha preaching to his mother in heaven was regularly cited to prove Buddhism included filial piety and it was retold in many Chinese texts.[71] Chinese versions of this story embellish upon the profundity of the mother and son connection in extremely visceral terms. When Māyā intuits her son's intention to visit, this causes her not only to lactate,[72] but her milk spurts across the cosmos between them and enters his mouth. The frozen iconographic image of Māyā as a beautiful, young mother comes alive in these stories, for she is eternally youthful in heaven, her breasts still heavy with milk. The adult Buddha's acceptance of her milk in his mouth, albeit without physical contact to her breast, signifies his acceptance of and participation in their bond, a bond that is continued when he preaches to her. Alan Cole has accurately characterized this as an exchange of breast milk for dharma,[73] a theme that he shows to be pervasive in Chinese Buddhist thought. It also contains an echo of Sujātā feeding Buddha the rice and milk that gave him the strength to achieve enlightenment. As strong as he is now, and even though the

Buddha is fully enlightened, accepting his mother's milk demonstrates belief in the enduring and sustaining ties of a mother to her son. If there is anyone who did not need his mother's help, it was the enlightened Buddha, yet he accepts her nurturance and acknowledges his enduring bond with her and his debt to her for having breast-fed him when he was an infant. In this sense it also harkens back to the *Pūrṇāvadāna* and the debt a son owes his parents, especially his mother for her breast milk. That this was no abstract ideal but rather an enacted obligation is suggested in the continuation of these beliefs in northern India, at least up to the 1970s. As part of the public acts of a traditional Hindu wedding ceremony, before the groom leaves for the bride's house, he enacts sucking from his mother's breast. In some cases the mother actually takes a breast out of her blouse, which the son then sucks.[74]

Our other example of a filial Buddhist son going to heaven to preach to his mother, that of Maudgalyāyana, also became well known in China as the story of Mu-lien, the Chinese translation of Maudgalyāyana's name. Chinese versions heighten the dramatic impact of this story in several ways and demonstrate their negative views of women. First, they have Mu-lien descend to hell rather than ascend to heaven in order to save his mother. Second, they focus on female pollution. In East Asia menstrual blood and the blood of childbirth were considered so polluting that they offended the deities. Chinese Buddhists augmented these beliefs by literally demonizing women's reproductive fluids. As a consequence, women inevitably ended up in the Hell of the Bloody Pond—to stew in their own juices as it were. The powerful impact of linking women's pollution with men's ability to act as saviors is demonstrated by the fact that the story of Mu-lien rescuing his mother from the Hell of the Bloody Pond became and remains an important part of women's funeral rites. This hell and its attendant rites will be discussed further in chapter 13.

Returning to the *Pūrṇāvadāna,* from which these Chinese and later Japanese versions arose, it must be remarked that overall it is an oddly patched text that particularly shows its seams when women appear. The first half is filled with jealous, snipping, thoughtless women as well as many negative statements about the nature of women—for instance, the frequent refrain that they divide families. Most peculiarly, it is not Pūrṇa who preaches to his mother; in fact, although she is a significant and self-motivated actor in the first part of the story, once she gives birth to Pūrṇa she completely disappears (though this is not the case in iconographic representations of the story).[75] In the beginning the story hinges on her. She is a devoted household slave who cared for Pūrṇa's father during an illness that made him so repulsive it drove away his wives and children. When he recovered, he offered her any reward she would like. She asked to have a child with him, and thus Pūrṇa was born. It is only later in the text, when Pūrṇa has grown up and converted to Buddhism, that Maudgalyāyana appears. Maudgalyāyana and Śariputra are among the Buddha's most important disciples and they frequently flank him in sculptures and paintings, so to have Maudgalyāyana appear has impact, but he preaches to his own mother, not Pūrna's. However, Pūrṇa preaching to his mother would have had equal impact, to say nothing of making the text more consistent. Clearly, Buddhist redactors pasted this teaching about mothers onto the end of a popular story; the only real connection between the two is the theme of conversion.

The disappearance of Pūrṇa's mother is not, however, completely irrelevant; it leaves one free to assume she is dead. It is particularly important to note that this lengthy articulation of the ideal mother-son relationship is about a dead woman and a living man, a clear reference to the adult Buddha preaching to his dead mother. This point is inescapable during funeral rites for mothers in which living sons reenact Maudgalyāyana's actions in the *Pūrṇāvadāna* to save their dead mothers from the Hell of the Bloody Pond, a hell they have fallen into simply by virtue of being female. But further, the mother's helpless desperation, compared with the adult status and expert ritualism of the son, completely conflates the child and the adult, rendering the former child all powerful in relation to the first person he had thought all powerful—only to find she had played him false.

In the foregoing texts, Buddhist filial piety emphasizes the mother and her conversion to Buddhism for her salvation, which lead to two possible scenarios. In cases where the mother has died unconverted, the son can convert her by ritually preaching to her. In cases where the mother, even though a Buddhist, is in hell because she menstruated and gave birth, the son can ritually take on those sins in order to expiate them. These themes will be explored further in chapter 13.

QUEEN CĀMA

A Buddhist text that celebrates motherhood in an entirely different vein is the Thai epic of Queen Cāma, traditionally said to have ruled in the seventh century C.E.[76] Most notably, Queen Cāma was already pregnant when she was asked to make the seven-month journey to Haripuñjaya and become its queen. She proved to be gloriously fertile when she gave birth to twin sons a few days after arriving in her new kingdom. Although she had been married, she was free to choose her own life because her husband had become a monk and she was a rich and powerful royal woman.

Celibate men continued to be an important feature in Cāma's story; her partner in creating the royal dynasty was the celibate sage (Thai: *isi*) Vāsudeva. He built the city of Haripuñjaya, invited her to rule, consecrated her queen and later consecrated her sons. Vāsudeva possessed the formidable powers of an ancient Indian *ṛṣi*, and he blended Buddhist and Hindu ascetic ideas: he had been a Buddhist monk, but found it too difficult and returned to the life of a householder. When he found this life dissatisfying as well, he then became a *ṛṣi*. Returning to married lay life suggests that it was not impotence that caused him to become a monk and later a celibate *ṛṣi*. As a *ṛṣī* his powers of fertility are stressed in a more obvious way when he fathers twin boys through a deer that drank some of his sperm-infused urine.

The epic of Queen Cāma is a richly layered text that balances the auspiciousness of the fertile woman, the mother or the potential mother, with the celibate yet sexually virile male. It also returns us to the voluptuous and thus fertile images of Māyā that opened this chapter, and points to the continuation of female auspiciousness as a meaningful element in Buddhist texts and iconography. Cāma's involvement with ascetic and celibate men also looks ahead to the chapters on courtesans and their complex involvement with celibate men and with Buddhism.

MOTHERS AND COMPASSION

An important valorization of the mother can be found in a famous poem of Theravāda Buddhists, one memorized by many: the *Metta Sutta* ("On Kindness"). In part, it says: "Just as a mother would protect her only child even at the risk of her own life, even so let one cultivate a boundless heart toward all beings."[77] This puts mothers at the center of the all-important Buddhist virtue of kindness or compassion, and it can be equated with the widespread Buddhist idea that at one time or another all sentient beings have been our mothers, therefore we should be compassionate to everyone. Gampopa (1079–1153) follows in the footsteps of such prominent Buddhist theoreticians as Asaṅga (fourth century C.E.) and Atīśa (d.1055) when he elaborates on this idea by placing mothers at the center of his exposition of compassion. His first recommendation for developing compassion toward all other beings is to reflect on the benefits we received as children due to the benevolence and self-sacrifice of our own mothers.[78]

Similarly, honoring motherhood is part of the *lo jong* (*blo sbyong*, mind training) practice that develops *bodhicitta*, the thought of enlightenment, which is essential for spiritual development.[79] In this context Buddhism takes the highly personal and individualized relationship of mother and child and universalizes it.

NOTES

1. Two valuable essays on Buddhist mothers are contained in I. B. Horner, *Women Under Primitive Buddhism* (1930. Delhi: Motilal Banarsidass, 1975), 1–18; and in Diana Paul, *Women and Buddhism: Images of the Feminine in the Mahāyāna Tradition*, 2d. ed. (Berkeley, CA: University of California Press, 1985), 60–73. For some discussion of the symbolical meaning of mothers and fathers, see José Ignacio Cabezón, "Mother Wisdom, Father Love: Gender-based Imagery in Mahȳāna Buddhist Thought," in Cabezón, ed., *Buddhism, Sexuality, and Gender* (Albany, NY: State University Press of New York, 1992), 181–99. Robert A. Paul, *The Tibetan Symbolic World: Psychoanalytic Explorations* (Chicago, IL: University of Chicago Press, 1982) should be consulted for its provocative psychoanalytic analysis of the mother-son relationship as well as that of fathers and sons, passim. Additional sources are discussed below.
2. In folktales the good, dead mother is often contrasted with the living, evil stepmother, e.g., Cinderella. Also, heroes are frequently orphans, for example Moses and Muhammed. This is one way of creating a sense of isolation that enables the hero to act as an outsider. Mary, the mother of Jesus, is an example of the all-good living mother. For a readable account, see Marina Warner, *Alone of All Her Sex* (New York: Alfred A. Knopf, 1976). A good discussion of another Christian mother is Clarissa W. Atkinson, " 'Your Servant, My Mother': The Figure of Saint Monica in the Ideology of Christian Motherhood," in *Immaculate and Powerful: The Female in Sacred Image and Social Reality*, ed. Clarisssa W. Atkinson, Constance H. Buchanan, and Margaret R. Miles (Boston, MA: Beacon Press, 1985), 139–72.
3. *Le Mahāvastu*, É. Senart, ed., 3 vols. (Paris: À L'imprimerie Nationale, 1890), hereinafter *MV*. English translation, J. J. Jones, *Mahāvastu*, 3 vols. (London: Pali Text Society, 1949–56). Jones argued that its long compilation period began in the second century B.C.E. and continued into the third or fourth century C.E., I.xi–xii.
4. *MV*, II.3. The *LV* says it is because when the time came for the Buddha to leave home his mother's heart would break, Bays, *Voice*, 147. See also June Campbell's analysis of the absent mother in Buddhism, *Traveller in Space: In Search of Female Identity in Tibetan Buddhism* (New York: George Braziller, 1996), chapter 5.
5. *MV*, II.6.
6. *LV*, 47.15; Bays, *Voice*, 103.
7. Saskia C. Kersenboom has a succinct discussion of female auspiciousness in "The Traditional Repertoire of the Tiruttaṅi Temple Dancers," in Julia Leslie, ed., *Roles and Rituals for Hindu Women* (Delhi: Motilal Banarsidass Publishers Pvt. Ltd., 1992), 137 and passim. But see also John B. Carman and Frédérique Apffel Marglin, eds., *Purity and Auspiciousness in Indian Society* (Leiden: E. J. Brill, 1985), passim.

8. Frédérique Apffel Marglin, *Wives of the God-King* (Delhi: Oxford University Press, 1985), 19, 53–57.
9. These are at Lumbini, Bodhgaya, Sarnath, and Kuśinagara, respectively, the sites of the Buddha's birth, enlightenment, first preaching, and death. See the excellent discussion of these and four additional early pilgrimage sites, which will be discussed below, in John C. Huntington's series of articles: "Pilgrimage as Image: The Cult of the Aṣṭamahāprātihārya," Part I, *Orientations*, 18.4 (April 1987): 55–63; Part II 18.8 (August 1987): 56–68; "Sowing the Seeds of the Lotus: A Journey to the Great Pilgrimage Sites of Buddhism," Part I, *Orientations* 16.11 (November 1985): 46–61; Part II 17.2 (February 1986): 28–43; Part III 17.3 (March 1986): 32–46; Part IV 17.7 (July 1986): 28–40; and Part V 17.9 (September 1986): 46–58.
10. The argument about exactly where and when the Buddha was first portrayed anthropomorphically is ongoing. John C. Huntington summarizes the argument between Foucher and Coomaraswamy and presents textual evidence for nonstone and therefore perishable images of the Buddha in "Origin of the Buddha's Image, Early Image Traditions and the Concept of Buddhadarsanapunya" in A. K. Narain, *Studies in Buddhist Art of South Asia* (New Delhi: Kanak Publications, 1985), 23–58. Gregory Schopen argues persuasively for epigraphic over textual evidence on this subject, see, "On Monks, Nuns, and 'Vulgar' Practices: The Introduction of the Image Cult into Indian Buddhism," in Schopen, *Bones, Stones, and Buddhist Monks: Collected Papers on the Archaeology, Epigraphy, and Texts of Monastic Buddhism in India* (Honolulu, HI: University of Hawai'i Press, 1997), 238–57.
11. This dream and its sources occurs in the *LV* VI.6–11; Bays, *Voice*, 95–99; *BC* I.4; *MSV* 1.40; *MV*, II.12; and *NK*, 154; among other texts, and are discussed at length in Young, *Dreaming in the Lotus*, 21–24.
12. See, e.g., Ernest Jones, *On the Nightmare* (New York: Liveright, 1951), 82–83.
13. Ibid., 92ff. The seventh-century Indian text the *Kādambarī* by Bāṇabhaṭṭa describes various acts performed by Queen Vilāsavatī in order to conceive a son, including sleeping in the temples of the goddess Caṇḍikā and telling her dreams to Brahmans; quoted by David N. Lorenzen, *The Kāpālikas and Kālāmukhas: Two Lost Saivite Sects*, 2d ed. (1972. Delhi: Motilal Banarsidass, 1991), 16–17. See also Bernard Faure, *The Red Thread: Buddhist Approaches to Sexuality* (Princeton, NJ: Princeton University Press, *1998)*, 182.
14. For some of the earliest representations of this dream, which may even occur in the Aśokan Rock Edicts, see Karl Khandalavala, "Heralds in Stone: Early Buddhist Iconography in the Aśokan Pillars and related Problems," 21–22 and also Biswanarayan Shastri, "The Philosophical Concepts and the Buddhist Pantheon," p. 56, both in *Buddhist Iconography* (Delhi: Tibet House, 1989). The dream may also be represented at pre-Aśokan sites in Andra Pradesh, see D. Sridhara Babu, "Reflections on Andra Buddhist Sculptures and Buddha Biography," in *Buddhist Iconography*, 100–01.

    Other early iconographic representations of this dream and its Interpretation are briefly discussed in Patricia Eichenbaum Karetzky, *The Life of the Buddha: Ancient Scriptural and Pictorial Traditions* (Lanham, MD: University Press of America, 1992), 11–15. See also her dissertation, Patricia D. Eichenbaum, *The Development of a Narrative Cycle Based on the Life of the Buddha in India, Central Asia, and the Far East: Literary and Pictorial Evidence* (Ann Arbor, MI: University Microfilm International, 1980), and the list in Dieter Schlingloff, *Studies in the Ajanta Painting; Identifications and Interpretations* (Delhi: Ajanta Publications (India): 1987), 17–18, 37–38, nn. 30, 32, and 33. See also the important discussion of iconographic representations of the life of the Buddha in Huntington, "Pilgrimage as Image," Part I, 55–63.

15. Susan Huntington, *The Art of Ancient India* (New York: Weatherhill, 1985), 68–69, has a lovely image of a *dohada* and discusses its meaning.
16. Marglin, *Wives of the God-King*, 56.
17. See Ananda K. Coomaraswamy, *Yakṣas* (Delhi: Munshiram Manoharlal Publishers, Ltd., 2001), who says that "there is no motif more fundamentally characteristic of Indian art from first to last than that of the Woman and Tree," 32, 35–36, where he briefly discusses women kicking trees. See also Gail Hinich Sutherland, *Yakṣa in Hinduism and Buddhism* (1991. Delhi: Manohar, 1992), 29, and esp. 136–47. Both of these works discuss the positive representation of *yakṣas* in art and their negative, frightening representation in Buddhist texts. See also the discussion in Vidya Dehejia, ed., *Devi: The Great Goddess* (Washington, D.C.: Arthur M. Sackler Gallery, 1999), 369–74.
18. For instance, Sanchi II (c. first century B.C.E.) has images of *yakṣīs* and of Lakṣmī, Vidya Dehejia, *Discourse in Early Buddhist Art: Visual Narratives of India* (New Delhi: Munshiram Manoharlal Publishers Pvt. Ltd., 1997), 77–78, and at Bharhut (c. 80 B.C.E.) eleven (of a total of sixteen) surviving entranceway columns indicate that terminus pillars were carved on three sides with figures of *yakṣīs* and *yakṣas*; ibid., p. 99. They are also beautifully depicted and Nāgārjunakoṇḍa and other sites.
19. This was also the case at Nāgārjunakoṇḍa and at Sanchi.
20. The Buddha's penis and its ability to function or not function is a subject of some interest to Buddhists, and is discussed in chapter 4 herein.
21. See Vishakha N. Desai, "Reflections on the History and Historiography of Male Sexuality in Early Indian Art," in Vidya Dehejia, *Representing the Body: Gender Issues in Indian Art* (New Delhi: Kali for Women, 1997), 42–55, for further discussion of these figures. For more information on this period see John M. Rosenfield, *The Dynastic Arts of the Kushans* (1967. New Delhi: Munshiram Manoharlal Publishers, 1993).
22. C. Sivaramamurti thinks of this as an "essential Indian principle . . . that no figure should be worked with sharp angular features supportive of physical strength"; *Amaravati Sculptures in the Chennai Government Museum, Bulletin of the Chennai Government Museum* (1942. Chennai: 1998), 45. He seems not to consider Gandhara as Indian, 65.
23. See fn. 17 above. Additionally, Faure cites the Chinese Buddhist belief of an evil *yakṣī* who causes wet dreams; *Red Thread*, 85.
24. Frank Reynolds, "The Many Lives of Buddha: A Study of Sacred Biography and Theravāda Buddhology," in Frank Reynolds and Donald Capps, eds., *The Biographical Process: Studies in the History and Psychology of Religion* (The Hague: Mouton, 1976), 37–61.
25. See, e.g., Dehejia's brief discussion of the influence of donors, *Discourse*, p. 34, and "The Collective and Popular Basis of Early Buddhist Patronage: Sacred Monuments, 100 BC–AD 250," in Barbara Stoler Miller, ed., *The Powers of Art Patronage in Indian Culture* (Delhi: Oxford University Press, 1992), 35–45; Étienne Lamotte, *History of Indian Buddhism: From the Origins to the Śaka Era*, trans. Sara Webb-Boin (Louvain-La-Neuve, Institute Orientaliste, 1988), 620ff. See also Huntington's discussion of the early textual references to images of the Buddha, which are all attributed to laymen, "Origin of the Buddha Image," passim. I will discuss Gregory Schopen's richly nuanced reading of these sites shortly.

26. Schopen, "Monks and the Relic Cult in the *Mahāparinibbāna-sutta*: An Old Misunderstanding in Regard to Monastic Buddhism," Schopen, *Bones, Stones*, 99–113.
27. For more information on the *stūpa* cult see Anna Libera Dallapiccola, et al., ed., *The Stūpa: Its Religious Historical and Architectural Significance* (Wiesbaden: Franz Steiner Verlag, 1980); and Adrian Snodgrass, *The Symbolism of the Stupa* (1985. Delhi, Motilal Banarsidass Publishers, 1992).
28. Among the most popular stories to be depicted were those of Vessantara, the Buddha's penultimate life, and of Sumati, when he vowed to achieve buddhahood in the presence of the then Buddha, Dipamkara. Lamotte lists the distribution of *jātakas* at the early sites, *History of Indian Buddhism*, 404–411.
29. Dehejia, *Discourse*, p. 7.
30. See, for example, some rituals and prayers of merchants in Joel Tatelman, *The Glorious Deeds of Pūrṇa: A Translation and Study of the Pūrṇāvadāna* (2000. New Delhi: Motilal Banarsidass, 2001), 57–58, 65.
31. Dehjia, *Representing the Body*, 8–9. See also Joel Tatelman's brief comparison of the *Pūrṇāvadāna* text and its iconography, where he found female characters to be more amply represented in the iconography than they are in the text; *The Glorious Deeds of Pūrṇa*, 170. See also Jacob N. Kinnard, *Imaging Wisdom: Seeing and Knowing in the Art of Indian Buddhism* (1999. Delhi: Motilal Banarsidass Publishers, 2001), who discusses the evolution of *prajñā* in text and icon where the early iconographic representations of Prajñāpāramitā are considerably later than the textual representation, e.g., 131–43, and the same is true for Mañjuśri. Additionally, Richard S. Cohen argues that several centuries passed before the ideology of the bodhisattva expressed in the earliest Māhāyana texts occurs in iconography, "Kinsmen of the Son: Śākyabhikṣus and the Institutionalization of the Bodhisattva Ideal," *History of Religions* 40.1 (August 2000): 1–31.
32. See especially Schopen, "Two Problems in the History of Indian Buddhism: The Layman/Monk Distinction and the Doctrines of the Transference of Merit," passim, and his other essays in *Bones, Stones*.
33. See Jacob N. Kinnard's interesting discussion of diverse viewers, "The Polyvalent *Pāda*s of Viṣṇu and the Buddha," *History of Religions* 40.1 (August 2000): 32–57.
34. Schopen, "Filial Piety and the Monk in the Practice of Indian Buddhism: A Question of 'Sinicization' Viewed from the Other Side," in Schopen, *Bones, Stones*, 64. Impressive as Schopen's work is, and it has made us rethink early Buddhism, he does not take up the issue of how much this cost or who had enough money to pay for such commissions. Further, he notes those whose donations are identified by inscriptions "were not just average monks," 33, 36 (and again in "On Monks, Nuns," 243); but rather doctrinal specialists. Perhaps these were monks who attracted a large enough following to be able to pay for iconographic commissions. Additionally, Schopen does not tell us how much of the iconography at any site is without inscriptions nor what percentage of the site is represented by his inscription sample. See, e.g., "Two Problems," 30–33, and "On Monks, Nuns," 240–42. He also mentions instances where an individual monk or nun set up images at more than one site, "On Monks, Nuns," 244–48, which suggests extensive control by a small, and as he shows, an interconnected elite. The fact that these monastics then, as now, may have been supported in their iconographic projects by donations from a laity who approved the projects somewhat undercuts his argument for greater monastic influence on iconography at these sites,

especially since he does not contextualize his figures in relation to the overall site. Significantly, Dehejia's breakdown of donative inscriptions shows a greater number were given by the laity; *Discourse*, passim. Of course, this needs to be looked at on a site by site basis.

Finally, Schopen does not incorporate his findings with other objects at these sites, for example, the vast amount of sculptures and freezes of deities such as Harītī and the *yakṣīs*.

35. Schopen, "Burial *Ad Sanctos* and the Physical Presence of the Buddha in Early Indian Buddhism: A Study in the Archaeology of Religions," particularly highlights the contradictions between textual and archaeological evidence on this point, passim, in Schopen, *Bones, Stones*, 114–47.
36. *Nidānakathā*, in *The Jātaka Together with Its Commentary*, ed. V. Fausboll (London: Trübner, 1877), hereafter *NK*. This text began as an introduction to the *jātakas*, but rapidly became the standard Theravāda biography of the Buddha. It is translated by T. W. Rhys Davids as *Buddhist Birth Stories* (1880. New Delhi: Asian Educational Services, 1999).
37. Dehejia, *Discourse*, p. 108.
38. See Rosenfield's discussion of these points, *Dynastic Arts*, 208–14. But see also Dehejia's discussion of early depictions of some aspects of Buddhist doctrine, such as the *triratna*, *Discourse*, 78–81, and passim.
39. See, e.g., the brief discussion of the influence of donors in Dehijia, *Discourse*, p. 34.
40. A. Foucher, *On the Iconography of the Buddha's Nativity*, *Memoirs of the Archaeological Survey of India*, No. 46, trans. H. Hargreaves (1934. New Delhi: Archaeological Survey of India, 1999), 20.
41. Huntington discusses her image in Gandhāra, *Art of Ancient India*, 146, but her image was much more widely spread over time and space. See below.
42. See the seventh-century Chinese pilgrim-monk, I-Tsing, *A Record of the Buddhist Religion as Practised in India and the Malay Archipelago: AD 671–695*, trans. J. Takakusu, (1896. Delhi: Munshiram Manoharlal Publishers Pvt. Ltd., 1998), 37.
43. I-Tsing attests to the daily offering of food made before her image, Takakusu, *Record of the Buddhist Religion*, 37.

The *Mahāvaṃsa* (XII.21), which calls her a *yakkhinī*, has a different version of her story, saying she was converted by the monk Majjhantika and that she, her husband called Paṇḍaka, and their five hundred sons become stream-enterers (*sotāpattiphala*), beings who are committed to the Buddhist path. *The Mahāvaṃsa or the Great Chronicle of Ceylon*, trans. Wilhelm Geiger (1912. London: The Pali Text Society, 1964). In the *Ratnakūṭa Sūtra* she is the Queen of the Pretas and converted by the Buddha Mohugalaputra; L. A. Waddell, *The Buddhism of Tibet or Lamaism*, 2d ed. (Cambridge: W. Heffer & Sons, Ltd., 1934, 1967), 99.

See also the story of two females who repeatedly reincarnate in human, animal, and demonic forms, and alternately devour the other's children in revenge for the previous incarnation until the Buddha reconciles them. The one who does the devouring becomes a benevolent forest deity who protects the crops. Eugene Watson Burlingame, trans., *Buddhist Legends*, vol. 3 (1921. New Delhi: Munshiram Manoharlal, 1999), 170–75.

44. See Ram Nath Misra, *Yaksha Cult and Iconography* (Delhi: Munshiram Manoharlal Publishers Pvt. Ltd, 1981), 73–80, for a discussion of texts that mention her.
45. Hiuen Tsiang, *Si-Yu-Ki: Buddhist Records of the Western World*, trans. Samuel Beal, reprint (New York, NY: Paragon Book Reprint Corp., 1968), 110–111.

46. Lowell W. Bloss, "The Buddha and the Nāga," *History of Religions* 13.1 (August 1973): 45.
47. Mary Storm, "Hāritī," in *EOW*, 392. A. D. H. Bivar attributes the proliferation of her image in Gandharan sculpture, and perhaps the expansion of her worship, to a smallpox epidemic in 166 C.E., "Hāritī and the Chronology of the Kuṣāṇas," *Bulletin of the School of Oriental and African Studies*, 33 (1970): 19–21.
48. See, e.g., Jitendra Nath Banerjea, *The Development of Hindu Iconography*, 4th ed. (Delhi: Munshiram Manoharlal Publishers Pvt. Ltd., 1985), 381; Alice Getty, *Gods of Northern Buddhism* (Oxford: Clarendon Press, 1914), 75–76; A. Foucher, "The Buddhist Madonna," in Foucher, *The Beginnings of Buddhist Art*, trans. L. A. Thomas and F. W. Thomas (1917. New Delhi: Asian Educational Services, 1994), 271–91; and Barbara E. Reed, "The Gender Symbolism of Kuan-yin Bodhisattva," in Cabezón, *Buddhism, Sexuality, and Gender*," 169–70. Susan Huntington divines an esoteric symbolism for Hāritī as the embodiment of the Mother of the Buddhas that is identical to Prajñāpāramitā, or at least to the *prajñāpāramitā* texts. She infers this from Ajimā shrines at Nepali temples, which are shrines of the Mother of the Buddhas; Huntington, *Art of Ancient India*, 148 and 633, n. 24.
49. Another example of lay interest is the presence of Sirimā Devatā, the goddess of fertility, at Bhārhut; Lamotte, *History of Indian Buddhism*, 407; and Dehejia, *Discourse*, 108 and fig. 83.

    Balkrishna Govind Gohkale, *Buddhism in Maharashtra: A History* (Bombay: Popular Prakashan: 1976), has a good discussion of lay influence on early Buddhism and especially of the *yakṣa* cult, 77–81.

    Geshe Lozang Jamspal informed me that in the 1940s and 1950s older monks at Tashilungpo Monastery in Tibet made offerings to Hāritī after their evening meal by throwing down some food. No image of her was necessary for this ritual. He also said that this practice is more widespread in Ladakh among all monks. Further, she has a shrine in Swayambhu, Kathmandu. Conversation, October 16, 2002.
50. Snodgrass, *Symbolism of the Stupa*, 189, 190–200 for additional meanings. See also Nur Yalman, "On the Purity of Women in the Castes of Ceylon and Malabar," *Journal of the Royal Anthropological Institute of Great Britain and Ireland*, 93.1 (1963): 30.
51. See Sivaramamurti, *Amaravati Sculptures*, 65.
52. Huntington, "Sowing the Seeds," Part V, 56. These are Sāṃkāśya, Śrāvastī, Rājagṛha, and Vaiśālī, sites of four supernatural events, respectively, the Buddha's descent from heaven, his display of magical powers, where he tamed a wild elephant, and where he was offered honey by a monkey.
53. Sivaramamurti, *Amaravarti Sculptures*, pl. xxxii, discussed 195.
54. *Divyāvadāna*, ed. E. B. Cowell and R. A. Neil (Cambridge: Cambridge University Press, 1886), 394ff. It was composed in northwestern India during the second century C.E.
55. Translated by Burlingame as *Buddhist Legends*, vol. 3, 47–52.
56. Fahien, *A Record of Buddhistic Kingdoms: Being an account by the Chinese Monk Fa-Hien of his travels in India and Ceylon (A.D. 399–414) in search of the Buddhist Books of Discipline*, trans. James Legge (1886. New York: Paragon Book Reprint Corp., 1965), 49.
57. A Sri Lankan variant on this story has it that Māyā had changed sex, had been reborn as the god Mātru in this heaven. R. Spence Hardy, *A Manual of Buddhism in its modern development* (London: Williams & Norgate, 1960),

306–307. A Chinese variant conflates this story with Maudgalyāyana's visit to his mother in heaven. See the discussion in chapter 12.

58. Cited by Huntington, "Origin of the Buddha Image," 42.
59. Additional examples of Buddhist stories about filial piety can be found in Horner, *Women*, 7–11.
60. This is not the case in East Asia. See, for example, the Shrine of Filial Piety and the Shrine of the Buddha of the Great Appropriate Means, which depict the Buddha's acts of filial piety in his life as Śakyamuni and in his past lives. Bai Ziran, *Dazu Grottoes* (Beijing Foreign Languages Press, 1984), no page numbers.
61. For example, it was depicted at Sanchi, in Gandhara, and twice at Ajanta; Dehejia, *Discourse*, 116, 148, 198, and 217. It is *jātaka* No. 540 in the Pali collection and is told in the *MV* (Jones, II.199–218) as well as in the *MSV*. For additional textual versions, see Schlingloff, *Studies in the Ajanta Paintings*, 64–73, and for his reading of this painted narrative in Cave 10, which he considers the earliest painted version (c. second century B.C.E.), and a later painting in Cave 17, as well as its carving at Sanchi, its representations at Gandhara, and various other representations, 67–71.
62. E. B. Cowell, ed., *Buddhist Mahāyāna Texts*, Part II (Oxford: Clarendon Press, 1894), 163.
63. This scene is depicted in the Dazu Caves, Bai Ziran, *Dazu Grottoes*, 12. The *Amitayus Sūtra* is further discussed in chapter 13 herein.
64. In the *Suttavibhaṅga* of the *Vinaya* Maudgalyāyana is able to see the suffering of the dead and to understand its causes; trans. I. B. Horner as *The Book of the Discipline*, vol. I (London: Pali Text Society, 1951, 1982), 181–88.
65. Tatelman, *The Glorious Deeds of Pūrṇa*, 77–80.
66. Similarly, the list of five unpardonable sins begins with matricide, followed by patricide, and then killing an arhat, and so on.
67. Tatelman, *The Glorious Deeds of Pūrṇa*, 77–78, emphasis added.
68. *Dīpavaṃsa*, trans. Hermann Oldenberg (1879. New Delhi: Asian Educational Services, 1992), 12.15 and the *Mahāvaṃsa* XIII.6–7.
69. Mable Bode, "Women Leaders of the Buddhist Reformation," *The Journal of the Royal Asiatic Society of Great Britain and Ireland* (1893): 517–66 and 763–98.
70. Alan Cole, *Mothers and Sons in Chinese Buddhism* (Stanford, CA: Stanford University Press, 1998), passim.
71. Ibid., 64–65, 116. See also the shrine to filial piety in the Dazu Caves, which focus on the mother's intimate physical relationship to her children. Illustrated in Bai Ziran, *Dazu Grottoes*, no page numbers.
72. Cole uses Bao Chang's early-sixth-century version of this story from *Details on Sutras and Vinayas*, which Dao She quoted in his seventh-century encyclopedia, *The Dharma Treasure Grove*; *Mothers and Sons*, 65.

    The ancient Indian medical text, the *Suśruta Saṁhitā*, states that "breast milk is secreted, and flows out at the touch, sight or thought of the child. . . . so the fondest love of a mother for her children brings about the secretion of her breast-milk. . . . constant love is the cause of secretion of milk from the breasts"; ed. and trans. Ram Karan Sharma and Viadya Bhagwan Dash (Varanasi: Chowkhamba Sanskrit Series Office, 1998), X.21–25. The fourth-century Chinese pilgrim-monk Fahien reports a past life of the Buddha in which upon seeing her adult sons a mother's breasts spurt milk into their mouths. The Buddha is said to have been one of her sons. Legge, *Record of Buddhist Kingdoms*, 73–74. I am grateful to Alan Cole for bringing this story to my attention.
73. Cole, *Mothers and Sons*, 66.

74. Ruth S. Freed and Stanley A. Freed, *Rites of Passage in Shanti Nagar,* Anthropological Papers of the American Museum of Natural History, New York, 1980, vol. 56, Part 3, 468. Stan Freed was kind enough to show me a photograph of such an event at a wedding he witnessed in the 1970s.
75. Tatelman, *The Glorious Deeds of Pūrna,* 170.
76. Donald K. Swearer & Sommai Premchit, *The Legend of Queen Cāma: Bodhiraṃsi's* Cāmadevivamsa, *A Translation and Commentary* (Albany, NY: State University of New York Press, 1998).
77. Richard Gombrich, "The Evolution of the Sangha," in *The World of Buddhism,* ed. Heinz Bechert and Richard Gombrich (London: Thomas and Hudson, 1984, 1995), 88.
78. Gampopa, *The Jewel Ornament of Liberation,* trans., Herbert V. Guenther, (Boston, MA: Shambhala, 1986), 91–98.
79. Geoffrey Samuel, *Civilized Shamans: Buddhism in Tibetan Societies* (Washington, D.C.: Smithsonian Institution Press, 1993), 269.

CHAPTER 3

MEDICAL EXCURSUS

When it comes to biological reproduction, Buddhism faces a dilemma. The Buddha advocated celibacy as necessary for achieving enlightenment because sex is connected to attachment, which does not lead to enlightenment, at least not in early Buddhism. Nevertheless, beings need to reincarnate in order to achieve enlightenment, and monastic institutions require the laity for financial support. Elaborate theories often arise from such incongruities, as can be seen in the following foray into Buddhist medical views of conception and the formation of sexual characteristics. The medical texts reveal an early scientific discourse on gender and reproduction, one that is shown to be fraught with deep social and religious ramifications.

The connections between Buddhism and medicine go back to early, frequent epithets of Buddha as the Great Physician and of his teachings as the King of Medicine,[1] as well as to the practice of medicine in Buddhist monasteries.[2] The Buddhist *Vinaya*, the rules for monks and nuns, reveals a deep interest in medicine, and by the mid-third century B.C.E. medicine was part of the course of study in Buddhist monasteries, which were extending medical care to the population at large.[3] Over time, medical skill became an important part of Buddhist missionary activity in India and elsewhere.[4] Epithets connecting the Buddha with medicine and medical activities proliferated in Mahāyāna Buddhism, where healing was valorized in pivotal works such as the *Lotus Sūtra*,[5] through the popularity of the Medicine Buddha, and in representations of primordial buddhas as the first physicians and the first teachers of healing.

The principal Tibetan medical text is the *Four Tantras* (*rGyud bZhi*),[6] said to have been written in Sanskrit around 400 C.E.,[7] and which now exists only in Tibetan and Mongolian translations. Actually it is a *terma*, a text rediscovered in the eleventh century, and attributed to the historical Buddha, who is believed to have manifested as the Medicine Buddha in order to teach this text. To a certain extent it is consistent with earlier Indian medical texts,[8] but it also shows indigenous Tibetan influences, as well as influences from Chinese, central Asian, Persian, and Greek practices.

Tibetan medicine is based on a theory of correspondences or sympathies between the human body, the natural world, and various spiritual realms. It both asserts this theoretical approach to the patient and utilizes practical experience, such as hands-on examinations of pulses and urine, along with questioning the patient. At the same time, the Tibetan experience of self includes: (1) the notion of past lives and the belief in future lives, (2) relationships with spiritual and natural beings of many different sorts, and (3) social arrangements that include family and clan members as an essential part of oneself. This expanded conception of self defines the field of possible influences on health: one's karma from past lives effects one's constitution, general health, and lifespan; demons and deities can influence health for good or ill; in the event that the patient cannot reach a doctor, their ailment can be diagnosed by examining the pulse of a close relative. The modern Western isolation of a diseased organ from the rest of the body,[9] to say nothing of its isolation from the mind and emotions of the patient, as well as from the influences of spirits and of the cosmos, is inconceivable to a traditional Tibetan doctor.

Medicine is believed to have had its origins in primordial time, in the realm of the Medicine Buddha Bhaiṣajyaguru, and therefore is not the end product of human experience and the ability to reason but rather a special discovery: the more spiritually advanced the practitioner the closer he or she is to understanding the workings of the cosmos and its relation to human beings. In this sense, even today many Tibetan doctors are believed to be *tulkus* (Tib: *sprul sku;* Skt: *nirmāṇakāya*), reincarnations of spiritually advanced beings. This means that to question the theory is to misunderstand reality; the theory is an eternal truth. Thus, the medical explanations put forth by the *Four Tantras* for the development of sexual characteristics offer profound insights into the Buddhist discourse on gender and sexuality. It begins by saying that the sex of the fetus is determined at several moments before and after conception, beginning with the three things necessary for conception: semen (*khu*), blood (*khrag*), and the consciousness (*rNam shes*) of the being about to reincarnate.[10] *The Blue Beryl* (*Vaiḍūrya sngon po*),[11] a leading commentary on the *Four Tantras*, adds that the incarnating consciousness has no "sense of belonging to a particular sex, regardless of its status in past lives."[12] Sex is determined by karma, which drives the incarnating consciousness toward a couple having sexual intercourse (Plate 3, second row). In a burst of pre-Freudian analysis, the text says that if the consciousness feels attachment to the mother and aversion to the father, it will be male; if it feels attachment to the father and aversion to the mother, it will be female.

Other factors determining sexual characteristics include that males are conceived on even days after the mother's menstrual cycle, females on odd days (Plate 3, fourth row, first two figures),[13] though Indian medical texts present this as advice on how to predetermine the sex of the child.[14] A physiological basis for the determination of sex characteristics is shown in the belief that males are formed through a preponderance of semen and females through a preponderance of blood in the embryonic mixture,[15] and that equal quantities lead to the birth of a hermaphrodite. The mother's blood is said to develop the blood, muscles, and viscera of the embryo, while the father's semen develops the bone, brain, and spinal cord (Plate 3, fourth row, figures four and five).[16] One aspect of the father's contribution, bone (*rus*), is considered more enduring over the generations than any of the mother's contributions, and the greater durability of bone is connected to privileging patrilineal descent over matrilineal descent and supporting patriarchal ideologies about family life. More will be said about this in chapter 10.

Further insights into the Buddhist discourse on gender are contained in the medical discussion of the postconception stages. Shortly before birth, mothers may dream of a male or a female figure depending on the sex of the child they are bearing (Plate 3, row nine, last two figures). Additionally, the male embryo curls up on the right side of the womb, the female on the left, while milk first appears in the right breast for a male and in the left for a female.[17] These left/right distinctions in the determination of sex introduce social and cultural assumptions about the relative value of the sexes, given the generally negative view of left in most early cultures, in that South Asian etiquette requires the right side, which is the pure side, be presented to any respected person or to any holy object that is circumambulated. Indeed, women are supposed to present only their right side to their husbands and other males.

The abundant number of factors influencing sexual characteristics at conception (karma, odd/even days, preponderance of semen or blood) and indications during gestation (dreams, left and right breasts and sides of womb) are an attempt to contain what appears to be a rather fluid category and suggests some anxiety about the stability of sexual characteristics. Such anxiety and instability are dramatized in stories of adult sexual transformation, the well known myth of a primordial androgynous state, and by ritual means to protect male babies from being transformed into female babies, as well as practices to assure the transformation of females into males in the next life.

What we see in the foregoing is the human proclivity to sustain various points-of-view simultaneously, even if they are contradictory. For instance, though karma is the first step in the determination of sex characteristics, karma can be altered by good deeds, such as making donations, and by performing religious acts such as circumambulations, and so on.[18] Additionally, parents can influence the sex of their children by choosing an odd or even day for conception, and there are ritual means to stabilize and protect sex characteristics, at least masculine ones.[19] The *Four Tantras* even contains a ritual for changing the sex of the embryo after conception:

> If someone wishes for a son, during the third and fourth week [after conception] the method of 'changing the centre' can be practiced. It can only be practiced before the child's sexual organs have developed. It can even be done during the first or second week. This method is very efficacious, and the centre is quite suddenly changed where the karma most certainly destines the child to become a girl, and quite easily when the karmic chances for a boy or a girl are equal. For anyone who wishes to have male descendants it is very important to practice this method. The best day is that on which the star rGyal [the eighth nakṣatra, *puṣyā*] and Jupiter meet, but at least it should be a day ruled by the star rGyal. On that day a perfect smith should make a good image of a baby boy four fingers high, either from one kind of black male iron or from three or five kinds of male inferior iron. On a subsequent day ruled by rGyal, one should heat the little figure in a charcoal fire for a little while, just until it changes its colour. Then one should take two handfuls of milk of a cow that has male calves and pour this into a vessel. One dips the little figure into the milk, once if it is made of one kind of iron, three times if made of three kinds of iron, and five times if made of five, always just so long that it makes a hissing sound. The husband takes one handful of this milk and gives it to his wife to drink. Then one takes equal amount of blood from a virgin girl and semen from a virgin boy and mixes them in molasses. If these cannot be procured, red *lhad-ts'er* (alloy application) and quicksilver, pulverized by burning, grinding and pounding, can be used instead. Equal amounts of each should be ground between millstones and thoroughly mixed, then mixed with the molasses and eaten. Following this, one should take wool from the right shoulder of one, three or five sheep, depending on how

> many kinds of iron were used for the figure. Then a virgin boy should make a rope with three stands of the wool and make either one, three or five knots in it, according to the number of sheep used. The mother should tie this round her waist so that the two ends hang from the spot where her navel is. The figure should be wrapped into a female calf's skin and tied to the mother's rope, taking care to keep it always upright. The combination of all these circumstances and materials specified, planets and constellations meeting together will certainly ensure a positive result.[20]

This ritual that utilizes astrology, alchemy, and sympathetic magic tells us that femaleness, the destiny of becoming female is tentative—it can be changed. Needless to say, the text does not provide a ritual to assure a female embryo. The message is that it is females who can and who need to change sex, who must acquire masculinity, in order to achieve spiritual and social status. This is confirmed by practices to assure the transformation of females into males in the next life. As we shall see in chapters 12 and 13, this is connected to the Buddhist notion that men are more capable of achieving enlightenment than women or, in some cases, the belief that women are totally incapable of achieving enlightenment.

The physiology behind these ideas is complex, even contradictory. On the one hand, the medical texts present the human body as a male body. In other words, the male body is the normative body—an idea we will meet in an assortment of Buddhist texts. To be female is to deviate from this norm due to bad karma and the dominant influence of the mother during conception, someone who by definition has received a lower form of birth. Except for pregnancy and a brief discussion of gynecological disorders, all the models in the medical texts are male, with women being a sidebar, or an afterthought (Plate 4), if they are mentioned at all. When one considers that the texts were written by men for male doctors and were studied in male monastic colleges, this becomes understandable, if not laudable. The medical texts are representative of an elite, literate, male practice that was distinguished from other forms of healing that concentrated on shamanic techniques and from the practices of midwives. Ideologically, though, the medical texts, their commentaries, and the iconographic display of their contents were immensely influential.

Returning to the contest between the mother's blood and the father's semen for the sex of the embryo, their mutual defeat in the conception of a hermaphrodite substantiates the notion that sex is fluid and that things can go very wrong indeed. It presents the category of a third sex, variously said to include hermaphrodites, eunuchs, homosexuals, and lesbians,[21] and evokes the idea of a human continuum, with male and female at opposite ends, and a whole range of variables in between. Nonetheless, maleness is the ideal to be aspired to by all variants. Yet a recurrent theme in Buddhist literature and practice is the vulnerability of maleness to the mutability of sexual characteristics. Masculinity can be weakened by sexual contact with women or through contact with menstruating women.

On the other hand, the medical texts clearly establish the difference between female and male as generated by different karma and in brief statements about women, such as defining them as those endowed with breasts and a womb and who menstruate and lactate.[22] This model presents women and men as binary opposites that are completely distinguishable—the presence of one is the absence of the other. It is a model that fits in nicely with the dualistic thinking presented in left/right, odd/even and the role of blood and semen in conception. These contradictory notions about sharply distinguishing the sexes as complete opposites, while noting their similarity as human beings, were widespread in many ancient cultures[23] and remain so to the present.

Underlying this early scientific discourse and ritual activities meant to ensure and maintain a male child are ideas about female pollution discussed at length in chapter 11. We have seen that the miraculous version of the Buddha's conception and birth involved having him ensconced in a protective casket during his time in the womb (Plate 2). A similar device is said to have been provided for the Tibetan reformer Tsongkhapa (1357–1419), while the Indian missionary to Tibet, Padmsambhava (eighth century) and the Tibetan epic hero Gesar were neither conceived nor born through wombs. These miraculous elements in pregnancies are quite suggestive of male anxiety about the *in utero* experience, about being immersed in femaleness, as if it were an infectious experience that could undo masculinity. The enactment of such beliefs is explored in chapter 11.

Overall, the womb is conceived of as a terrible place, a point detailed from a religious and a medical perspective by the Tibetan saint Gampopa (sGam po pa, 1079–1153), who had been a doctor. He analyzes the period of gestation in the womb as painful and unpleasant. For instance:

> In the eleventh week . . . pain is felt as if an open wound was probed with a finger.
>
> This misery of staying in a womb may be illustrated in another way. . . . When a mother indulges too often in sexual intercourse during her pregnancy, the embryo feels as if it were beaten with thorns.

> In the thirty-seventh week, while still in the uterus, the consciousness of the foetus, grieved by the state of dirtiness, stench, darkness and imprisonment, conceives the idea of escaping.
>
> In the thirty-eighth week, there arises in the mother's womb the so-called "flower gathering" (*me.tog sdud.pa*) wind. This turns the foetus around and pushes it near the mouth of the womb. It feels pain as if being damaged by iron machines.[24]

Such a restatement of basic ideas contained in the medical texts only serves to highlight the negativity of Buddhist views about reproduction.

However, despite this emphasis on the male body and the male medical expert, the paintings contain many female deities as healers and protectors of the medical tradition, such as the culture heroine Yid Thogma (Yid 'phrog ma), who traveled the world studying with human and divine medical teachers and whose knowledge was passed on to the semilegendary first doctor of Tibet, Yuthog.[25] The presence of human and divine females in these mythical accounts suggests that some male practitioners gained their medical knowledge from women. Charlotte Furth notes a similar female source for Chinese medical practices, especially those specific to women, such as gynecological practices.[26] Nonetheless, both the scientific and the mythological medical discourse of Tibetan Buddhism reified the secondary status of women.

The influence of these views on Buddhist fathers is the subject of the following chapter.

NOTES

1. Raoul Birnbaum, *The Healing Buddha* (Boulder, CO: Shambhala, 1979), 3–19. This study of the celestial Medicine Buddha Bhaiṣajyaguru is essential reading for the understanding of healing in Mahāyāna Buddhism. His cult was widespread in Tibet; see Anthony Aris, ed., *Tibetan Medical Paintings*, 2 vols., (New York, NY: Harry N. Abrams, 1992), vol. 1, 17–18 and vol. 2, 173–74.
2. Kenneth Zysk, *Asceticism and Healing in Ancient India: Medicine in the Buddhist Monastery* (New York: Oxford University Press, 1991), 43–48.
3. Ibid., 43–48.
4. Ibid., 51. An explicit example of this can be found in the preamble to the biography of the Tibetan doctor Yuthog Yontan Gonpo, trans. in Rechung Rinpoche, *Tibetan Medicine* (1973. Berkeley: University of California Press, 1976), 179–82.
5. Discussed in Birnbaum, *The Healing Buddha*, especially 26–34.
6. *rGyud bZhi, A Reproduction of a set of prints from the 18th century Zuṅ-cu ze Blocks from the Collections of Prof. Raghu Vira*, by O-rgyan Namgyal (Leh: S. W. Tashigangpa, 1975). Rechung Rinpoche, *Tibetan Medicine*, 48, has translated part of this text, though he drew on a slightly different manuscript than I have used. Another partial transation is *The Quintessence Tantras of Tibetan Medicine*, trans. Barry Clark (Ithaca, NY: Snow Lion, 1995).

Todd Fenner discusses its role in Tibetan medical practice and its Western translation; see "The Origin of the *rGyud bzhi*: A Tibetan Medical Tantra," in José Ignacio Cabezón and Roger R. Jackson, *Tibetan Literature: Studies in Genre* (Ithaca, NY: Snow Lion, 1996), 458–69.

7. Zysk, *Asceticism and Healing*, 3.
8. Zysk, *Asceticism and Healing*, has persuasively argued for the early Buddhist influence on the ancient Indian medical texts, 21–24.
9. On this point see Michel Foucault, *The Birth of the Clinic: An Archaeology of Medical Perception*, trans. A. M. Sheridan (1973. New York: Random House, 1973, 1994), passim.
10. Rechung, *Tibetan Medicine*, 32. See also Paul, *Women in Buddhism*, 171–72, for more on the establishment of sex at conception. Two good articles that emphasize the karmic dimensions of this process are Mitchell G. Weiss, "*Caraka Saṃhitā* on the Doctrine of Karma," and William Stablein, "Medical Soteriology of Karma in the Buddhist Tantric Traditions," both in Wendy Doniger O'Flaherty, ed., *Karma and Rebirth in Classical Indian Traditions* (Berkeley, CA: University of California Press, 1980), 90–115, and 193–216, respectively.
11. Even though Monier-Williams glosses *vaiḍūrya* as "a cat's-eye gem," and the translators of Sangye Gyatso's commentary as "beryl," I am influenced in taking this as lapis lazuli by Raoul Birnbaum's discussion of lapis lazuli in *The Healing Buddha*, 80–81, and his translations of this term from Chinese texts, passim. I will, however, continue to use *The Blue Beryl* since that is the title of the only English translation in Aris, *Tibetan Medical Paintings*.

    Aris has translated much of what follows somewhat out of sequence with the Leh edition that I used (*Vaiḍūrya snon po*, ed. T. Y. Tashiganpa [Leh: 1973], vol. I, f. 222, l. 5), and he incorporated material from the *rGyud bZhi*, *Tibetan Medical Paintings*, vol. I, 25, and vol. II, 181.

    For more information on the author of this text, Sangye Gyatso (*Sangs rgyas rGya mtsho*, 1653–1705), regent of the Fifth Dalai Lama, an extremely important and very enigmatic figure, see D. L. Snellgrove and Hugh E. Richardson, *A Cultural History of Tibet* (Boston, MA: Shambhala, 1986), 204–08.
12. Aris, *Tibetan Medical Paintings*, vol. I, 25, col. 1.
13. Aris, *Tibetan Medical Paintings*, vol. 1, 25, col. 2. The same idea exists in medieval Chinese medical texts; Charlotte Furth, *A Floruishing Yin: Gender in China's Medical History, 960–1665* (Berkeley, CA: University of California Press, 1999), 210, and in Indian medical texts, *Suśruta Saṁhitā*, II.12–18.
14. *Suśruta Saṁhitā*, II.10 and *Caraka Saṁhitā*, ed. & trans. Kaviraj Kunjalal Bhishagratna (Varanasi: Chowkhamba Sanskrit Series Office, 1977), VII.5. *Manu* voices the same ideas, III.48–49.
15. The idea of a battle between female and male elements for the sex of the embryo is contained in several other medical traditions, for instance, the *Indian Bundahisn*, Bruce Lincoln, *Death, War, and Sacrifice: Studies in Ideology and Practice* (Chicago, IL: The University of Chicago Press, 1991), 219; medieval Europe, Joan Cadden, *Meanings of Sex Difference in the Middle Ages: Medicine, science and culture* (Cambridge: Cambridge University Press, 1993), 132; while Chinese medical texts say that the sex of the embryo is determined at conception through the predominance of *yin* or *yang* energies; Charlotte Furth, *A Floruishing Yin: Gender in China's Medical History, 960–1665* (Berkeley, CA: University of California Press, 1999), 54, but see also 206–16.
16. Aris, *Tibetan Medical Paintings*, vol. I, 25, and *Suśruta Saṁhitā*, II.32. Significantly, these represent the two lineages that define Tibetan kinship structure

and the permitted and forbidden marriage groups. Claude Lévi-Strauss, *The Elementary Structures of Kinship* (Boston, MA: Beacon Press, 1969), 373–76. See also 393 ff for similar ideas in India and China.

17. Aris, *Tibetan Medical Paintings*, vol. I, 25. See also *Suśruta Saṁhitā*, III.33 and *Caraka Saṁhitā*, II.23–25. Left/right distinctions are also represented in the Hippocratic corpus as determining the sex of the embryo. Helen King, *Hippocrates' Woman: Reading the Female Body in Ancient Greece* (Routledge: London and New York, 1998), 8, which continued into medieval medical thinking; Cadden, *Meanings of Sex Difference*, 130.
18. See Samuel's discussion in *Civilized Shamans*, 199–222.
19. Some of these will be discussed in chapter 12 herein.
20. Rechung, *Tibetan Medicine*, 33–34. This ritual is remarkably similar to the *puṃsavaṇa* rite in the *Caraka*, 4.8.19.
21. See, e.g., Leonard Zwilling and Michael J. Sweet, " 'Like a City Ablaze': The Third Sex and the Creation of Sexuality in Jain Religious Literature, *Journal of the History of Sexuality* 6.3 (1996): 359–84; Walter Penrose, "Hidden in History: Female Homoeroticism and Women of a 'Third Nature' in the South Asian Past," *Journal of the History of Sexuality* 10.1 (2001): 3–39; and Gilbert Herdt, ed., *Third Sex, Third Gender: Beyond Sexual Dimorphism in Culture and History* (New York: Zone Books, 1994).
22. Aris, *Tibetan Medical Painting*, vol II, 263, col. 1.
23. See Thomas Laquer, *Making Sex: Body and Gender from the Greeks to Freud* (Cambridge, MA: Harvard University Press, 1990), whose work I have found very helpful in thinking through these ideas. Primarily, though, I am influenced by conversations with Jo Ann McNamara who suggested the two sexual ideologies of a human continuum and binary opposites.
24. Gampopa, *The Jewel Ornament of Liberation*, 64–65.
25. Both their biographies are contained in Rechungpa, *Tibetan Medicine*, 141– 327. Yid Thogma is discussed further herein, chapter 9.
26. Furth, *A Flourishing Yin*, 68.

CHAPTER 4

FATHERS AND HEIRS[1]

KING ŚUDDHODANA

While iconographic images of Queen Māyā are spread across the Buddhist landscape, those of the Buddha's father, King Śuddhodana, are far and few between. When he does appear, it is usually with Queen Māyā, seated on a throne, listening to her dream being interpreted.[2] As we have seen, Queen Māyā's iconography is associated with two major events in the Buddha's life that are commemorated at two of his eight pilgrimage sites: his birth at Lumbini and his descent at Sāṃkāśya after having preached to her in Trāyastriṃśa heaven. Throughout South Asia these eight sites were frequently grouped together in single carvings, with Māyā grasping a tree to illustrate the birth, and three ladders representing the Buddha's descent from Trāyastriṃśa heaven. Śuddhodana receives no such iconographic attention nor is he featured at any of the Buddha's pilgrimage sites, yet he is a larger presence in the texts than the Buddha's mother. This is not simply a matter of his having lived longer than Queen Māyā.

Even though South Asian beliefs about conception emphasize the dominant influence of the father in male children and attribute to men a greater overall influence on all their descendants, several biographies of the Buddha deny that Śuddhodana was his physical father, though he clearly remained the Buddha's social father or adoptive father. Queen Māyā's conception dream was and remains a popular motif in both texts and iconography, and a close reading of this dream in the *NK*, *LV*, and *MV* suggests that the dream elephant is the progenitor of the Buddha, not King Śuddhodana.[3] The *NK* says that Queen Māyā had this dream while sleeping apart from her husband and specifies that the Buddha took the form of the elephant, so he incarnated himself.[4] In the *MV* Queen Māyā pointedly asked Śuddhodana's permission to remain celibate for one night, the night she has the dream,[5] while the *LV* states she had been separated from the king for thirty-two months in order to practice asceticism.[6] As mentioned in chapter 2, miraculous conceptions are a common motif in world religions, and many ancient people believed that women could conceive through dreams, as is evidenced by women who slept in temples in order to have dreams cure their infertility.

Stories and images of the Buddha's miraculous conception serve to distance King Śuddhodana from his son. Though the texts accord him all the respect due Indian fathers, at the same time they emphasize his opposition to the Buddha's choice of a spiritual life from the moment of his conception through his adulthood. The *LV*, however, goes further than other biographies in not only negating Śuddhodana as a father, but also negating the Buddha as a father, in that Rāhula, the Buddha's son, generally said to have been born on the night he left home,[7] is completely absent from the text, except for a remark that all the bodhisattvas of the past married and had a son.[8] Rāhula is well known in the Buddhist tradition through other canonical sources, and from tender depictions of the Buddha bidding farewell to his sleeping wife with Rāhula in her arms, so his absence from this text is remarkable. The absence of Rāhula's birth curiously parallels Śuddhodana's absence in the Buddha's conception. In the *LV* the Buddha is neither fathered nor does any fathering. This is the text that most clearly introduces the Buddhist problem with male reproductive power, a problem that weaves in and out of other early biographies, and one that we will see continues in later Buddhist biographies.

As mentioned several times above, the *BC* consistently privileges men over women, and thus its portrayal of Śuddhodana is more extensive than in other biographies. Further, it limits the Buddha's preaching to his mother in Trāyastriṃśa heaven to two stanzas (XX.56–57), yet extends almost an entire chapter (XIX) to the Buddha teaching his father.[9] The *BC* is modeled on courtly dramas and thus it begins with King Śuddhodana and makes him a very royal figure. Nor does this text deny his siring the Buddha. It says Queen Māyā dreamed of the elephant before she conceived, and that she conceived "without defilement" (I.3). Unlike his son, who is described as "a captive to the women" of the harem (II.32), the *BC* tells us that King Śuddhodana practiced self-restraint and behaved as an ideal South Asian king (III.33–56), hoping that when the Buddha saw his own son he would stay in the world. The text forewarns that this will not happen and justifies the Buddha's desertion of his child by claiming a tradition in which all previous bodhisattvas left home when their sons were born (II.56). So, the *BC* asserts Śuddhodana's paternity at the same time it justifies the Buddha's rejection of his paternity of Rāhula.

In effect, in the *BC* King Śuddhodana is fulfilling what became traditional Buddhist instructions on how parents should look after their children: "they restrain them from evil, they encourage them to do good, they give them education and professional training, they arrange suitable marriages for the children, and hand over property as inheritance to them at the proper time."[10] Yet, the Buddha does *not* minister to his father as traditional Buddhist instructions say a son should: "My parents have supported me, I shall support them in turn; I shall manage affairs on their behalf; I shall maintain the honour and tradition of the family; I shall make myself worthy of the inheritance; and furthermore, I shall offer alms on behalf of the departed parents."[11] Nor is he properly attending to his son. The Buddha's position is that he can give enlightenment, which is the best care anyone can receive, and eventually he converts his father and his son. Still, it is intriguing to see the Buddha, while still a layman, flaunt what became Buddhist guidelines for the laity. Before turning to that, though, it is useful to recall that as we saw in the chapter on motherhood, any lack of filial piety was modified in Chinese Buddhism. In addition to the texts about and rituals for deceased mothers, Chinese Buddhists elaborated on the Buddha's relationship with his father. For instance, they said that the Buddha, his half-brother Nanda, and son Rāhula were at King Śuddhodana's bedside when he died and that the Buddha helped carry his coffin.[12]

BUDDHA AS FATHER

Initially, the Buddha rejected his son Rāhula, who in most of the biographies was born on the night the Buddha left home. Years later, after the Buddha achieved enlightenment, he returned home, converted his father and other family members, and took Rāhula into the order of Buddhist monks.[13] In this he doubly thwarted his father, first by having removed himself from the patrilineal succession and secondly by causing his son to do the same. He went even further when he converted and ordained his half-brother Nanda, presumably Śuddhodana's only other son. Now there would be no male descendants to maintain the offerings to the ancestors.

Early Buddhism subverted biological fatherhood in this and other ways, such as co-opting fatherhood into a mentoring system between younger and older monks referred to as the father/son connection. This idea goes back to the early days of Buddhism, in fact to the first rule attributed to the Buddha when he had individual senior monks undertake teaching novices. The rule, in part, states: "the preceptor, monks, should arouse in the one who shares his cell the attitude of a son; the one who shares his cell should arouse in the preceptor the attitude of a father. Thus these, living with reverence with deference, with courtesy towards one another, will come to growth, to increase, to maturity in this *dhamma* and discipline."[14] Yet, after having inducted Nanda into the order of monks, he respected his father's request that from then on monks would require the permission of their parents before joining the order.[15]

There is a deep ambivalence in early Buddhism toward biological fatherhood, both having a father and being a father. This is brought out in the best known past life of the Buddha as Prince Vessantara, who proved his status as a supreme bodhisattva, as one who would become a buddha, by his unstinting generosity, when he gave away his children.[16] Images of this *jātaka* are spread throughout Asia and the story has been retold in many languages.[17] Seemingly, it turned out well in the end because he got the children back, but it remains a stark model of a bodhisattva's generosity and lack of attachment. Vessantara also gave his wife away in this tale, so it is a preamble to the Buddha's departure from home, when he once again abandoned his wife and child.

The Buddhist message is clear. In order to achieve enlightenment one must move beyond attachment, including attachment to family. Buddhism reconfigured fatherhood by incorporating its authority with the teachings of the Buddha and the order of monks and actually apotheosized it in the notion of the spiritual father—on earth the guru and in the heavens the celestial buddhas and bodhisattvas. Throughout this process Buddhism never questioned the patriarchal social order, it incorporated it—but it did this at the expense of male fertility.

In contrast to the foregoing texts, the compilers of the *MSV* placed Rāhula's conception, not his birth, on the night of the Buddha's departure from home. Further, they extended the pregnancy of the Buddha's wife, Yaśodharā, into six long years, during which the Buddha pursued enlightenment. Yaśodharā's pregnancy will be discussed further in chapter 5, but for now, the *MSV* version stresses that both the Buddha and his wife had tremendous, even magical, powers of fertility that were directed toward their appropriate end, the birth of a son.

A short digression here will bring together some threads from earlier chapters. The *MSV* is a Sanskrit text compiled in northern India

Pl. 1 Buddha, earth-touching pose. Courtesy of the Division of Anthropology, American Museum of Natural History, 70.0/6937.

Pl. 2 Infant Buddha in jewel casket (detail of Plate 1).

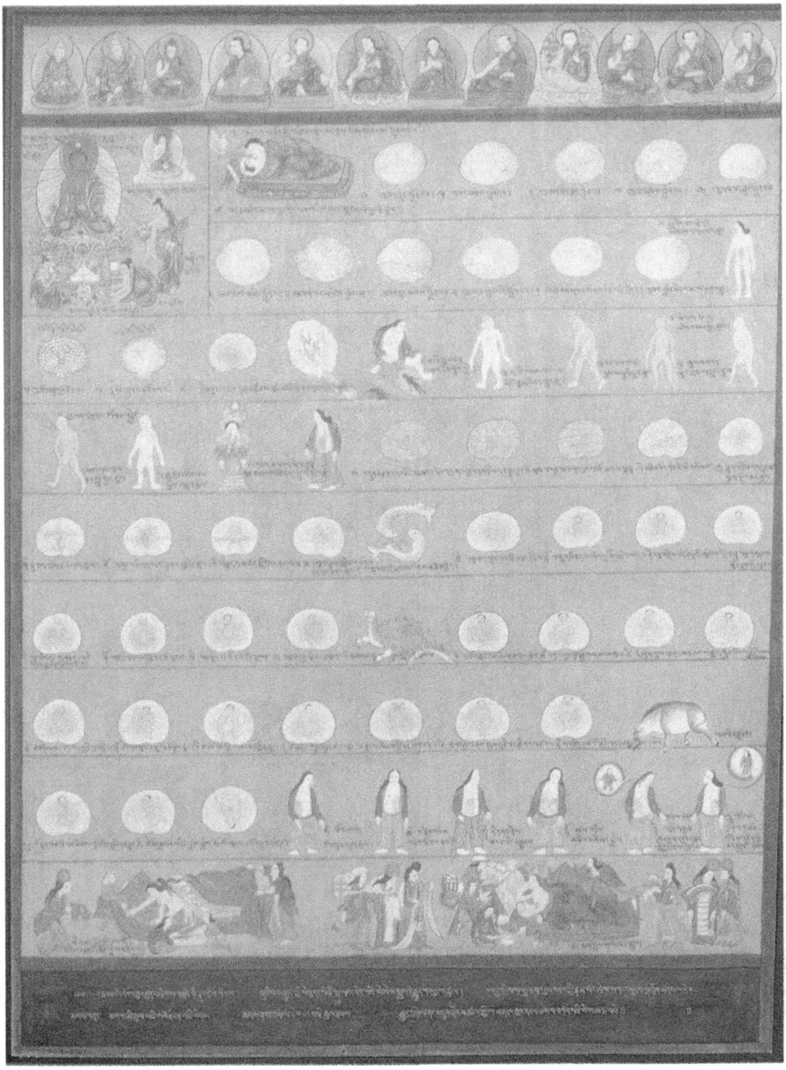

Pl. 3 Fetal development. Courtesy of the Division of Anthropology, American Museum of Natural History, 70.3/5468. Late twentieth century, from the atelier of Romio Shrestha, Kathmandu, Nepal.

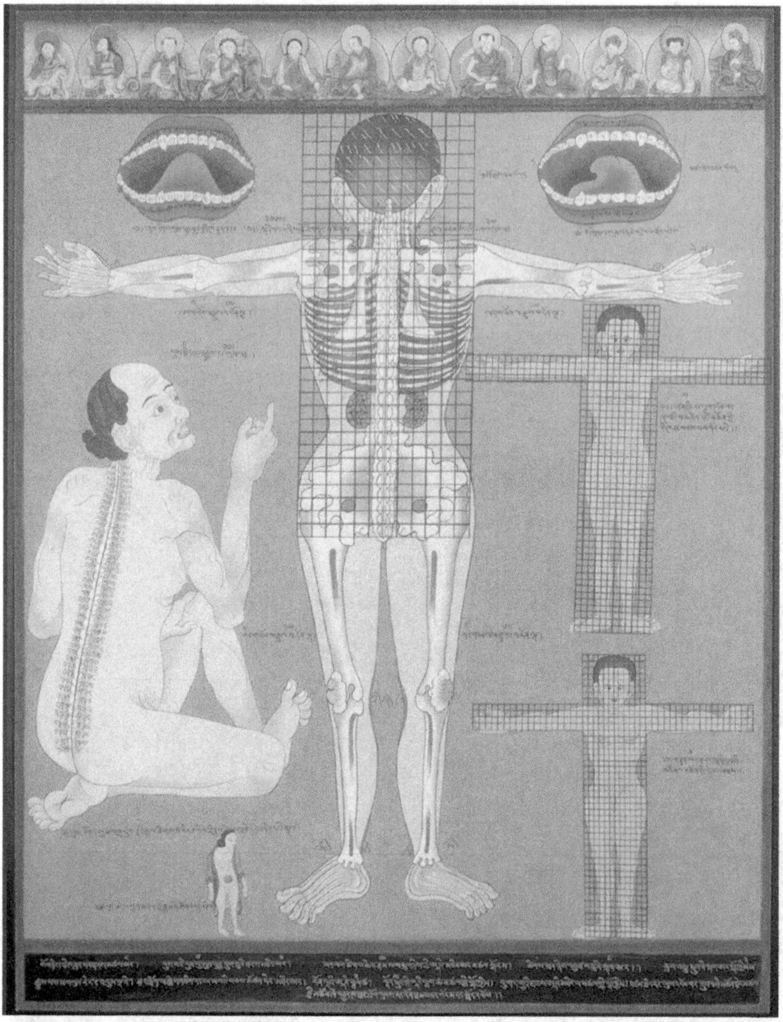

Pl. 4 Woman as medical sidebar. Courtesy of the Division of Anthropology, American Museum of Natural History, 70.3/5471. Late twentieth century, from the atelier of Romio Shrestha, Kathmandu, Nepal.

Pl. 5 Sexuality in medical text. Courtesy of the Division of Anthropology, American Museum of Natural History, 70.3/5483. Late twentieth century, from the atelier of Romio Shrestha, Kathmandu, Nepal.

Pl. 6 Kālacakra in *yab/yum*. Courtesy of the Division of Anthropology, American Museum of Natural History, 70.0/7198.

Pl. 7 Vairocana in *yab/yum*. Courtesy of the Division of Anthropology, American Museum of Natural History, 70.2/3222.

Pl. 8 Tārā in dominant position with her consort, the celestial Buddha Amoghasiddhi. They are surrounded by four other celestial buddhas and their consorts. Western Tibet, fifteenth century. Image #779. Courtesy of the Shelley & Donald Rubin Collection. http://www.himalayanart.org

Pl. 9 The goddess of wealth Vasudhārā with her consort, the god of wealth Jambhala, on her left thigh. Gyantse, Tibet, fifteenth century. Photograph by Franco Ricca.

Pl. 10 Mahāsiddha Virupa with standing barmaid. Tibet, thirteenth century, The Kronos Collections.

Pl. 11 Vajravārāhī with *khaṭvāṅga*. Central Tibet, c. 1200. Courtesy of the Division of Anthropology, American Museum of Natural History, 70.0/6958.

Pl. 12 The celestial Buddha Vairochana flanked by the female celestial bodhisattvas Green Tārā and Vajradhateshvara. Tibet, fourteenth century, Private Collection. Used with permission.

Pl. 13 Woman siddha in *yab/yum*. Courtesy of the Division of Anthropology, American Museum of Natural History, 70.2/3486C.

Pl. 14 Padmasambhava, Yeshe Tsogyel, and Mandāravā on Copper Mountain Heaven. Tibet, late eighteenth to early nineteenth century, The Collection of the Newark Museum, 69.35. Purchase 1969 the Member's Fund.

Pl. 15 Amitābha in Sukhāvatī, Taima Mandara, seventeenth century, Edo period Japan, ink, color, gold on silk, 43.25" × 37". Denver Art Museum Collection, given in honor of Isaac Newton Phelps Stokes by John Davis Hatch, 1971.64. Photography by the Denver Art Museum.

Pl. 16 Rebirth in Lotuses (detail of Plate 15).

and completed around the third century C.E., a date that coincides with the Kushan Dynasty of northern India (c. first to third century C.E.). It will be recalled that during this dynasty Buddhist iconography briefly celebrated male powers of fertility. As mentioned in the chapter on mothers, standing male figures from this period display penises under the folds of their garments, even statues of the Buddha. These statues have a distinct articulation of muscle and strength that express male power. As noted, this articulation of the male form disappeared rather quickly; indeed, male forms become somewhat feminized, or at least lost any suggestion of overt masculinity.

It seems reasonable to assume that given their geographical and temporal proximity, the compilers of the *MSV* were familiar with the Kushan sculptures that emphasized the Buddha's masculinity, which led them to reflect on the issue of the Buddha's sexuality in ways far different from that of other texts. E. Frauwallner has argued that the *MSV* originated in Mathurā,[18] a center of Kushan art, a point contested by scholars such as Étienne Lamotte, who suggested Kashmir, a region also under Kushan rule, as the place of its final redaction.[19] In either case, the visual field created by the Kushan sculptures was still relevant to the compilers of the *MSV*.

The Buddha's penis and its ability to function or not function was a subject of some interest to Buddhists. The textual discussion centers on the thirty-two physical marks of the Buddha, which include a sheathed or hidden penis (*kośopagatavastiguhyo*),[20] in other words, a penis that was not readily discernible.[21] In the context of the Kushan sculptures that do not have a sheathed penis but instead a prominent penis, one sees an interesting collision of the textual and iconographic gaze. As mentioned above in relation to the undoing of Queen Māyā's fertile powers, Dehejia has made the point that early Buddhist texts were written down after the iconography was created and they were meant to explain the art.[22] Beginning as an oral tradition, there was some fluidity in Buddhist storytelling, which endures to this day in the discourses of Buddhist monks at pilgrimage sites and which eventually became the texts we now have. When ancient authors contrasted the many statues of Buddha without a prominent penis with statues of divinities and other male beings that did indicate the penis, some explanation was required. Hence in texts it became a special feature of all buddhas; they have a penis, but one that is sheathed, hidden from view.

Even though the *MSV* added the sheathed penis to the list of the thirty-two marks of a Buddha, its compilers were gazing at the Buddha's prominent penis in Kushan sculpture, which perhaps raised questions in their minds about it and its functioning that led them to place Rāhula's conception, rather than his birth, on the night of the Buddha's departure. The Kushan buddhas bristle with a masculinity reminiscent of the virile semidivine *yakṣa* figures who were deeply associated, as were their female counterparts, the *yakṣīs*, with powers of fecundity. Indeed, the first stone images of the Buddha were modeled on *yakṣas*. It was apparent to the men collecting stories for the *MSV* version of the Buddha's life that any question about his potency was answered by these sculptures. Although at this time there was no textual tradition that described the sex life of the Buddha and his wife, Rāhula's existence indicated that they had had sex at least once, and the final editor of the *MSV* placed that event on the night of the Buddha's departure, which also enabled him to incorporate the wonderful parallel between Yaśodharā's pregnancy and the Buddha's quest for enlightenment. Such an explicit relationship between the Buddha and his wife will not be seen again until the rise of Tantric Buddhism.

TIBET

Conception dreams such as Queen Māyā's are a consistent element in Tibetan sacred biographies, but they do not necessarily negate the biological role of the father. Examples can be found in the biographies of Milarepa (1040–1123), Tsongkhapa (1357–1419), Yeshe Tsogyel, Mandāravā (both eighth century C.E.), and others.[23] In all their cases dreams announced that conception had taken place rather than caused the conception. Two important exceptions are Padmasambhava and the epic hero Gesar. Padmasambhava (eighth-century C.E.) is referred to as the Second Buddha for his role in spreading Buddhism in Tibet, and, like Buddha, he also had a miraculous birth. He is a self-manifested emanation of the celestial Buddha Amitābha. A dream directed King Indrabhūti, Padmasambhava's eventual foster father, to a beautiful lake where he discovered an eight-year-old boy sitting in a lotus. When questioned, the boy claimed to be without a human father or mother and thus he was named *padma* (lotus) *sambhava* (self-born).

Gesar is a greatly admired heroic figure throughout the Tibetan cultural world, and there are many versions of his epic. He is an underdog who rose to become a great warrior and king, roundly defeated neighboring heretical kings and thus spread Buddhism. He also had a miraculous and fatherless birth when his mother conceived by drinking blessed water.[24] Significantly, Gesar's conception begins in heaven as the work of Padmsambhava, assisted by Gesar, who imprinted his image by gazing at himself in the water that was then transported to his mother-to-be on earth.[25] With Padmasambhava's divine assistance, he is his own father in much the same way the self-born Padmasambhava is his own father, a form of impregnation that goes back to the Buddha fathering himself through his mother's dream of an elephant. Just before he is born, Gesar speaks to his mother from within her body, telling her he will not be born in the natural way, but instead will emerge from her head without harming her. An egg then emerges from a white vein at the top of her head, which she wraps up and puts in her waistband. It soon breaks of itself and Gesar is born. This odd birth, like Padmasambhava's, pointedly avoids female pollution and completely negates female biology, and consequently the role of mothers. The fact that it is specifically a white vein, and thus according to medical views, a water vein,[26] a nonblood, nonfemale vein, emphasizes its masculinity. The egg suggests nonhuman birth and also acts as a protective device from the pollution of a woman's body in much the same way as the containers do in the wombs of Buddha's and Tsongkhapa's mothers. Birth from the head further avoids the pollution of the birth canal. Gesar's mother then acted like a hen sitting on her egg, keeping it warm and close to her belly until a chick is born.[27]

The unusual conceptions and births of these two Buddhist heroes had important consequences for Tibetan Buddhism. Both are self-generated and thus fatherless, while Padmasambhava is motherless, and Gesar's birth all but negates the need for a mother. In what follows I argue that these supernatural conceptions and births played into a new understanding of what constitutes a spiritual and specifically all-male lineage.

In general, Tibetan parents and stepparents disappear from the biographies of their children quite early. This is true for Padmasambhava, Milarepa, Tsongkhapa, Yeshe Tsogyel, and Mandāravā, among others. It is as if once the spiritual path is attained, all connection with the past is abandoned, especially biological connections, though spiritual connections, such as with an early guru, are maintained. A notable exception that proves this rule is the biography of Machig Lapdron (1055–1153), whose mother accompanied her on the early stages of the spiritual path. Nonetheless, her mother is not prominent in the biography. Ironically, it is Nangsa's (traditionally eleventh century C.E.) unwanted husband and his family who join her hermitage, not her parents. These biographies are all discussed below.

Milarepa's biography is particularly interesting with regard to parents. His father died while he was a child, leaving him in difficult, unprotected circumstances that included a problematic mother who directed Milarepa to study black magic so she could exact revenge against the relatives who stole his patrimony. She disappears from the biography quite early, but her evil influence lingered, causing Milarepa to collapse his evil uncle's house, killing everyone inside. Milarepa soon repented of his harmful actions and sought a true teacher.

Milarepa did not become a monk; he was instead a wandering yogi who pursued the tantric path to realization. His guru Marpa was essential to his spiritual development, and their relationship is at the heart of the biography. Marpa and his wife Dakmema had dreams the night before Milarepa arrived seeking teachings. Marpa's dream contains masculine imagery: he dreamed of his guru Nāropa and a vajra, the ritual object representing the male aspect of trantric practice. Dakmema dreamed of two *ḍākinīs* carrying a *stūpa*,[28] a womblike receptacle.[29] These dreams establish Dakmema and Marpa as Milarepa's true parents, parents who nurture and give him a new life, a rebirth, through Buddhism. Indeed, Marpa and Milarepa often refer to each other as father and son throughout the biography, while Dakmema and Milarepa refer to each other as mother and son.

In the early days of their relationship Marpa treated Milarepa very harshly and set him the trying task of building a house. Each time Milarepa completed a house, Marpa ordered him to tear it down for one reason or another, only to begin again. This activity is meant to burn off Milarepa's bad karma and make him fit to receive the tantric teachings. At the same time the constant building and tearing down of houses reenacted the destruction of his uncle's house and family and symbolizes the process of building a new family house, the family of Milarepa, Marpa, and Dakmema, whose fruit will be the Kargyud (*bKa rgyud*) lineage passed from Marpa to Milarepa and from Milarepa to his disciples, whom he called sons and who called him father. Milarepa destroyed his biological family through murder and his own celibacy, but then replaced it with a spiritual family.

Robert Paul's discussion of this biography and, indeed, his understanding of hereditary and spiritual lineages is thought provoking in connection with Milarepa's filial relationship with Marpa and Dakmema. Paul sets out the dilemma in the following way: "the doctrines of karma versus descent in Sherpa [Tibetan Buddhists of Nepal] culture express the contradictory view that fathers and sons both are and are not related to each other."[30] His point is that one is physically connected to one's biological family (descent), but karmically driven to incarnate. However, one is also spiritually (karmically) connected to the biological family, and spiritually connected to others outside the biological family unit. Even though the relationship of guru and disciple parallels the relationship of father and son, more significantly, Milarepa in all ways rejected a biological family by surviving the death of his biological parents (the earlier generation), rejecting his planned marriage (any later generations are proscribed), and by establishing himself as the guru of his remaining family: his aunt and sister. In other words, he transformed his biological family into part of his spiritual family. In this process, especially with Milarepa's move to celibacy, one can see a male appropriation of the spiritual path that excludes women (they can be taught but they cannot be teachers), and that elevates "true masculinity to a spiritual rather than a material, conditioned, and sexual state,"[31] leaving the latter three states to women. This is brought out in the tradition of male lineages, to which we now turn.

Male Lineage

Male lineages play an important part in Buddhism from the earliest period and they were soon accompanied by successful efforts to undermine the order of nuns.[32] In both texts and iconography, there is a celebration and articulation of buddhas of the past,[33] none of whom were women, and of male celestial buddhas. Additionally, monks are well represented in the Buddha's biographies and its iconography, while nuns are not, and the attentive reader will have noticed the absence of any discussion of daughters[34] and the consequent emphasis on sons. The almost complete exclusion of women in spiritual lineages can be seen as a logical development from their virtual exclusion in physical kinship lineages. As was shown in the medical literature, women are the field for male patrilineal descent. A woman's contribution is considered dominant when it produces a daughter rather than a son because her blood is deemed to have been stronger than her male partner's semen. But daughters do not have a very enduring part in patrilineal descent systems after they carry and deliver their fetuses, so patrilineal spiritual descent systems, which negate the need for sexual reproduction, can and do follow social and scientific thinking and completely negate any need for women. The absence of women is supported by the low social status of women, the belief in their polluted nature, the medical discourse on their contribution to the fetus, and by systematically undercutting female spiritual authority as represented by nuns.

Male spiritual lineages are of two kinds. First, there is the lineage of guru/disciple transmission, the passing on of esoteric spiritual teachings from one individual to another. Women quite rarely participate in this.[35] A second male lineage is the *tulku* (*sprul sku*) system, meaning the emanation body and signifying the incarnation of a divine being or the self-controlled reincarnation of highly advanced human beings.[36] The best-known example is that of the Dalai Lamas, who are believed to be incarnations of the celestial bodhisattva Avalokiteśvara, and who choose to continue to reincarnate as future Dalai Lamas. The belief in *tulku*s is based on the Buddhist ideal of the bodhisattva, enlightened beings who postpone achieving *nirvāṇa* in order to assist other beings by continuing to reincarnate. While precedents for the beliefs in *tulku*s can be found earlier in Indian Buddhism, its origins are generally ascribed to the Karmapa lineage beginning in the late twelfth century with the death of the first Karmapa.[37] Writing in the 1970s, Barbara Aziz estimated there were about two hundred living tulkus.[38] While a few of these were female tulkus, such as the abbess of Samding, this is a male institution. The chances of a highly evolved male incarnating as a female are nil.

Both types of male-only lineages take reproduction out of the physical realm and place it in the spiritual; the first by displacing reproduction onto the transmission of knowledge from male to male (master to disciple), and the second by emphasizing the male ability to continually reincarnate in the same monastic office, if not as exactly the same person. One is succession and perpetuation by the transmission of spiritual power (*dbang*) and the other succession by reincarnation. Both types of male lineages are strengthened, indeed held together, by the absence of women as productive agents and by emphasizing female powers of pollution.[39] As will be discussed in the chapters on tantric consorts, monastic tantric ritual sexuality is supposed to be a visualization (referred to as right-handed practice), rather than an actual sexual engagement with a woman (left-handed practice), because more than simply rejecting sex with a woman, they are co-opting procreative sexuality; and their product, that which they reproduce, is male-only lineages.

Robert Paul has a revealing discussion of the terms used for spiritual lineages, which are the same terms used for groups related by biological descent: *brgyud, rigs*, and *rabs*.[40] He states that:

> In both cases there is an apical ancestor, in one system an original sire, in the other a founding lama, from whom a direct line of descent across generations is traced. In the case of religious lineages, the ancestor is a lama who originates some innovation in ritual, liturgy, or doctrine, or who rises to great spiritual heights. While he himself is in some sense self-originating, he passes his new doctrine intact along with the essence of his spiritual power through

> disciples whose aim it is to reproduce exactly in each generation what the master taught.[41]

Historically, this goes back to the father/son relationship between a senior and a junior monk in which a novice shared his cell with a senior monk who acted as his mentor. Additionally, the similar physical appearance of the nuns and monks with their shaved heads and matching, shapeless robes were designed to obscure gender, which allowed monks to assume more feminine characteristics. Indeed, feminine characteristics such as gentleness, compassion, shyness, slenderness, submissiveness, and reticence were the monastic models for men and women. This is coupled with the feminization of male buddhas and bodhisattvas in iconography, while the curvaceous female figure continued from ancient times to the present.

Several processes are at work here. In biological reproduction Buddhist medical theory diminishes the role of women in order to emphasize patrilineal descent and patrilineal ancestors. In spiritual reproduction women are similarly marginalized through exclusion, beginning with the lower status of female religious experts, such as nuns and female yogis, and their general lack of access to advanced teachings. Finally, in Buddhist iconography male buddhas, bodhisattvas, and monks are feminized. In other words, there is a co-optation of feminine attributes, including those of reproduction, accompanied by the rejection of actual women. This movement offers some resolution for the problem of male reproductive power by spiritualizing it, sublimating it, or at least disguising it through feminine attributes.

Male-only lineages allow Buddhism to reproduce itself through the trivialization of women's reproductive abilities, the exaggeration of female pollution, and the portrayal of women as sexual threats to celibate males. The result is a childlike avoidance of the actual politics of sexuality and of the gendered society that maintains celibate males in their pristine state, ironically a state authored by a spiritual rhetoric that denies the relevance of gender. Paul aptly sums up the situation:

> The reincarnate lama, then, represents the living proof of the legitimacy of the monks' claim to the possibility of asexual reproduction, the eternal dream of the male sex. He represents immortality not of the species but of the individual. In quite a literal sense, he is the monastery's "baby," the assertion of their ability to create a self-sufficient male world and thus obviate the need for the divisive presence of women.
>
> Skeptics may object that even a reincarnate lama is, after all, born of a woman. But, as I argued earlier, symbolism can only reduce or conceal, not eliminate, the real paradoxes of existence. The

> reincarnate comes as close as humanly possible to being self-generating, immortal, and asexual. . . .[42]

True masculinity is thus defined as an eternal spirituality detached from the material world but in control of fertility, a fertility wrested from women, and devoid of women, who are relegated to the non-spiritual, the material, the polluted, and the temporal.

NOTES

1. This is the general topic of Paul, *Tibetan Symbolic World*, passim. See also Cabezón, "Mother Wisdom, Father Love," passim.
2. Such images appear in Gandhara, Amaravātī, and Ajanta, among other sites.
3. This dream and additional sources on it are discussed in Young, *Dreaming in the Lotus*, 21–24.
4. *NK*, Fausboll, I.50.
5. *MV*, Senart, I.145–146, II.5–6.
6. Bays, *Voice*, 48.
7. For example, *BC* II.46 and *NK*, 169.
8. Bays, *Voice*, 213.
9. In addition to the *BC*, this story is contained in the *NK*, 215–24. It is depicted at Sanchi, among other places.
10. *Ten Suttas from Dīgha Nikāya, Siṅgāla Sutta* (Sarnath: Central Institute of Higher Tibetan Studies: 1987), 267, 442.
11. Ibid., 267, 441–42.
12. Faure, *Red Thread*, 24.
13. Cohen discusses the *MSV*'s presentation of the Buddha as a father to Rāhula and to Buddhist monks, "Kinsmen of the Son," 4–31.
14. *Vinaya Piṭaka*, ed. Oldenberg, Hermann (1879. London: Pali Text Society, 1969), I.45; trans. by Horner in *The Book of Discipline*, 4:58–59. Cohen takes a very original and informative approach to the use of kinship terms among the Buddhist laity and monastics; "Kinsemen of the Son," passim.
15. Rhys Davids, *Buddhist Birth Stories*, 227.
16. Paul refers to a Tibetan drama based on this *jātaka* as "perhaps the most popular of all Tibetan plays," *Tibetan Symbolic World*, 198. An English translation is available in Marion H. Duncan, *More Harvest Festival Dramas of Tibet* (London: The Mitre Press, 1967), 63–123.
17. See Margaret Cone and Richard Gombrich, *The Perfect Generosity of Prince Vessantara: A Buddhist Epic* (Oxford: Oxford University Press, 1977), xxxv–xliv, for the diffusion of this story and 109–110 for a list of versions in other languages; see xxxv–xxxvii for some of its iconographic representations.
18. E. Frauwallner, *The Earliest Vinaya and the Beginnings of Buddhist Literature* (Roma: Is. M.E. O., 1956), 37.
19. Lamotte, *History of Indian Buddhism*, 178.
20. Desai lists them in, but does not cite, the *Mahayana Sutralamkaras, Kalinga Bodhi Jataka, LV* and *Chitrasutra*, "The History and Historiography of Male Sexuality," 52. In an appendix to their translation of the *Dharmasaṁgrahaḥ (Excellent Collection of Doctrine) of Ācārya Nāgārjuna*, Tashi Zangmo and Dechen Chime quote the lists in Sanskrit, Tibetan, and English, but do not cite, from the *LV, Arthaviniścayasūtram, Bodhisattvabhūmi, Abhisamayālaṅkārālokah*, and *Mahāvyupattih* (Sarnath, Varanasi: Central Institute of Higher

Tibetan Studies: 1993), 95–109. See also E. Waldschmidt, *Mahāvadānasūtra*, 101ff.

They are listed in the *LV*, Vaidya, 105.21 and 429.20; *MSV*, I.49; and *MV*, Senart, II.305.10, among other biographical texts.

21. Faure tells some interesting stories about the Buddha's penis, unfortunately without citation, but presumably from East Asian sources, *Red Thread*, 60.
22. Lecture, Columbia University, October 7, 2002.
23. See Young, *Dreaming in the Lotus*, 75–85.
24. Paul discusses this and another version of Gesar's conception through a rain of hail, *Tibetan Symbolic World*, 246–51.
25. Alexandra David-Neel and Lama Yongden, *The Superhuman Life of Gesar of Ling* (Boston, MA: Shambhala, 1987), 71–72.
26. Aris, *Tibetan Medical Paintings*, 41.
27. David-Neel and Yongden, *Gesar*, 76–77.
28. Gtsaṅ smyon He ru ka, *Mi la ras pa'i rnam thar*, ed. J. W. de Jong, ('s-Gravenhage: Mouton, 1959), 53.13–54.9, translated by Lobsang P. Lhalungpa as *The Life of Milarepa* (Boulder, CO: Shambhala, 1984), 43–44. These dreams are discussed in Young, *Dreaming in the Lotus*, 81–85.
29. See Snodgrass, *The Symbolism of the Stupa*, 189, for a brief discussion of womb symbolism in *stūpas*, and Young, *Dreaming in the Lotus*, 83, and herein, chapter 2.
30. Paul, *Tibetan Symbolic World*, 29.
31. Paul makes this point in a different context, ibid., 148.
32. See, for example, Nancy Auer Falk, "The Case of the Vanishing Nuns: The Fruits of Ambivalence in Ancient Indian Buddhism," in Nancy Auer Falk and Rita M. Gross, eds., *Unspoken Worlds: Women's Religious Lives* (San Francisco, CA: Harper & Row, Publishers, 1980), 207–24.
33. For example, all the gates at Sanchi are topped by images of seven buddhas of the past and the trees under which they liberated.
34. Horner has a short chapter on daughters, *Women Under Primitive Buddhism*.
35. Some exceptions are contained in Taranatha, *Seven Lineage*, discussed in chapter 8 herein.
36. Samuel has a good discussion of the complexities of this system, *Civilized Shamans*, 281–86 and 493–98.
37. Nik Douglas and Meryl White, *Karmapa: The Black Hat Lama of Tibet* (London: Luzac & Company, 1976), passim. See also Samuel, *Civilized Shamans*, 493–98.
38. Barbara Aziz, "Reincarnation Reconsidered: Or the Reincarnate Lama as Shaman," in *Spirit Possession in the Nepal Himalayas*, ed. John T. Hitchcock and Rex L. Jones (1976. New Delhi: Vikas Publishing House Pvt Ltd, 1996), 346. Franz Michael says at the turn of the twentieth century there were more than 10,000 such incarnations in Tibet. *Rule by Incarnation: Tibetan Buddhism and Its Role in Society and Sate* (Boulder, CO: Westview Press, 1982), 43. An accessible collection of the multiple lives of one *tulku* is Karma Thinley, *The History of the Sixteen Karmapas of Tibet* (Boulder, CO: *Prajñā*, 1980). Michael Aris has written an important study of the flaws in the *tulku* system, *Hidden Treasures and Secret Lives: A Study of Pemalingpa (1450–1521) and the Sixth Dalai Lama (1683–1706)* (Shimla: Indian Institute of Advanced Study, 1988). See also Campbell's critique of the system, though it is a perspective very influenced by Robert Paul's work; *Traveller in Space*, chapters 4 and 5.
39. I am influenced in this discussion by Rey Chow's essay "Male Narcissism and National Culture: Subjectivity in Chen Kaige's *King of the Children*," especially 106–114, and by Constance Penley's and Sharon Willis's discussion

of this article in their Introduction to *Male Trouble* (Minneapolis: University of Minnesota Press, 1993), xi.

40. Paul, *Tibetan Symbolical World*, 30–31.
41. Ibid., 30.
42. Ibid., 96.

PART III

Sexualities

CHAPTER 5

WIVES AND HUSBANDS[1]

Despite the great emphasis placed on monasticism, the very first followers of the Buddha were lay people. As we have seen, a lay woman, Sujātā, made the first food offerings to the Buddha, which gave him the strength to attain enlightenment and which sustained him for seven weeks thereafter until he received food offerings from two laymen, Tapassu and Bhallika.[2] Many more people soon became lay followers of the Buddha, while others became nuns or monks, and rules of conduct were established for both groups. Early basic precepts for the laity required them to refrain from killing, stealing, lying, drinking liquor, or misconduct in sexual activity. Commentaries, which were written from the male perspective, explain that misconduct in sexual activity means a man cannot have intercourse with a forbidden woman, such as: "The wife of another, a woman under the care of a guardian, a betrothed woman, a nun, a woman under a vow of celibacy."[3] Relevant to the discussion of courtesans that follows this chapter, courtesans are not in the category of forbidden women unless they are engaged to be married. So early Buddhism defined laymen as independent agents who do not break precepts when they have sex with their wives, prostitutes, or any woman not defined by her relationship with another man or under a religious vow. During his life as a householder the Buddha was represented as having had sexual access to many women, which made it rather difficult for later Buddhists to uphold monogamy, as this would suggest the Buddha's behavior had been incorrect. Additional precepts say men cannot have intercourse with their wives "by a 'forbidden passage' (the anus), in an unsuitable place (that is, a public place or a shrine), or at an unsuitable time (that is, when she is pregnant, is nursing, or has taken a vow of abstinence.)"[4] Other sources include fellatio and cunnilingus as forbidden passages.[5]

The vast majority of women are not understood to be independent agents, and their sexual partners are much more limited. Again, they are defined from the male point of view, so rather than saying unmarried women living with their parents cannot have sex, or that married women can only have sex with their husbands, it says all men are forbidden sexual access to unmarried women living with their natal families, and all men but her husband are forbidden sexual access to the married woman. Only one category of women is relatively unconstrained in her choice of male sexual partners; an unmarried woman living independently—the only men forbidden to her are those observing religious vows of celibacy.[6] Such women were rare in ancient India. The only examples that come to mind are prostitutes, courtesans, and destitute women. These precepts are obviously ideals dictated by monks and do not encapsulate practice. Most notably neither lesbianism nor homosexuality is mentioned, activities railed against in the *Vinaya*. Nor are class and caste factored in despite evidence that lower caste women had more sexual license, whether by choice, necessity, or coersion. The text does demonstrate that early Buddhism maintained the prevailing double standards of Indian society for women and men, and must have assumed, rather than stated, other sexual rules, such as no sex during certain holy days or while a woman is menstruating.[7] The rule against having sex with menstruating women is stated in Sangye Gyamtso's commentary on the Tibetan medical text, the *rGyud bZhi*, discussed in chapter 3, along with prohibitions against sex with a married woman, an unpleasant woman (*mi sdug pa*), a pregnant woman, or a woman who is weak and panged by hunger (Plate 5, row 3, images 2–6, the last being a menstruating woman). It states further that one should not have sex in front of a sacred image, in broad daylight, with an animal, or with a woman other than one's own wife (Plate 5, row 5, images 8 and 9; row 3, image 1; row 6, images 1 and 2).[8] Thus, Tibetan Buddhism significantly narrows the earlier field of sexually available women, which may have been a reaction to more relaxed sexual habits. Research among contemporary Tibetan groups indicate much looser codes of behavior that in all likelihood are consistent with earlier practices.[9] Note that the painting used to illustrate these precepts (Plate 5) depicts the missionary position. The reluctance to portray women in dominant sexual positions will be discussed further in the chapters on tantric consorts.

Along with sexual practices current at the time of the Buddha, Buddhists also followed the prevailing norm that wives and children were the property of the male head of household, who could dispose of them as he chose. We will see an example of this shortly in a past life story of the Buddha as Prince Vessantara, who actually gave away his wife and children.

Buddhism never defined marriage, preferring instead to accept whatever forms of marriage it met with as it spread through various Asian societies, among them monogamy, polyandry, and polygamy. Nor did it ever condemn concubinage or prostitution, though as we shall see, it did condemn individual prostitutes—but not their clients. The Buddhist attitude toward marriage is best summed up by the fact that Buddhist monastics never officiated at marriages until fairly recently.[10] But perhaps most important, in his own life the Buddha deserted his wife and child. Significantly, the Buddhist ordination ceremony reenacts the Buddha's departure from home, his abandonment of lay life. Once clear of his father's palace, the Buddha cut off his hair, changed into the clothes of an ascetic, and took up a begging bowl. To this day, the Buddhist ordination ceremony involves shaving the candidates' heads, dressing them in monastic robes, and giving them a begging bowl. Buddhists get around the denigration of marriage and the family by distinguishing two groups within the Buddhist community, monastics and lay people, and giving them separate rules of conduct. Ideally, monastics are celibate, but the laity is not, and therefore guidelines for sexually active Buddhists had to be established. Inevitably, these rules were shaped by the customs of whatever culture Buddhists missionized.

As we saw in the discussion of parents, the *Siṅgāla Sutta* is a moral guide for the laity, defining the ideal relationship between parent and child. It also contains a description of five reciprocal ways a wife and a husband should minister to each other. The wife: (1) "should perform all her duties well; (2) be hospitable to the kin of both; (3) be faithful to her husband; (4) watch over the goods he brings; and (5) be skillful and industrious in discharging all her tasks."[11] In turn, a husband should minister to his wife in the following five ways: (1) "by praising her and upholding the relationship; (2) by not looking down on her; (3) by not being unfaithful; (4) by letting her be in charge of the home and family; (5) by giving her clothing and presents." This ideal view of the marital relationship is presented as one of mutual dependence and responsibility and mutual sexual fidelity.

The *Siṅgāla Sutta* is concerned with maintaining harmonious relationships, and it establishes both rights and obligations for individuals on a fairly even basis. In reality, though, a wife's life was not easy.

The nun Isidāsī had three unhappy marriages before joining the order. She describes the first as follows:

My salutation morn and eve I brought
To both the parents of my husband, low
Bowing my head and kneeling at their feet,
According to the training given me.
My husband's sisters and his brothers too,
And all his kin, scarce were they entered when
I rose in timid zeal and gave them place.
And as to food, or boiled or dried, and drink,
That which was to be stored I set aside,
And served it out and gave to whom twas due.
Rising betimes, I went about the house,
Then with my hands and feet well cleansed I went
To bring respectful greeting to my lord,
And taking comb and mirror, unguents, soap,
I dressed and groomed him as a handmaid might.
I boiled the rice, I washed the pots and pans;
And as a mother on her only child,
So did I minister to my good man.
For me, who with toil infinite thus worked,
And rendered service with a humble mind,
Rose early, ever diligent and good,
For me he nothing felt save sore dislike.
Nay, to his mother and his father he
Thus spake: "Give me leave and I will go,
For not with Isidāsī will I live
Beneath one roof, nor ever dwell with her."[12]

Wrenched from her own natal family, the bride had to please everyone in her husband's family. As Isidāsī's story shows, power resided with the husband. And, despite the *Siṅgāla Sutta*'s description of how a Buddhist should treat his parents, children, and wife, in his own life the Buddha did not fulfill his obligations to his father, his son, or his wife. He deserted them all as part of his rejection of worldly life in favor of the ascetic life, and most of the sixty men who joined the order of monks in the first few months of its existence also deserted wives and families.[13] Of course, all this occurred long before the Buddha was credited with establishing a Buddhist code of behavior for monastics and the laity. Even so, he did breach prevailing brahmanical social codes in that a man was not supposed to retire into the forest until his son was grown and married with a son of his own. The biographies of the Buddha are caught between Buddhism's attempt to reconcile itself with lay life and maintain its emphasis on celibate monasticism, and the Buddha's initial rejection of women.

The Buddha's wife is described as having been an exemplary woman, one who fulfilled all her wifely obligations, especially that of having given birth to a son. Of course, this is meant to show the strength of the Buddha's resolve to pursue the spiritual life—leaving a plain, barren, and unpleasant woman would have been too easy. Yet, as we shall see, their relationship, which extended over many lifetimes, remains a model for married life. Most tellingly, men who wished to become monks could and did leave their wives, while wives were required to have the permission of their husband and/or their parents before they could become nuns.[14] The *Vinaya* records that the Buddha was accused of destroying families and making widows.[15] The prelude to *jātaka* no. 485 says the Buddha's wife lived like a widow while he practiced asceticism, for which the Buddha praised her, saying she should continue to love him, be faithful to him, and be led by him.

There are many tales of wives trying to tempt their monk-husbands to come back home[16] that have been presented as a sign of women as sexually threatening. Such stories are better understood as a reasonable response on the part of women to end their ambiguous status as pseudowidows. Being a wife completely defined a woman's life in ways being a husband did not, and being a widow, but not a widower, was considered so inauspicious that Buddhist women deserted by their husbands were left in a highly questionable and vulnerable state. Tear back the veil of male hubris that clouds tales of women's seductive power and you will see women fighting for their lives through the only means available to them. Without a husband a woman was nothing; she was blamed by his family for not keeping him at home, and due to her possible inauspiciousness she was excluded from the round of celebratory events that make up family life. Knowing the hardships of life as a Buddhist monk, any thoughtful woman would have given her husband enough time to miss the comforts of home life before she made a personal appeal to him to return, often bringing their young son along to strengthen her position. Indeed, even the Buddha's wife attempts to win him back by sending their son Rāhula to him.[17] The Buddhist texts are perfectly silent about the lives of such deserted women, except for those instances when they mustered the courage to approach their monk-husbands. Their lives can be imagined, however, from what we do know about the lives of non-Buddhist Indian widows.

The *Therāgāthā* commentary specifically mentions several men who left their wives, mostly after they had given birth to a son (viii, x, xviii, xxxiv, cxciv, cliv, clxxxix, cxlvi, ccxxiii), though certainly there were many more abandoned wives than this, given that marriages were arranged by parents while their children were quite young. Several of these stories portray the wives trying to convince their husbands to come back home. *Jātaka* tales on this topic are said to have been told in response to visits by or longing for former wives. These past-life stories feature men escaping the snares of women (No. 423) or being destroyed by women (Nos. 13, 318) or simply succumbing to them (No. 526), and they are all suggestive of women's potential to have more power than men, something that was unthinkable.

A successful seduction of a monk by his former wife is preserved in the *Vinaya*,[18] and it reveals some details about the life of a deserted wife. After Sudinna became a monk, his wife continued to live with his parents. At their instigation and with their planning she went into the forest to ask her former husband to give her a child so that the family's considerable estate would not revert to the state. Neither her wishes in the matter, nor her name, are ever revealed. As is so often the case, the female seductress acts at the behest of those who control her life. Sudinna acquiesces, and the wife becomes pregnant. The wife's story does not end here, for the text adds that she gave birth to a boy and later both she and her son entered the order and became arhats. This suggests that she may have sincerely wanted to become a Buddhist nun all along, but had been held back by Sudinna's parents because they wanted a grandchild. Of course, she was then held back by her infant son, but eventually got her way. Viewed from a woman's perspective, this hardly reads like the actions of a heartless seductress.

The first abandoned wife in Buddhism is the Buddha's, to whom we now turn.

THE WIVES OF THE BUDDHA

The biographies of the Buddha give him variously one, two or three wives, and call them by different names, such as Gopā in the *LV*,[19] Yaśodharā in the *BC* and *MV*, and simply "the mother of Rāhula" in the *NK*. The *Abhiniṣkramaṇasūtra*, hereinafter the AS, has two wives, Yaśodharā and Gotamī,[20] and the *MSV* three, Yaśodharā, Gopā, and Mṛgajā. Where there is more than one wife, Yaśodharā seems to be the chief wife in that she is the one who had premonitory dreams about the Buddha's abandoning her,[21] though Gopā, being the only wife in the *LV*, has similar dreams. In what follows it will be easier to think of Yaśodharā and Gopā as the same person, which indeed she is—the Buddha's wife. Multiple wives were the privilege of the wealthy, and the Buddha's father is said to have been married both to Māyā and her sister, Mahāprajāpatī.[22]

Name variations aside, she is consistently if somewhat contradictorily described as unique among women, yet she is deeply enmeshed in the negative pull of all the women in the Buddha's household. For example, the *LV* makes it plain that she is part of the entanglements meant to keep the Buddha in the world. When his marriage is being planned by the Śākya elders, they say: "once he is married and surrounded by women, he will know such pleasure that he will not leave his family."[23] The Buddha's wife and the harem women are parallel figures in terms of their beauty and sexuality, which are represented as negative and controlling elements in the Buddha's life.

Initially, the Buddha agreed to marry when he reflected that all previous bodhisattvas had married and had a son, and he made a list of the virtues his future wife must have. This daunting list represents the ideal virtues of the Hindu wife. The first few lines read:

> "May she be in the flower of youth and beauty,
> and yet without pride.
> May she act with benevolent spirit like a mother or a sister.
> Accustomed to giving gifts to ascetics and brahmans,
> may she take pleasure in renunciation."[24]

The consistent virtue in the full list is the absence of pride, which is mentioned four times. Upon hearing this list of virtues Gopā did, however, speak up to say that she possessed all of them.[25]

Their courtship involved a series of tests that add dimension to their individual characters. When the Buddha hands out jewelry to all the young women at court, Gopā does not take any. For his part, the Buddha must prove himself in the manly arts by winning her in a tournament.[26] As it is a Buddhist text, no living beings can be harmed, and the tournament included skills such as writing and mathematics, as well as physical sports such as jumping, swimming, running, wrestling, and archery.[27] Once they are married, Gopā is criticized for being seen unveiled. She successfully defended herself in a long speech in which she argued that virtue does not need a veil.[28] Indian heroines are often quite high spirited and they speak out, especially about womanly virtues.[29] In both the *LV* and the *BC* the Buddha's wife is given long and passionate speeches. She is a crucial figure in the biographies because the Buddha's eventual desertion of her went completely against prevailing notions of morality, or *dharma*. The texts worked hard to justify this dereliction of duty, especially the *BC*, which contains long exchanges between the Buddha and various people on the subject of his departure from home (IX and X). In it

Yaśodharā makes an impassioned speech emphasizing that his duty, his dharma, is to stay with her or at least to take her into the forest with him as other great sages have done (VIII.60–68).

All the biographies refer to the Buddha's wife as being devastated by his abandonment. In the *LV*, when Gopā learns of his departure she vows to live as an ascetic,[30] and in a very moving scene, she embraces the neck of the Buddha's horse and sings a three-page lament, which concludes with her wish for his enlightenment.[31] Chandaka, the servant who helped the Buddha to leave home, attempts to console her and he predicts that because she served the Buddha she in turn will become a buddha herself.[32] In this part of the text Gopā is drawn with sympathy and is promised the ultimate accomplishment of Buddhism, to be enlightened.

The wife of the Buddha must be unique, but still she is female, and therefore problematic. Any tradition that emphasizes celibacy will have problems with the founder's wife and this is the case in Buddhism. Most of the texts responded to this problem by spiritualizing the Buddha's marriage, by having him marry "only in order to conform to social custom, as he is free from passion."[33] None of the biographies actually dwell on the Buddha's marriage, rather they are focused on his abandonment of family life. An exception is the *MSV*, which has the Buddha reflect that some people might interpret his abandonment of wives and harem women as a sign of impotence, so he made love to Yaśodharā on the night he left home, impregnating her with Rāhula.[34] This is in contrast to other biographies, which have her give birth to Rāhula on the day of the Buddha's departure. As mentioned in the chapter on fathers, the *MSV* originated in northern India where it may have been influenced by the explicitness of Kushan art, which depicted the Buddha as a virile man with a prominent penis.

Even though she is pregnant, like Gopā in the *LV*, in the *MSV* Yaśodharā practices an asceticism that parallels that of the Buddha: "She too began to eat meals of one sesame seed, one grain of rice, one jujube, one pulse pod, one bean, and she slept on a bed of straw."[35] During the six years the Buddha was away seeking enlightenment, Yaśodharā not only did the same things he did, but she continued to carry his child, the seed of his decision to abandon home and family life. And, in the *MSV*, on the night he achieved enlightenment she delivered Rāhula.[36] Surely here is an eloquent image of the powerful productivity of an auspicious female, as Yaśodharā's prolonged pregnancy resonates with the power of the Buddha's withheld male fertility; eventually, he gives birth to enlightenment and she to a son. In the *MSV*, her pregnancy, the evidence of her powerful female fertility, does not simply parallel the Buddha's asceticism, it actively sustains him in his efforts. The later Tantric tradition goes further when it bases the Buddha's achievement of enlightenment on their sexual relationship:

> Along with Gopā, he [the Buddha] experienced bliss.
> By uniting the diamond scepter [penis] and lotus [vagina],
> He attained the fruit of bliss.
> Buddhahood is obtained from bliss, and
> Apart from women there will not be bliss.[37]

The profound cojoining of their lives brought out by the *MSV* stretches back, deep into the past, to the many past lives they shared.

Jātaka *Wives*

The biographies of previous buddhas create a background for the life of the Buddha, such as his decision to marry because this is what past bodhisattvas, men who eventually became buddhas, have done. The Buddha's wife is part of this past. The Pali *jātaka*s alone contain more than five hundred tales about past lives of the Buddha, during which he is said to have migrated through time with the same people, such as his faithful disciple Ānanda, his enemy Devadatta, and his wife.

In order to became a buddha, one first has to meet a buddha before whom one makes the vow to pursue the path to buddhahood through as many lifetimes as it may take. The historical Buddha, Śakyamuni, did this eons ago in the presence of the Buddha Dipaṃkara. In this life the Buddha was a learned young brahman called Sumati, who won several prizes, including a young woman. Being celibate, he refused to keep the woman, who moved to another city. Here they soon meet again when the Buddha Dipaṃkara visits her city. As it is customary to make an offering of flowers to a guru, the king had bought up all the flowers in the city and surrounding areas. When the woman tried to buy flowers for her offering to Dipaṃkara, a flower seller said he did not have any left. She told him to go back to the lotus pond, where, because of her merit, seven blue lotuses, the rarest flowers, appeared. In order not to offend the king she hid them in a pot of water and later carried them into the city where she once again met Sumati. As she had such merit, the lotuses miraculously rose up out of the pot and Sumati asked for some for his offering to Dipaṃkara. She answers that she will give him five lotuses (keeping two for her own offering), if, when he offers them, he will make the earnest wish to have her as his wife in all his future lives, to which he agrees. Together they go to see Dipaṃkara, but the crowd is so great they cannot get near him. Dipaṃkara senses this and causes a tumultuous rainstorm that disperses the crowd. They are then able to approach him and make their offerings. Sumati bows before him, spreading out his long hair, and asks Dipaṃkara to confirm his vow to become a Buddha by putting his feet on the hair. Dipaṃkara does so, and Sumati rises in the air to a great height, whereupon his hair falls out and is replaced by even better hair. When she makes her offering, the woman vows to become Sumati's wife in all future lives.[38]

Needless to say, this story contains abundant fertility symbols and sexual images, not the least of which is the turning around of Sumati's celibacy by his acceptance of a wife, even if it is in the future, a scenario made explicit by Sumati's miraculous loss of his long ascetic's locks and their restoration with even better hair. Hair is almost universally equated with virility,[39] and this better hair represents his acceptance of sexuality. It is a scene that parallels the Buddha's acceptance of food from Sujātā before he walked to the tree of enlightenment. Lotuses, like most flowers, are frequently symbols for wombs. This symbolism is heightened by putting the lotuses in a pot, another symbol for the womb, and having it filled with water signifying embryonic fluid. The offering, though, is enlightenment, also symbolized by the lotus. As in his life as Śakyamuni, Sumati has rejected women, but had to reconcile with them before he could make this all-important vow, the first step that will lead to his eventual enlightenment. His rejection of a desirable woman is shown to be a mistake, so much so that Dipaṃkara himself creates the rainstorm that allows them both to approach him and to make the vows that will connect them throughout the centuries to come. Rain, of course, is fraught with sexual meaning, especially in terms of desire and its release, a theme emphasized in Indian poetic conventions and in Indian beliefs that connect rain and semen.

So while Yaśodharā is rarely represented in iconography,[40] she is evoked through the frequent depictions of the Buddha as Sumati, shown spreading his hair before Dipaṃkara with the woman who vowed to become his wife standing to the side holding her pot of lotuses.[41] She is also represented in any depictions of Buddha's lives that contained a wife, most notably in the exceedingly popular depictions of the Buddha's penultimate past life as Prince Vessantara when she was his wife Maddi, which will be discussed shortly.

Dreams of Buddha's Wives

In an earlier work I explored the meaning of dreams in Buddhist biographies, beginning with those of the Buddha.[42] I found there was a consistent pattern of dismissing women's dreams that suggested some anxiety about women who used dreams to intuit men's intentions. Although the texts privilege this voice—women's oracular speech is the only female speech that broke free of convention—their prophetic words are inevitably ignored or manipulated by the men around them.[43] For instance, on the night that the Buddha left her, Gopā was awakened by a nightmare. The beginning of her very long dream in the *LV* is as follows:

> While Gopā and the prince are sleeping, in a dream at midnight she sees the whole earth, including oceans and mountain peaks, shaken, and trees broken by the wind. The sun, moon, and stars fall from the sky.
>
> She sees her hair cut off by her left hand and her crown fallen. Then her hands and feet are cut off, and she is naked, her pearl necklaces and her jewels broken and strewn about.[44]

The Buddha interpreted this dream, in part, by saying:

> Be joyful, these dreams are not evil. Beings who have previously practiced good works [*kṛtapuṇyapūrvacaritā*] have such dreams. Miserable people have no such dreams.
>
> Seeing the earth shaken, and the mountain peaks fallen to earth [means that] the gods, the *nāgas*, the *rākṣasas*, and the *bhutas* will render you the greatest homage.
>
> Seeing trees uprooted, and your hair cut off with your left hand [means that] soon you will cut the nets of the passions and you will remove the veil of false views that obscures the conditioned world.
>
> Seeing the sun, moon, stars and planets fallen [means that] soon, having conquered the passions, you will be praised and honored. . . .
>
> Be joyful and not sad; be content and satisfied. Soon you will be delighted and content. Be patient, Gopā; the omens are auspicious.[45]

The Buddha's positive interpretation of this dream (one that Brahmanical Hindus would see as negative because of its images of a woman whose hair is shorn and who is naked and without jewels), the length of the dream, and the repetition of its images in the interpretation suggest an attempt to establish a new dream terminology that reverses the world-affirming values of Brahmanical Hinduism. Actually, a Hindu interpretation of Gopā's dream would be appropriate here because the Buddha's desertion of her does wreck her life:

Hindu widows cut their hair and do not wear jewelry. The positive interpretation of Gopā's dream helps gloss over the consequences of the Buddha's desertion of his duties to his wife and child. The Buddha's dismissal of Gopā's fears and his interpretation of her dream undermine her prophetic powers and silence any protest. He does the same in the *AS* and the *MSV*.

In the *AS* Yaśodharā has a dream quite similar to Gopa's and of the same length. Again, the Buddha understands the meaning of her dream, but he tells her to ignore it.[46] In the *MSV* Yaśodharā has a brief dream: "She saw her own maternal line broken, her marvelous couch broken, her bracelets broken, her teeth falling out, the braid of her hair undone, happiness departed from her house, the moon eclipsed by Rahu, and the sun rising in the east and then setting there again" (I.82). When she tells the Buddha her dreams, just as in the *LV*, he denies their prophetic meaning and explains them away through a piece of sophistry. He argues that everything she lost in her dreams is actually still there (I.85). She then extracts a promise from him to take her wherever he goes. Of course, he does not take her with him, and the text glosses this as meaning he promised to take her along to *nirvāṇa* (I.83).

This process is repeated in the *Vessantara Jātaka*, the Buddha's past life as Prince Vessantara and Yaśodharā's as his wife Maddi, who has important, frightening, and ultimately prophetic dreams. While living in the forest with Vessantara, who in order to prove his generosity has given away the wealth of his kingdom and become an ascetic, Maddi asked him to interpret her dream:

> A black man clothed in two yellow robes, with red flowers in his ears, came and entered the hut of leaves, grasped Maddi's hair and dragged her out, threw her down on the ground, and amidst her cries tore out her two eyes, cut off her two arms, split her chest, and tearing out her heart dripping with blood went away. She woke up filled with fear, thinking, "I have seen an inauspicious dream; I will ask Vessantara to interpret my dream." . . . [Vessantara] understood the dream: "The perfection of my giving," he thought, "is to be fulfilled: tomorrow someone will come to beg for my children. I will console Maddi. . . ." So he said, "Your mind must have been agitated by uneasy sleep or by indigestion; do not be afraid." With this deceit [*mohetvā*] he consoled her. . . .[47]

Interestingly, in a very popular Tibetan play based on this *jātaka* his wife did not dream, but the text maintains Vessantara's use of deception by having him send her away to gather fruits because he knew she would not agree to his giving her children away.[48]

It is clear that these women knew what was going on, what was going to happen, and they voice their fears and their protest in the only acceptable way they can, through their dreams. Like women in trance, they are not ultimately responsible for their words; dream narrations are a safe way to protest male authority over their lives.[49] Hence the consistent pattern of women who dream, who fully understand the meaning of their dreams, and yet who ask their husbands to interpret them is shown to be a way of obliquely having direct discourse with their husbands. That the Buddha was consistently deceptive in dealing with his wives' dreams robbed them of their autonomy and their subjectivity. Needless to say, he also showed complete disregard for their feelings and their earthly welfare. Of course, the dreams also function as prophecies of what will inevitably follow, but that does not excuse deception. Dreaming wives and falsely interpreting husbands served to underscore women as passive receptors and men as autonomous actors. The fact that their dream prophecies come true is completely ignored. These attempts by women to have discourse with their husbands have been used to silence women and return them to the background of the male drama. This is a theme that continues in Tibetan biographies as well.[50]

In an extraordinary poem, a modern Buddhist woman presents a different perspective of the Buddha's departure from home, one that captures an actual woman's experience of desertion. The poem wonderfully parallels the fearful images in Gopā's dream by describing the way she lived after her husband was gone. The Buddha's symbolizing and dismissal of these fears in his interpretation is conveyed in the poem's accusation of the silence surrounding her life. Both Gopā's dream of 2,500 years ago and the contemporary poem present fissures in traditional representations of the Buddha's life. They present the faint echoes of a woman's interpretation of these events within a cacophony of male interpretation and editorial control.

The poet, Hira Bansode, is a well-known *dalit* (untouchable) woman of the Buddhist community of Maharashtra in northern India. Throughout the poem she emphasizes Yaśodharā's heroic and unsung sacrifice of giving up her marriage to the Buddha so that he could achieve enlightenment. In the last two stanzas she contrasts the silence of the Buddhist tradition about her with the glorification of the wives of Hindu holy men. The poem, entitled "Yasodhara," follows in its entirety.

Oh Yashodhara!
You are like a dream of sharp pain, life-long sorrow.
I don't have the audacity to look at you.

We were brightened by Buddha's light, but you absorbed the dark
Until your life was mottled blue and black, a fragmented life, burned out,
Oh Yashodhara!

The tender sky comes to you for refuge
Seeing your shining but fruitless life, and the pained stars shed tears.
My heart breaks,
Seeing your matchless beauty, separated from your love, dimming like twilight.
Listening to your silent sighs
I feel the promise of heavenly happiness is hollow.

Tell me one thing, Yashodhara, how did you contain the raging storm in your small hands?
Just the idea of your life shakes the earth and sends the screaming waves dashing against the shore.
You would have remembered while your life slipped by
The last kiss of Siddharth's final farewell, those tender lips.
But weren't you aware, dear, of the heart-melting fire
And the fearful awakening power of that kiss?
Lightning fell, and you didn't know it.
He was moving toward a great splendor, far from the place you lay . . .
He went, he conquered, he shone.
While you listened to the songs of his triumph
Your womanliness must have wept.
You who lost husband and son must have felt uprooted like the tender banana plant.

But history doesn't talk about the great story of your sacrifice.
If Siddharth had gone through the charade of *samādhi* [perhaps meaning Hindu liberation]
A great epic would have been written about you!
You would have become famous in *puraṇa* [myth] and palm leaf like Sita and Savitri.
Oh Yashodhara!
I am ashamed of the injustice.
You are not to be found in a single Buddhist *vihāra* [monastery]
Were you really of no account?
But wait—don't suffer so.
I have seen your beautiful face.
You are between the closed eyelids of Siddhartha.
Yashu, just you.[51]

The last stanza refers to the absence of iconographic images of Yaśodharā, an absence the poet seems to feel represents the general invisibility of women in Buddhism. She is able to turn this absence into a powerful presence when she alludes to the ubiquitous presence of Buddha images, many of which depict him with lowered eyelids, usually thought to represent the meditative state but here evoking the sealed memory of Yaśodharā's image.

THE *SAUNDARĀNANDA*

In chapter 4 we saw that the Buddha's postenlightenment visit to his home terminated the family line when he took his son Rāhula as well as his handsome half-brother Nanda into the order of monks. The initially coerced conversion of Nanda is told in a beautiful Sanskrit epic composed by Aśvaghoṣa, the same Buddhist monk who authored the *BC*. Even more than in the *BC*, in the *Saundarānanda* Aśvaghoṣa utilized the physical beauty and sexuality of women in order to denigrate them. This story was translated into many languages and widely depicted throughout Asia at sites such as Gandhara, Ajanta, Amarāvatī, Nāgārjunakoṇḍa, and so on.[52]

The story opens with and revolves around the relationship of Nanda and his beautiful wife Sundarī, who are madly in love. Indeed, they are shown to be so involved with each other that they do not hear the Buddha arrive to beg for alms. Nanda is terribly upset about this failure of hospitality and respect for his older brother, so he set out after the Buddha. In this way he ends up among the monks, as a monk, but a reluctant one. Nanda never ceases to long for his beautiful wife. In an attempt to free Nanda from her charms, the Buddha takes him to Trāyastriṃśa heaven. On the way they see an ugly female monkey, and the Buddha asks Nanda whether Sundarī is more beautiful than the monkey, to which Nanda emphatically answers yes. Once in Indra's heaven they see divine women, the *apsaras*, Indra's celestial courtesans, and Nanda thinks that the difference between them and his wife is just as great as that between her and the ugly monkey. He develops an ardent desire for the *apsaras* and, returning to earth, devotes himself to ascetic practices in order to ultimately reach this heaven and those divine women. Slowly, he comes to understand that even heavenly pleasures are empty and vain. He retires into the forest, practices the four great meditations, and becomes an arhat.

We are already familiar with Aśvaghoṣa's antiwoman stance from the *BC*, where he went much further than other biographies of the Buddha by devoting several chapters to negative, seductive female images. Aśvaghoṣa uses women not only to represent the pleasures and ensnarement of sexuality, but to speak against women in general, a theme he developed even further in Nanda's story. For Aśvaghoṣa rejecting women is the ultimate sign of spiritual attainment. As an author he has only two interests in women, their seductiveness and their rejection, after which he loses all interest in his female characters. This can be seen in his complete dismissal of Sundarī after the opening chapters. He never tells us what becomes of this deserted wife. Other authors of this tale, who composed with a more sympathetic view of women, say that the Buddha helped her, encouraging her to become a nun and even went so far as to create a phantom woman to illustrate the ephemeral nature of beauty, so that she too became an arhat.[53]

Appropriately enough, the rejection and disparagement of wives and the householder's life finds a reciprocal note about husbands among Buddhist nuns, as in the following poem from the *Therīgāthā*, attributed to the nun Muttā.

> I am well released, properly released by my release by means of the three crooked things, by the mortar, pestle, and my crooked husband. I am released from birth and death; that which leads to renewed existence has been rooted out.[54]

The commentary on this poem seems to reveal a male inability to see a husband as unpleasant or as men who might cheat and lie when it says for no apparent reason that he was a hunchback ("my crooked husband").[55]

Another poem is by Sumangla's Mother:

> O woman well set free! how free am I,
> How thoroughly free from kitchen drudgery!
> Me stained and squalid among my cooking-pots
> My brutal husband ranked as even less
> Than the sunshades he sits and weaves always.
> Purged now of all my former lust and hate,
> I dwell, musing at ease beneath the shade
> Of spreading boughs—O, but tis well with me![56]

The nun Bhaddā Kuṇḍalakesā had fallen in love with a condemned thief before she joined the order, and had convinced her father to rescue him from being executed so that she could marry him. Later she realized he planned to kill her for her jewels, but this enterprising woman foiled his plot and saved herself by pushing him over a precipice, the fate he had planned for her. After this she realized that she could not go home, so she became a Jain nun and later converted to Buddhism, eventually becoming an arhat.[57]

POSITIVE IMAGES OF WIVES

There are some very positive, even touching representations of wives in Buddhism, such as Queen Vaidehī, the chief wife of King Bimbisāra and a devout follower of the Buddha, whose story was briefly discussed in chapter 2. When Bimbisāra's son Ajataśtru usurped the throne he jailed his father and attempted to starve him to death. Ajataśtru's mother, Queen Vaidehī, disregarded her son's order and managed to feed her husband through various stratagems, such as hiding food on her person by concealing the juice of grapes in her flower garlands, and coating her body with honey and ghee mixed with corn flour which he could then lick off, an act that speaks wonderfully of their intimacy and mutual affection. She did this knowing full well the ruthlessness of her hot-tempered son, and indeed, when he finds out what she has been doing it is with great difficulty that his ministers talk him out of killing her. Instead he imprisoned her as well. Queen Vaidehī's devotion to the Buddha and to her wifely duty to protect her husband, and her gentle feminine wiles are depicted positively. In fact, while she was in prison, the Buddha visited her and personally preached to her alone the *Amitāyus Dhyāna Sūtra*,[58] one of the core texts of Pure Land Buddhism that will be discussed in chapter 13.

The story of Mahākassapa and his wife Bhaddā also rides above the wake of the earlier negative stories of men abandoning wives and children in order to become monks. Like the Buddha and Yaśodharā, they were married to each other in many past lives. In their present life neither wished to marry, preferring to join the Buddhist order, but they had no choice. Discovering they were of the same mind, they did not consummate their marriage. Previously Mahākassapa had vowed to care for his parents until they died, at which time he would enter the order. When they did die, he and Bhaddā decided to join the Buddhist orders, and eventually both became arhats.[59]

The *Therīgāthā* records several other instances of wives following their husbands into the order (xxii, lxviii). Without a doubt, some women actively chose to become nuns, and the order was certainly a refuge for widows, but for some it was also a convenient place to dump unwanted women (xix, xlv).

A final story that salutes, rather than denigrates, Buddhist wives is that of Atiraï, a devout Buddhist wife who remained married and is shown to possess all the auspicious powers of fertile womanhood, powers that she used in specifically Buddhist ways to benefit others. Her story is told in the *Manimekhalaï*, a Buddhist epic about a courtesan that will be discussed at length in chapter 7. Briefly, the heroine of the *Manimekhalaï* is a reluctant courtesan, while Atiraï is the most virtuous wife in the city.[60] When Manimekhalaï becomes a nun and receives a magical begging bowl, Atiraï is chosen to put the first food donation in her bowl, food that thenceforth endlessly multiplies. Atiraï's auspicious fecundity is so strong that she has the power to make rain fall in its proper season, a power she earned through enduring devotion to her husband, despite the fact that he left her for a courtesan and squandered all his wealth. The *Manimekhalaï* counters the destructive sexuality of the courtesan, which can impoverish men, with the constructive sexuality of the virtuous wife, which is regularized through marriage.

As we have seen and as we shall continue to see in the chapters that follow, Buddhist attitudes toward sexuality gather in some diverse ideas. First, they locate sexuality within women, as the repositories of the desirable, and this defines women's nature—they are filled with power, which they can use negatively, for example as seductresses, to destroy men, or positively, as faithful wives bringing their auspicious fertility to their husbands' families and to the very country they live in, for example by controlling the rain. Second, the celibate monastic life remains the ideal because sexuality is believed to entangle one within the world, preventing liberation. However, Buddhist monastics are dependant on the laity for sustenance, so South Asian ideas about the powers of the virtuous wife are maintained. As a general rule, Buddhism tended not to disturb cultural practices unless they were in direct conflict with Buddhist ethics.

Lastly, I have postponed discussing marriage in terms of disengaging the bride from her natal family and transferring her to her husband's family, with their consequent involvement of dowries, inheritance rules, and rituals until chapter 10, which focuses on the economic basis of marriage and other types of sexual arrangements. It is to these other forms of sexual arrangements that we now turn in the chapters that follow.

NOTES

1. Horner has a chapter on wives; *Women Under Primitive Buddhism;* and Elizabeth Wilson has a very good article on husbands in early Buddhism, "Henpecked Husbands and Renouncers Home on the Range: Celibacy As Social Disengagement in South Asian Buddhism," *Union Seminary Quarterly Review* 48. 3–4 (1994): 7–28.

2. For example, *NK*, 205.
3. Richard H. Robinson and Williard L. Johnson, *The Buddhist Religion: A Historical Introduction*, 4th ed. (Belmont, CA: Wadsworth Publishing Company, 1997), 78.
4. Ibid., 78.
5. Faure, *Red Thread*, 67, citing Louis de La Vallée Poussin.
6. Robinson and Johnson, *The Buddhist Religion*, 78.
7. *The Laws of Manu*, III.45–47, IV.40–43, and 128.
8. Aris, *Tibetan Medical Paintings*, 211.
9. See, for example, Barbara Nimri Aziz, *Tibetan Frontier Families: Reflections of Three Generations from D'ing-ri* (New Delhi: Vikas Publishing House Pvt. Ltd., 1978), 60–66, 137–38, 177, 179, and 183–85.
10. According to Richard Gombrich and Gananath Obeyesekere, *Buddhism Transformed: Religious Change in Sri Lanka* (Princeton, NJ: Princeton University Press, 1988), especially 249–73, the Buddhist attitude toward marriage is changing in modern Sri Lanka, a change they correctly attribute to the influence of Christian missionaries, as monks are participating in wedding ceremonies, something unheard of before the late twentieth century. Additionally, now only monogamous marriage is legal; older forms such as polyandry and polygyny are outlawed and divorce has been made more difficult (256). They point out that this change can also be seen among Western converts to Buddhism who want to sacramentalize their marriages (267).
11. I have slightly modified T. W. and C. A. F. Rhys Davids's translation in *Dialogues of the Buddha*, Sacred Books of the Buddhists Series, Part 3 (London: Oxford University Press, 1921), 182. *Dīgha Nikāya* III.180. Buddhaghosa called this the *Vinaya* of the laity.
12. *Therīgāthā* lxxii, trans. Mrs. Rhys Davids as *Psalms of the Early Buddhists*, Part I (London: Pali Text Society, 1909, 1980), 158–59.
13. Wilson, "Henpecked Husbands," 11.
14. *Vinaya, Suttavibhaṅga* lxxx; *Therāgāthā*, trans. Rhys Davids as *Psalms of the Early Buddhists*, clxi; *Therīgāthā* i, xii, xvii, and lii.
15. *Vinaya* I.43.
16. John Strong briefly discusses the popular theme of a monk longing for his wife, *The Legend and Cult of Upagupta* (1992. Delhi: Motilal Banarsidass Publishers, 1994), 126–27, 131–32.
17. *MSV* 2:31–32 and *NK*, 226.
18. *Suttavibhaṅga*, Pārājika I.4–5.
19. Elsewhere the *LV* calls her Yaśavatī, 142.
20. The *Abhiniṣkramaṇasūtra*, trans. by Samuel Beal from the Chinese edition as *The Romantic Legend of Śākya Buddha* (1875. Delhi: Motilal Banarsidass, 1985), hereinafter the *AS*, 101–02, n. 1, and 127–28. In *The Blue Annals* the Buddha also has two wives, called Yaśodharā and Gopā; 'Gos Lo tsa ba Gźon nu dpal; *The Blue Annals*, trans. George N. Roerich (1949; Delhi: Motilal Banarsidass, 1976), 18. See also André Bareau, "Un personnage bien mysterieux: l'épouse du Buddha," in *Indological and Buddhist Studies, Volume in Honour of Professor J. W. de Jong on His Sixtieth Birthday*, ed. L. A. Hercus et al. (Canberra: Australian National University, 1982), 31–59.

    The *Mahāvaṃsa* calls her Bhaddakaccānā (II.24), which is also the name of the progenitrix of the Sri Lankan kings (VIII.17). This is also her name in *AN* 1.14.25, which is a list of the leading monks and nuns who lived at the time of the Buddha along with their main accomplishments. The accomplishment of the Buddha's wife is that she is chief among those who attained supernormal powers.

21. The textual sources for these dreams are discussed in Young, *Dreaming in the Lotus*, 33–41.
22. *Mahāvaṃsa*, II.24.
23. Bays, *Voice*, 211.
24. Ibid., 213.
25. Ibid., 216.
26. This is a common mythological theme. Some examples from Indian epics are Rāma and Sītā, Nala and Damyantī, Ambā and Bhīma, and so on.
27. A full list of the skills is summarized Bays, *Voice*, 234–35.
28. Ibid., 235–37.
29. Śakuntalā is a good example. Of course, they are always eventually put in their proper place.
30. Bays, *Voice*, 344.
31. Ibid., 347–49.
32. *Tvaṃ ahi bheṣyasi yathā narottamaṃ, LV*, 173.8. Edgerton lists *narottamaṃ*, which means highest of men, as a standard epithet for the Buddha, *Buddhist Hybrid Sanskrit Dictionary*, 291, col. a. Hints of her future enlightenment can also be read into the Buddha's interpretation of her dream, discussed below.
33. Har Dayal, *The Bodhisattva Doctrine in Buddhist Sanskrit Literature* (1932. Delhi: Motilal Banarsidass, 1970, 1975), 305.
34. *MSV* I.120.
35. Strong, *Experience of Buddhism*, 16.
36. Ibid., 18.
37. The *Caṇḍamahāroṣaṇa Tantra*, cited and translated by Miranda Shaw, *Passionate Enlightenment: Women in Tantric Buddhism* (Princeton, NJ: Princeton University Press, 1994), 143.
38. This version comes from the *Divyāvadāna*, ed. Cowell and Neil, 246–53. Strong has a translation of this, *Experience of Buddhism*, 19–23.
39. Howard Eilberg-Schwartz and Wendy Doniger, eds., *Off With Her Head! The Denial of Women's Identity in Myth, Religion, and Culture* (Berkeley, CA: University of California: 1995) has several excellent essays on hair.
40. She is depicted at Ajanta, and the British Museum has a carving from Gandhara depicting the Buddha's departure from home that shows him sitting on the bed where Yaśodharā is sleeping (OA 1900. 4–14.1).
41. See, for example, Fig. 15 in Dehejia, *Discourse*. Dipaṃkara is also a popular subject of Tibetan art but often he is not shown making his vow, which also excludes the presence of his future wife, but rather as a buddha. For example, see 70.0/6865 of American Museum of Natural History's Collection.
42. Young, *Dreaming in the Lotus*.
43. Similarly, Bruce Lincoln, *Authority: Construction and Corrosion* (Chicago: University of Chicago Press, 1994), 96–101, has presented some relevant and pervasive examples of dream discourse as one of the few authoritative voices available to women in the Roman world, albeit an easily challenged one.
44. Bays, *Voice*, 293.
45. *LV*, 141.9–142.28.
46. *AS*, 127–18.
47. No. 547, *The Jātaka Together with Its Commentary*, ed. V. Fausboll (London: Trübner, 1887). Translated as *The Jātaka*, ed. E. B. Cowell (1895. London: Pali Text Society, 1973). *Jātaka*, Fausboll, 6:540–41.
48. Duncan, *More Harvest Festivals*, 98. Paul discusses this play, *Tibetan Symbolic World*, 198–202.
49. For further discussion of women's important and complicated relation to alternate states of consciousness, see Lincoln, *Authority*, 96–101; I. M. Lewis,

Ecstatic Religion: An Anthropological Study of Spirit Possession and Shamanism (Middlesex, U.K.: Penguin, 1971); Janice Boddy, *Wombs and Alien Spirits: Women, Men and the Zār Cult in Northern Sudan* (Madison, WI: University of Wisconsin Press, 1989); and Laurel Kendall, *Shamans, Housewives, and Other Restless Spirits: Women in Korean Ritual Life* (Honolulu, HI: University of Hawai'i Press, 1985), esp. 23–25.

50. See Young, *Dreaming in the Lotus*, chapter 10.
51. Quoted by Eleanor Zelliot, "Buddhist Women of the Contemporary Maharashtrian Conversion Movement," Cabezón, *Buddhism, Sexuality, and Gender*, 104–105. See this essay for further discussion of the poem as well as for the background of Maharastrian Buddhism. Zelliot gives the following publishing and translation information for the poem: "Yashodhara" was first published in *Strī* (Devali issue, 1981), and reprinted in a collection of Hira Bansode's poems, *Phiryād* [Petition, Complaint] (Pune: Samaj Prabodhan Sanstha Prakashan, 1984), translated by Jayant Karve, Philip Engblom, and Eleanor Zelliot, 106, n. 21.
52. *Saundarāananda Mahākāvya of Ācārya Aśvaghoṣa with Tibetan and Hindi Translations*, trans. Ācārya Shri L. Jamspal (Sarnath: Central Institute of Higher Tibetan Studies: 1999). An English translation is by E. H. Johnston, *The Saundarananda or Nanda the Fair* (Oxford: Oxford University Press, 1932). See Schlingloff for textual and iconographic versions of this story, *Studies in Ajanta Paintings*, 50, and Leslie Grey, *Concordance of Buddhist Birth Stories* (Oxford: The Pali Text Society, 1994), 265–66. This story is also discussed by Winternitz, *Indian Literature*, II.263ff.
53. Burlingham, *Buddhist Legends*, II.336–339.
54. *Therīgāthā, The Elders' Verses*, trans. K. R. Norman (London: Pali Text Society, 1971), 2.
55. Rhys Davids, *Psalms*, Part I, 15.
56. Trans., Rhys Davids, *Psalms*, Part I, 25.
57. *Therīgāthā* xlvi.
58. Cowell, *Buddhist Mahāyāna Texts*, 161ff.
59. *Therīgāthā* cclxi; *Therīgāthā* xxxvii.
60. Shattan, *Manimekhalaï*, 62.

CHAPTER 6

SOUTH ASIAN COURTESANS

Courtesans have long been a staple of South Asian myth, literature, drama, and ritual life. Plays featuring courtesans were frequently performed during spring fertility festivals to help promote the fruitfulness of humans, animals, and crops.[1] In keeping with this connection between courtesans and fecundity, there are many tales in which a king can only end a drought by sending a courtesan to seduce a celibate sage. This theme was enacted in an annual ritual by *devadāsīs*, the sacred courtesans at the temple of Jagannātha in Puri in order to hasten the monsoon rains.[2] The connections between semen and rain have a long history in the ancient world, and both are also connected to fecundity and thus to power. By withholding his semen a sage can blight the land, unless the king has a greater command over the powers of fertility, or unless he can command the auspicious powers of a beautiful and fertile woman. In similar scenarios the god Indra sends heavenly courtesans (*apśaras*) to seduce celibate sages whose spiritual power threatens his own.[3]

Buddhist stories utilize these same motifs, most famously as when the god Māra attempts to prevent the Buddha's enlightenment by sending his daughters to seduce him. Stories in which courtesans fail in their attempts at seduction serve several purposes: the encounter between ascetic and courtesan is often a literary device to highlight an ascetic's control of his sexuality, as when the harem women fail to seduce the Buddha, but they also serve as warnings about the dangers of sexuality to spiritual power and define women as sexual temptresses. For instance, as we saw in chapter 5, there are several stories of monks whose former wives attempted to seduce them back into married life, sometimes with success. For the most part, early Buddhist texts were under the control of monks committed to celibacy, among whom seduction stories were quite popular. Early Buddhist biographies also tended to focus on women as temptresses and on failed seductions, emphasizing the oppositions of *dharma* and *kāma*, religious obligation and pleasure, where *dharma* is clearly associated with men and *kāma* with women. Yet stories about courtesans with *dharma*, not *kāma*, in their hearts also appear, and these will be discussed shortly.

What follows is not meant to be the final word on courtesans in Buddhist texts; after all, their success in life depended on maintaining a subtle balance between availability and elusiveness. In much the same way, they slip in and out of early Indian texts, sometimes harnessed to the text's purpose and at other times intimating more complex meanings. Often they act as a necessary female counterpoint to the male ascetic, not only by contrasting their sexuality with his celibacy, but in being almost as free from social restraint as the ascetic: she moving below conventional morality just as he moves above it.[4] This idea was captured in an early play, *The Farce of the Pious Courtesan* (*Bhagavadajjuka Prahasanam*) by King Mahendravarma I (early seventh century C.E.), in which the souls of a holy man (*bhagavad*) and a courtesan named Ajjuka are accidentally exchanged.[5] Significantly, courtesans, like monastic communities, could not exist without the disposable wealth of princes and merchants.

Courtesans lived in their own section of town, as in caste-driven India most occupational groups had their own neighborhoods.[6] It was a "red light" district of sorts, but one in which arts other than the art of love also flourished. Many courtesans were accomplished singers, musicians, dancers, poets, and wits; these often highly educated women were in full command of the arts of costume, cosmetics, and setting.[7] In the classical plays the courtesan district is often presented as separate from the mundane world, a place of art and refinement, populated by beautiful, sexually available women. The entrance fee, of course, could be high, and it is perhaps a testament to the skills of these women that the plays and stories often tell of men who met financial ruin in their pursuit of the many pleasures they offered.[8]

The *Manimekhalaï*, a South Indian Buddhist epic composed in Tamil and dated between the second and sixth centuries B.C.E.[9] describes a courtesan's accomplishments:

> [She] knew both kinds of dance, dances suitable for the royal palace and those for the common public, poems set to music, the

> art of dramatic posture . . . to emphasize the rhythm of the poetic meter, the various musical rhythms . . . , and how to play the harp.
>
> She knew by heart the poems chanted during the dances and had mastered the language of gesture . . . by which love . . . , virtue, and glory . . . are expressed. She knew how to play the great drum and how to adjust the tightness of its skin to regulate the sound. She knew how to play the melodious flute, as also the art of playing ball, of preparing dishes according to the recipes of the best cuisines as well as the preparing of scented powders of diverse colors, the manner of bathing in the various seasons, the body's sixty-four positions in making love, the art of anticipating men's desires, of speaking charmingly, and of seeming reluctant (the better to excite her lovers), of writing elegantly with a cut reed, or arranging magnificent bouquets of flowers chosen for their form and color, the choice of dress and jewels according to circumstances, and the art of fashioning necklaces of pearls or precious stones.
>
> She had also studied astrology and the art of measuring time, and other similar sciences, the art of drawing and painting.[10]

Some of these accomplishments recall the seductive arts of the Buddha's harem women.

SEXUAL CATEGORIES

South Asian languages have a rich vocabulary of terms to place women in various sexual categories. For example, there is the distinction between the *kula-strī* (a wife, a woman from a good family) and *vāra-strī* (a courtesan, a restraining woman). One of the main characters in Śrudraka's drama the *Padmaprābhṛtakam* (fourth or fifth century C.E.) is a courtesan, and the play uses a rich variety of terms for them and for prostitutes, such as: *gaṇika* (the calculating one), *veśya* (one who disguises herself), *puṃścalī* (agitator of men), *vṛṣali* (a low-caste woman), and *bandhakam* (a binder, a fetter).[11] Despite the negative connotations of these words, other early texts associated prostitutes and courtesans with auspiciousness, harkening back to the tales that their sexual activity stimulated the fertility of the earth.[12] This idea continued into the twentieth century, as is shown by an Indian king's coronation ceremony that involved filling a vessel with water from various sources as well as different kinds of earth, including some taken from the house of a courtesan (Oriya: *beśyā* = Skt: *veśyā*).[13] A vessel with the same contents is also part of the royal wedding ceremony,[14] and *devadāsīs* sang auspicious songs during both ceremonies.

Devadāsīs, female servants of god, served in the courts of kings and in Hindu temples as ritual specialists and as concubines. They capture the ambiguities of the sexually active woman in that they are both distinguished from the foregoing sexual categories and yet encapsulated by them; Marglin found that the terms *gaṇika* and *veśya* were also used for them.[15] In this instance these two terms seem to be related more to sacred than secular prostitution. Sarat Chandra Das lists them as equivalents for two Tibetan terms for prostitutes: *tshogs mo can* and *tshogs can ma*, both of which are connected to the word for the sacred tantric feast, *tshogs 'khor* (Skt: *gaṇacakra*),[16] a ritual that can incorporate sexual yoga and sometimes involved prostitutes. (This ritual will be discussed further in the chapters on tantric consorts.)

In his attempt to summarize these women the Indologist A. L. Basham ends up showing just how slippery all these terms can be:

> The position of the courtesan merged with that of the concubine. Kings and chiefs retained numerous prostitutes in their palaces, who were salaried servants, and who often had other duties to perform, such as attending on the king's person. The status of these women is somewhat obscure, but apparently they were not only at the service of the king, but also of any courtier on whom he might choose temporarily to bestow them, and thus they were not on a par with the regular inhabitants of his harem. Prostitutes of this type accompanied the king wherever he went, and even awaited him in the rear when he went into battle.[17]

James Davidson discusses an equally rich range of Greek terms for female sexual categories, and he notes the distinction to be made between the gift-exchange practice of the *hetaera*s (courtesans) that establish a relationship of patronage and friendship, and the commodity-exchange practice of the prostitute, which does not.[18] This distinction between presents and payments seems useful for ancient and medieval India as well, especially in the case of the *devadāsī*s, who were supported by their temples and by the kings; thus they did not require the financial support of their lovers, with whom they often maintained enduring relationships and from whom they received gifts.[19] Courtesans, too, established relationships with men who gave them gifts, and can be distinguished from prostitutes who traded sex for money and did not have a courtesan's education. As the English word *courtesan* suggests, they were first and foremost associated with royal courts that had the money, leisure, and interest to enjoy their various talents.

DEVADĀSĪS

As already suggested, *devadāsī*s present the most complex picture of South Asian women who have been classified as courtesans. This complexity is connected to the sacredness of their temple office, and thus to their relationship with divine beings, and to kings, who in India, as in many parts of the world, were considered divine. Indeed, *devadāsī*s brought together the courtesan and the sacred by often classifying themselves as *apśara*s, divine courtesans.[20]

One became a *devadāsī* either by inheriting the office, for instance being the daughter of a *devadāsī*'s brother,[21] or being adopted by a *devadāsī*, as *devadāsī*s were not supposed to give birth to children. They were ceremonially dedicated to the temple before they reached puberty (a tradition that was outlawed in 1947 by the Devadasi Act), and from that moment they were considered married to the ruling deity of the temple. Since the gods do not die, this meant that *devadāsī*s could never become widows; they were *nityasumaṅgalī*, forever auspicious. While still children their temple duty was to dance at the morning devotional ritual. After their first menstruation they went through another ceremony that allowed them to sing and dance in the evening devotional ritual, and which led to the consummation of their marriage. Since the king was considered to be the living incarnation of the god Jagganātha (Viṣṇu in his incarnation as Kriṣṇa), a tradition existed that the king consummated the marriage. Frédérique Apffel Marglin, however, found that the king's role was often taken by a brahman priest of the temple.[22] If she wanted, a *devadāsī* could then establish a *liaison*, but only with an upper-caste man who lived in the area served by the temple. In the temple that Marglin studied, this meant the entire city of Puri. These were usually long-term relationships, and as already mentioned, the *devadāsī*s were not financially dependent on their lovers since they were supported by the king and the temple. There is nothing to indicate that they exchanged sex for gifts or money.[23]

*Devadāsī*s also presided at rites involving newborns, such as the name-giving ceremony and the ear- and nose-piercing ceremony, and at wedding ceremonies that focus on the bride and take place at her natal home. Traditional South Asian wedding ceremonies extend over several days and take place at both the bride's and the groom's natal homes. *Devadāsī*s decorated the bride and sang a variety of songs, some auspicious, some that mocked the groom, and bawdy ones as well.[24] As perpetually auspicious women they were able to bestow their excess of auspiciousness on others, in this case the bride. Since they were not allowed to have children of their own, *devadāsī*s were like ascetics who build up spiritual power (*tapas*) by abstaining from sexuality. *Devadāsī*s, of course, were sexual, but they did not procreate. Procreative power is the root of their auspiciousness; they stored up their procreative powers by not conceiving and heightened them by their sexual activity, passing some on to brides, to the infants they blessed, and the entire kingdom through their ritual functions.

In addition to their daily temple service during the morning and evening rituals, *devadāsīs* participated in the three most important and public temple rituals, as well as other temple rituals performed throughout the year. They danced at the annual ceremony of bathing the deities and they danced and sang while accompanying the statue of the goddess Lakṣmī during the annual festival that was believed to renew the deities, the king, the people, and the land. Once every twelve years, new images of the deities were carved and the old images discarded. During the time of their carving, the *devadāsīs* sang auspicious songs.[25] These are all rituals focused on renewal, regeneration, and rebirth that are enhanced by the presence of the *devadāsīs* and their ritual acts.

Their presence was also required at auspicious palace occasions, such as royal life-cycle ceremonies and palace festivals. They were a ubiquitous presence at the seven- to ten-day royal wedding ceremonies, during which they sang auspicious songs and/or stood next to two "filled pots," common symbols for auspiciousness.[26] Their presence was also required at three royal festivals: the coronation and its yearly renewal; the ceremony that marks the beginning of the dynasty's new regnal year; and the Durgā *pūjā*. They sang auspicious songs at the first two and both sang and danced at the latter.[27] Here, too, they added their auspicious powers to rituals of renewal, regeneration, and rebirth.

The origins of the *devadāsīs* are lost in history, but they enacted ancient ideas about female auspiciousness and the sacred power of female sexuality. On the one hand, they were considered the living embodiment of Lakṣmī, the wife of Jagannātha/Viṣṇu, the bestower of prosperity.[28] They were supremely auspicious women who had the power to bring abundance, sustain life, and ward off evil. On the other hand, they were considered to be *gopīs*, the cow-herding girls who were Kriṣṇa's lovers. This is brought out in the evening ritual during which the *devadāsīs* sang erotic songs, especially from the *Gita Govinda*, a twelfth-century poem devoted to the love between Kriṣṇa and the *gopīs*. The evening ritual can only be performed by *devadāsīs* who have reached puberty, those who are sexually mature, for their evening songs are their participation in the sexual activity of the god. Through these activities they represent the role of the divine in maintaining life and creating fecundity, and dramatize the auspicious power of sexuality. This is no virgin priesthood. It is a sexually active one that participates in the divine through their embodiment of Lakṣmī and their sexual relations with Kriṣṇa; in the semidivine through their relations with the king; in sacred humanity in their relations with brahman priests; and in the fully human through their relations with the laity and with their lay lovers. Their auspicious powers did not arise from sexual activity with many beings, but from sexual activity in so many realms.

MALE COURTESANS

The *Kāma Sūtra*, a text compiled in the fourth century C.E. by incorporating much earlier works,[29] introduces additional terms for prostitutes when it discusses male courtesans, who are included among people of the third nature, often taken to mean a third sex (*tritīya prakriti*),[30] such as hermaphrodites, transvestites, and homosexual prostitutes, who are forerunners of those *hijrā*s today who partially support themselves through prostitution by having sex with other men for money. While I am not suggesting that the *hijrā*s as we now know them existed from such an early date—their origins are lost in mythic time—the complexity of sexual and religious ideas and activities that define them are quite ancient[31] and reveal other aspects of South Asian concerns about the relation of sexuality and spiritual power, about the uses and abuses of fertility for secular and religious ends.

*Hijrā*s are a religious community of sexually charged and sexually ambiguous men who dress and act like women. A brief look at their ritual roles sheds light on the sexuality and fertility ethos of South Asia, and evokes the complementary tension between the courtesan and the ascetic, for *hijrā*s are religious ascetics required to be celibate servants of the goddess Bahucharā Mātā and many have undergone castration,[32] yet some work as homosexual prostitutes. One of the stories told about Bahucharā Mātā, is that she cut off her own breasts to avoid being raped by thieves, which suggests her male priests castrate themselves in imitation of her primal act.[33] Of equal religious significance is that *hijrā*s identify with the sexually ambivalent god Śiva, who is both the great ascetic and the virile husband, particularly in his *ardhanārīśvara* form of half-man/half-woman[34] and in the legend of his self-castration.[35]

In many ways *hijrā*s seem to mimic *devadāsī*s. In the past *devadāsī*s had male equivalents, young men who dressed as women and danced outside the temple while the *devadāsī*s danced inside the temple,[36] and *hijrā*s may have had some connection to these transvestites. Regardless, like *devadāsī*s, the ritual roles of *hijrā*s center around temple festivals, births, and marriages. In the temples of Bahucharā Mātā they act as her servants, tell stories about her, and bless worshippers. After the birth of a male child *hijrās* visit the child's home to sing and dance, examine the child's genitals, and demand money for blessing him with fertility, prosperity, and a long life. They also dance with exaggerated female sexuality for the small boys who are present, and whose genitals they touch. For this they receive traditional gifts of cash and goods.[37] Only male babies are involved, which suggests that their sexuality has to be assured and protected. As will be discussed in chapter 12, anxiety about the stability of male sexual characteristics is found throughout the world.[38] Seemingly, *hijrās* who have lost masculinity, or who represent the third sex and are associated with hermaphrodites, are perceived as individuals who would have intimate knowledge of changeable or inadequate sex organs. Their ambiguous sexual characteristics and/or sexual natures reflect the deities they worship: a breastless mother goddess and a god who is half-woman/half-man. This gives them the ability when they examine the infant's genitals to know if they are ill defined, if they are those of a hermaphrodite, and if so, the right to claim the baby as one of them. To the families they serve, *hijrās* embody fears about losing masculinity, and yet they have the power to give what they do not have: the power of creating new life. They receive this power from the mother goddess Bahucharā Mātā, but, like *yakṣīs*, their powers cut both ways; they can curse as well as bless, and their curses are greatly feared.

At weddings they bless the married couple for fertility. Unlike *devadāsīs*, who go to the bride's house, *hijrās* make all arrangements with the groom's family and perform at the groom's house, although, like the *devadāsīs*, some of their songs make fun of the groom and his family. While they sing and dance the *hijrās* tell various family members "you will have a son," or "you will have a grandson."[39] Often the bride is not allowed to be present.[40] *Hijrās* are presented as a masculine concern, a concern of the patrilineal family that must have sons who will be capable of siring sons of their own. Brides are outsiders, the vehicles for male fertility.

First and foremost, *hijrās* are ritually connected to maintaining patrilineal descent. It is as if having surrendered their own masculine fertility they can confer it onto others, and the powerfulness of their austere asceticism is enough to assure male, definitely not female, babies. Indeed, their actual or rumored homosexuality, while frowned upon, increases their contact with semen, thereby increasing their power to confer patrilineal fertility. Many people believe that loss of semen reduces a man's power. Male South Asian ascetics act on this belief by building up their spiritual power through celibacy. Castrated *hijrās* cannot ejaculate even if they want to, or by accident, such as nightly emission. They are ascetics par excellence, yet some of them are also prostitutes; they encapsulate within themselves the sexual/ascetic tension depicted in stories about the courtesan and the ascetic, and they use that tension, that power, to bless or curse the fertility of others.

TRANSITIONS

As we shall see in the two chapters on tantric consorts, the later tradition of Tantric Buddhism joins the female courtesan and the male ascetic, and reverts to the pattern of successful seduction stories by reinterpreting the courtesan as the tantric consort, and placing both the tantric practitioner and the consort above conventional morality. Indeed, tantric consorts were sometimes prostitutes.[41] In Tantra, the ancient idea that sexuality has the power to stimulate other forms of fertility is harnessed by practitioners who use sexuality to generate and empower their spiritual advancement. As we have seen, the early biographies of the Buddha reveal a similar acceptance of women and fertility as part of the path toward enlightenment.

Consequently, I am arguing that while monastic Buddhism rejected sexuality in favor of celibacy from the earliest period—thereby problematizing womanhood—there was another, equally early current within Buddhism that accepted both women and sexuality, and further, that this current survived and was later rearticulated within a tantric context. Stated differently, the erotic female imagery of Tantra does not mark a huge break with the earlier tradition. There is both textual and iconographic evidence for this. As we have seen, the earliest iconography celebrates the auspiciousness of female fertility and sexuality in life-size female statues depicted with voluptuously curved, almost nude bodies in unself-conscious postures. These female images were believed to imbue monuments and sites with their life-sustaining auspiciousness, thereby assuring that the sites would flourish. Among these are the justly famous *śālabhañjikā* (woman and the tree) pose (Figures 2.4 and 2.5), which was used to represent Queen Māyā giving birth to the Buddha. This pose, as discussed earlier, expresses the belief that an auspicious woman who kicks or touches a tree with her foot causes it to bloom and that tree spirits (*yakṣīs*) can confer fertility.[42] The female figures stand under a blooming tree, one hand stretched overhead, grasping a branch, with one leg bent back at the knee, toward the tree, the foot raised to touch the trunk, or with one leg twined around the tree trunk. The latter pose is a clear allusion to a sexual encounter in that the literary tradition often described the sexual embrace as a woman encircling a man like a vine encircles a tree trunk. Significantly, Monier-Williams glosses *śālabhañjikā* as a term for courtesans,[43] which echoes the practice of marrying courtesans to trees,[44] while Vidya Dehejia translates it as "auspicious women",[45] thus suggesting a broad application of female fertility and auspiciousness to a wide variety of divine and human women from different social stations. Vogel translates it as "she who plucks *śāla* flowers," a reference to a festival during which women climbed these trees to pluck their blossoms.[46]

These *yakṣī*-like figures have their male counterparts, the *yakṣas*, male fertility deities, who at least in the early periods of Buddhist stone iconography were depicted as powerfully built, sensual men. As mentioned above, the first anthropomorphic Buddha images were modeled on *yakṣa*s, and some of the finest examples were made during the Kushan Dynasty (Figure 2.8). Later, the *yakṣa*s become dwarflike figures but still retained their great physical strength, as is shown by their use as supports for columns and other objects, and retained their powers of fecundity. Additionally, loving couples became a frequent motif quite early at Buddhist sites such as Nāgārjunakoṇḍa. These are beautifully carved figures of voluptuous women and virile men often depicted in a loving embrace (Figures 6.1, 6.2, and 6.3).

Textually, as we have seen above, one of the most important incidents in the Buddha's life is his departure from home and abandonment of his wife and the harem women who used various sexual ploys in their fruitless attempt to prevent him from leaving. Scenes depicting these harem women are often found in early Buddhist iconography, representing both his rejection of women and sexuality and yet preserving the beauty of the women. The Buddha then spends seven years practicing such severe asceticism that he is close to death, until his dead mother descends from heaven and persuades him to relent, thus beginning his reconciliation with women. The Buddha then has a series of positive encounters with females, both divine and human, including accepting food from the woman Sujātā, culminating in his calling upon the earth goddess to act as witness to his merit during his battle with the demon Māra on the night of enlightenment. After achieving enlightenment the Buddha began a public life as a teacher and lived for almost fifty more years. It is during this period that women of all sorts, including courtesans, actively reenter his life.

Fig. 6.1 Intoxicated courtesan. American Institute of Indian Studies A1-86. Mathurā (Maholi), late second century C.E.

Fig. 6.2 Loving couple. American Institute of Indian Studies 106.84, Patna, second century B.C.E.

Fig. 6.3 Couples. Karli, photograph by John C. Huntington, courtesy of the Huntington Archive.

NOTES

1. One of the earliest fragments of Buddhist drama from the first century C.E. has a courtesan as a character; Winternitz, *A History of Indian Literature*, III.199; see also the *Avadāna Śataka* that has the story of Kuvalayā, a dancer who achieved enlightenment (Winternitz, III.197); and several other early plays in which courtesans are major characters, for example, Śrudraka, *The Padmaprābhṛtakam*, trans. and ed., Johannes R. A. Loman (Amsterdam: Uitgeverij de Driehoek, 1956); and his *The Toy Cart*, trans. P. Lal in *Great Sanskrit Plays* (New York: New Directions Books, 1957, 1964).

   In general, see Winternitz on the enduring connections between religion and drama in South Asia, III.178ff.; and Moti Chandra, *The World of Courtesans* (Delhi: Vikas, 1973) for their history in Sanskrit literature. See also J. Gonda, "Ascetics and Courtesans," in J. Gonda, *Selected Studies*, vol. iv, *History of Ancient Indian Religion* (Leiden: E. J. Brill, 1975), 223–47.
2. Marglin, *Wives of the God-King*, 101–08.
3. See, for example, Annapurna Garimella,"Apsaras," in *EOW*, vol. I, 48–50. Marglin discusses some of these stories (*Wives of the God-King*), as does Wendy Doniger O'Flaherty, citing some Buddhist sources among others, in *Asceticism and Eroticism in the Mythology of Śiva* (1973. Delhi: Oxford University Press, 1975), 42–52. See also her Index of Motifs, no. 21ea, ibid., 377. O'Flaherty suggests they may be connected with ancient sexual rites, 45 and 52. In some tales of this type they are *apśaras*, in others earthly courtesans, or women, frequently a king's daughter. When a courtesan, she is abandoned after the seduction, when a princess, the ascetic marries her. A famous exam-

ple of the latter are the many stories of Pārvatī's seduction of Śiva, see, e.g., ibid., 151–55 and passim. Aśvaghoṣa, *Buddhacarita,* summarizes some of these stories in Udāyin's speech to the Buddha, IV.8ff., discussed in chapter 2 herein. It appears, though, that Buddhist tales did not go along with this princess/courtesan distinction: in the *Naḷinkā Jātaka,* after a princess's successful seduction of an ascetic he rejects her. Cowell, *Jātakas,* no. 526.

4. O'Flaherty, *Śiva,* 52. See also Marglin for some of the subtleties of relationship between the ascetic and erotic, *Wives of the God-King,* 202–03.
5. King Mahendravarma I, *Bhagavadajjuka Prahasanam,* ed. and trans. by Michael Lockwood and A. Vishnu Bhat (Madras: Diocesan Press, 1991).
6. Merchant-Prince Shattan, *Manimekhalaï (The Dancer with The Magic Bowl),* trans., Alain Daniélou (New York: New Directions Books, 1989), 142–43.
7. See, for instance, the *Simhāsana Dvātriṃśikā: Thirty-Two Tales of the Throne,* trans. A. N. D. Haksar (New Delhi: Penquin Books India, 1998), 64–65, which describes King Vikrama relaxing among courtesans and other women.
   Some courtesans were also prolific authors. Susie Tharu and K. Lalita begin their introduction to *Women Writing in India: 600 B.C. to the Present* (1991. Delhi: Oxford University Press, 1995), with the story of Bangalore Nagaratnamma, a courtesan who corrected and reprinted the eighteenth-century classic, *Radhika Santwanam,* an epic by the courtesan Muddupalani (c. 1730–1790), vol. I, 1ff.
8. See, for example, J. A. B. van Buitenen, who translated several stories that feature courtesans in *Tales of Ancient India* (Chicago, IL: The University of Chicago Press, 1959), 65–71, 72–78, 180–205, and 218–58.
9. Daniélou dates it to the second century; Shattan, *Manimekhalaï,* p. xvi, and Richman to the sixth century. Paula Richman also gives the author as Cāttanār, "The Portrayal of a Female Renouncer in a Tamil Buddhist Text," *Gender and Religion: On the Complexity of Symbols,* ed. Caroline Walker Bynum, Stevan Harrell, and Paula Richman (Boston: Beacon Press, 1986), ed. Bynum, et al, 144.
10. Shattan, *Manimekhalaï,* 5.
11. The *MSV* adds *rūpājīvinī,* subsisting by beauty of form, Gnoli, 207, while the *BC* (III.52) uses *vāramukya* (an obstruction).
12. Marglin, *Wives of the God-King,* 98.
13. Ibid., 158–59.
14. Ibid., 163.
15. Ibid., 9–10.
16. Sarat Chandra Das, *A Tibetan-English Dictionary* (Calcutta: Bengal Secretariat Book Depot, 1903), 1033.
17. Basham, *Wonder,* 184.
18. James Davidson, *Courtesans & Fishcakes: The Consuming Passions of Classical Athens* (1997. New York: HarperCollins, 1999), respectively, 73–74 and 109–36. See also Alain Daniélou, trans., *The Complete Kāma Sūtra* (Rochester, VT: Inner Traditions India Home Office: 1994), Part 6, "About Courtesans," especially 400–01, which discuss the courtesan's gifts to her client, and 422–28, which discuss ways of getting money from the client.
19. Marglin, *Wives of the God-King,* 90–91.
20. Ibid., 91, 145
21. Ibid., 79.
22. For their dedication ceremonies see ibid., 67–78.
23. On this point see ibid., 90–91.
24. Kersenboom, "The Traditional Repertoire," 145–46. Also see this article for their activities in a different temple, 137–47.

25. Marglin, *Wives of the God-King*, 250–65.
26. Ibid., 146–53.
27. Marglin describes these festivals, ibid., 156–70.
28. Ibid., 172–84.
29. *Kāma Sūtra*, trans. Daniélou, 3–4.
30. *Kāma Sūtra*, IX.1, 183.
31. For instance, Shattan's *Manimekhalaï* describes male transvestite dancers, 11. See also Alf Hiltebeitel, "Śiva, the Goddess, and the Disguises of the Pāṇḍavas and Draupadī," *History of Religions* 20.1–2 (August and November 1980): 164.
32. In many ways they are similar to the castrated transvestite *galli* priests of Cybele and Attis, as well as to the priests of Inanna and Ishtar. See Will Roscoe, "Priests of the Goddess: Gender Transgression in Ancient Religion," *History of Religions* 35.3 (February 1996): 195–230.
33. Roscoe, "Priests of the Goddess," 219. Serena Nanda also discusses Bahucharā Mātā's legend and its relation to the castration of *hijrās*, *Neither Man nor Woman: The Hijras of India* (Belmont, Ca: Wadsworth Publishing Company, 1990), 24–37.
34. Nanda, *Neither Man nor Woman*, 20.
35. Hiltebeitel discusses Arjuna's disguise as a eunuch in relation to Śiva; "Śiva, the Goddess, and the Disguises," 147–74.
36. Marglin, *Wives of the God-King*, 28.
37. Nanda, *Neither Man nor Woman*, 1–3. Hiltebeitel points out that they sing and dance, making a nuisance of themselves, until they get money; "Śiva, the Goddess, and the Disguises," 164.
38. Roscoe has a brief discussion of this; "Priests of the Goddess," 220–21, as does Hiltebeitel, "Śiva, the Goddess, and the Disguises," 165–68.
39. Nanda, *Neither Man nor Woman*, 4.
40. Ibid., 4.
41. Marglin, *Wives of the God-King*, 222, 230; and Eliade, *Yoga*, 261.
42. See Coomaraswamy, *Yakṣas*, who says that "there is no motif more fundamentally characteristic of Indian art from first to last than that of the Woman and Tree," 32, and 35–36, where he briefly discusses women kicking trees. See also Sutherland, *Yakṣa*, 29, and esp. 136–47. Both these works discuss the positive representation of *yakṣas* in art and their negative, frightening representation in Buddhist texts. In chapter 2 we saw that *yakṣīs* and Queen Māyā in a *yakṣī*-like pose are depicted at famous early Buddhist sites such as Bhārhut, Sanchi, Mathurā, Amarāvatī, Nāgārjunakoṇḍa, and so on. See also the discussion in Dehejia, ed., *Devi*, 369–74.
43. Sir Monier Monier-Williams, *A Sanskrit-English Dictionary* (Oxford: Clarendon Press, 1899, 1976) 1067, col. b.
44. Cowell, *Jātaka*, V.294 and William Crooke, *The Popular Religion and Folklore of Northern India* (1896. Delhi: Munshiram Manoharlal, 1968), II.115.
45. Dehejia, *Devi*, 369.
46. Cited by Coomaraswamy, *Yaksas*, II, 11.

CHAPTER 7

COURTESANS IN BUDDHIST LITERATURE

The conversion of a courtesan is a popular motif in Buddhist literature,[1] one that provides dramatic impact. The presence of a beautiful courtesan demonstrates the Buddha's utter indifference to the sexual charms of women, since a rich and successful courtesan will be the most attractive of women.[2] This suggests to the male audience that they, too, should be beyond such attractions. At the same time, though, these stories about courtesans and ascetics still retain their associations with the power and auspiciousness of female sexuality.

In Buddhist literature courtesans act as lightning rods for Buddhist teachings about sexuality, the nature of women, and the impermanence of the body.[3] The central obstacle to the Buddhist path of renunciation and the main cause of human suffering is desire, and courtesans are experts in desire—the male desire of their customers and their own greed. Indian literature represents the courtesan as one ruled by desire, both for sex and wealth, whose primary goal is to arouse desire in others.[4] When courtesans are converted, they reinforce the Buddhist teaching that all people can become Buddhists, even great sinners, and that not only women but even the worst women can be equal practitioners. Moreover, some converted courtesans also maintain their auspicious powers of fecundity.

ŚYĀMĀ JĀTAKA

In one of his past lives the Buddha was involved with a courtesan. In this tale from the *MV* (II.162–70), the *Śyāmā Jātaka*, the Buddha is a caravan leader, named Vajrasena, who is wrongfully accused of committing a crime and sentenced to death. On his way to the execution ground the rich and beautiful courtesan Śyāmā sees him, and because of the many past lives they spent together, falls madly in love with him. She arranges to set him free by tricking a young man, who has been a paying guest in her house for ten years, to unwittingly take Vajrasena's place. Śyāmā and Vajrasena then became lovers, and all is well until he began to worry that one day she would similarly dispose of him. He runs away to another city, and when some time later she sends him word that she still loves him, he rejects her again. The surprising element in the story is that while the Buddha was Vajrasena in this life, Śyāmā was his wife Yaśodharā. As is usual with past life stories, an explanation is given as to when and why it was told. The Buddha is said to have told this story on the night of his departure from home when asked how he could leave Yaśodharā. The story is meant to show that he had done this before, indeed many times before; he is in the habit of leaving her.

At least two things about women are of interest in this tale. First, even the Buddha's devoted wife, the noble Yaśodharā, had been a courtesan.[5] Second, as Vajrasena, the reason the Buddha runs away from Śyāmā is all about exchange (*nimineyā*). As a courtesan Śyāmā exchanges men at will, and this unhinges even the Buddha. Men can exchange women whenever they want, but when women do so, the whole sexual economy is shaken. As will be discussed in chapter 10, men exchange women as a way of establishing relationships, particularly kinship relationships with other men, mainly fathers by giving daughters in marriage. Or they change women at and for their own pleasure. Courtesans, on the other hand, exchange men for gifts and can maintain highly profitable relationships with more than one man. Even though in relation to Vajrasena, Śyāmā acted out of love, the story emphasizes her ruthlessness in that she exchanges her first lover by sending him to his death in order to save the man she now loves. Vajrasena repeatedly refers to this exchange: it is the impulse for his escape and the reason he does not return to her. We will look at an even darker exchange by a courtesan in the story of Vāsavadattā below.

AMRAPĀLĪ

The most famous courtesan in the Buddha's biographies is the beautiful and rich Amrapālī, known throughout India for her intelligence and accomplishments.[6] She is described as "beautiful, good to look upon, charming, she was possessed of the utmost beauty of complexion, was clever at dancing and singing and lute-playing, much visited by desirous people and she went for a night for 50 [*kahāpaṇ*as, a very high sum of money], and through her [the city of] Vesālī shown forth all the more."[7] In her story the ascetic and the courtesan receive a new twist: it is the ascetic who seduces the courtesan into abandoning worldly life, for Amrapālī later becomes a Buddhist nun and achieves enlightenment.[8]

Amrapālī first appeared in the Buddha's life when he came to preach in her city. She approached him, received teachings, and then invited him and his disciples to dine at her house. Shortly after that the leaders of the city also invited the Buddha to a feast, but much to their annoyance he declined in order to keep his appointment with Amrapālī.

There are several messages contained in this anecdote that are central to early Buddhism: a flaunting of food taboos, as well as caste and social status, and, as in the story of Sujātā, this story emphasizes the virtue of generosity and the acceptance of women—in Amrapālī's case even women on the fringes of society. It is a famous story, one that is told in several texts[9] and in iconography.[10] Amrapālī and the virtuous woman Sujātā, despite their different status, enact one of the primary roles accorded to women in Buddhism, to sustain the monastic order through food offerings. The relevance of this blend of courtesans, virtuous women, and food offerings received its finest articulation in the story of the young courtesan Manimekhalaï, to which we now turn.

THE *MANIMEKHALAÏ*

A lengthy literary treatment of a Buddhist courtesan occurs in the *Manimekhalaï*,[11] a South Indian epic composed sometime before the sixth century C.E.[12] The young heroine of the title does not yet work as a courtesan—she is on the brink of this fate, being pushed into it by virtue of her birth into a family of courtesans, by her grandmother, by the desire of a powerful prince, and by the citizens of her city (Puhâr), who consider her an important asset—her fame as a dancer and courtesan will attract many rich men to their city. Manimekhalaï, however, has different plans. Through the influence of her mother she is attracted to the teachings of the Buddha and the ascetic, nonsexual life he recommended. Her desire for the religious life allows the author to explore a continuum of female sexualities, from celibate women to virtuous married women and sexually available women, as well as to display women's auspicious powers of fertility and plentitude, particularly as represented by food offerings.

With the whole city set against her decision to become a Buddhist nun, it takes divine intervention to move the story forward. Manimekhalaï's namesake, the goddess of the sea,[13] a wonderful model of the productive and destructive female powers that are the epic's subject, transports her to a deserted island where she teaches her many things, including mantras that will enable her to shape-shift, to fly, and to eliminate hunger pangs.[14] But of most importance, she is given a magic bowl. That this bowl appears on the anniversary of the Buddha's birth is particularly auspicious, evoking as it does the image of another beautiful woman whose fertile powers were a blessing to the world—Queen Māyā giving birth to the Buddha. A begging bowl is one of the main accouterments of Buddhist monastics, which they use in begging food for their single meal of the day, and it symbolizes, among other things, divine acceptance of Manimekhalaï's decision to become a Buddhist monastic. The magic quality of the bowl is that it will always be filled with food, thereby enabling her, even as a nun, to feed everyone rather than being fed by everyone. This is an enthralling inversion, not unlike the sexual inversion she is trying to make. Bowls are a frequent symbol for wombs, especially in South Asia, and here, rather than being indiscriminately filled, it indiscriminately empties.[15] Manimekhalaï's grandmother employs this symbolism when she describes the life of courtesans: "It is our privilege to eat from all hands,"[16] meaning to have sex with all.[17] This bowl enables Manimekhalaï to transform her value: no one will be deprived because of her asceticism, in fact everyone will profit. At the end of the epic, the text says she "appeared as a dispenser of prosperity."[18] In other words, she remains an auspicious woman, a bringer of prosperity and plenty, but one whose auspicious powers have been diverted from sexuality for the enduring benefit of all.

This text, with a nod toward Buddhist lay followers, also acknowledges the auspicious fertility of regularized female sexuality in the figure of Atiraï, the most virtuous wife in the city,[19] who is chosen to put the first food donation in Manimekhalaï's bowl, food that thenceforth endlessly multiplies.[20] As discussed briefly in chapter 5, Atiraï is so virtuous that she has the power to make rain fall in its proper season,[21] a power she earned through enduring devotion to her husband, despite the fact that he left her for a courtesan upon whom he had squandered all his wealth.[22] Here the text counters the destructive sexuality of the courtesan, which can impoverish men, with the constructive sexuality of the virtuous wife, a wife who was brought to the brink of death because of a courtesan,[23] and yet is instrumental in redirecting the fertility of another courtesan, Manimekhalaï, toward celibacy and giving life to all.

As previously mentioned, Buddhist attitudes toward sexuality gather in some diverse ideas. First, they locate sexuality within women, as repositories of the desirable, and this defines women's nature—they are filled with power, which they can use negatively, such as courtesans, to destroy men,[24] or positively, as faithful wives bringing their auspicious fertility to their families and to the very country they live in, for example by controlling the rain. Second, the celibate monastic life remains the ideal. Sexuality is believed to entangle one with the world, a point well made in this text by the prince who is blinded by his desire for Manimekhalaï and eventually destroyed by it. Enlightenment involves abandoning desire and abandoning attachment to the world. Yet Buddhist monastics are dependant on the laity for sustenance, so South Asian ideas about the powers of the virtuous wife endured.

The *Manimekhalaï* is a unique Buddhist text not only for having a woman as its main character, but for the rich range of female characterizations that surround her, including two mild villianesses (her grandmother and the queen),[25] and the fact that the primary actors are almost all female, including the goddess. Except for a male guru and the amorous prince, both of whom remain in the background, all the action and all the dialogue is between women throughout the first half of the text. Of course, husbands are mentioned continually, but for the most part they do not act until the middle of the text.[26] In fact, it is not the king but rather the queen who attempts to avenge the death of their son, whose inappropriate desire for Manimekhalï led to his death, and all the main female characters assemble before her, not the king, to resolve the situation.[27] The sympathy that exists between Manimekhalaï and her mother, and indeed the support of her mother, adds to the text's female orientation, which continues with the first person Manimekhalaï feeds from her magic bowl: a woman who has been cursed with an insatiable hunger that Manimekhalaï's food cures.[28] The text's emphasis on women echoes Manimekhalaï's female lineage: as a courtesan her father is irrelevant[29]—in her case we know he died long ago—it is her mother and grandmother who represent her family, one that her grandmother claims goes back to the *apśara* (celestial courtesan) Urvasī.[30] It also reflects the matrilineal practices of south India, where the text was composed, and those of the *devadāsīs* (temple courtesans).

The text is clearly directed to women. Emphasizing women as independent beings and placing them at the center of the text demonstrates the importance of women to the Buddhist community. It is a text that affirms Buddhist women and that encourages non-Buddhist women to convert. At the same time it is an alluring, romantic tale filled with adventure and magic that held great interest for women as well as men.[31] Perhaps most important, it subverts all the earlier tales of women as seductresses in realistically portraying the torment a woman endures, especially a defenseless woman, from the unwanted sexual attentions of men.

Having said all this, it is regrettable to add that Manimekhalaï does not achieve enlightenment. Instead she is given a prophecy that in the future she will always be born as a man and will thus achieve enlightenment.[32] Among the powers the goddess bestowed on Manimekhalaï was the ability to shape-shift, to change sex, which Manimekhalaï did on two occasions. Once, briefly, she changed to protect herself from rape.[33] The second time was for an extended period while she traveled around studying with various religious teachers.[34] Compounding the gender contradictions of this text, she returned to her female form when she met the Buddhist guru Aravana Adiagal, and she became a nun. Manimekhalaï's gender shifting was shown to be a form of expediency in her present life and her female form was affirmed by her Buddhist teacher. Yet, the text says that in order to achieve enlightenment she will need to be reborn as a man. The issue of whether or not women can achieve enlightenment will be taken up at length in chapters 12 and 13.

Returning to the magic bowl, it powerfully links wives with Buddhist nuns, for both Buddhist nuns and monks begged their daily food mostly from housewives, as they continue to do throughout Southeast Asia. The virtuous housewife Atiraï is the first to offer food in Manimekhalaï's bowl, and magically this food multiplies. As we saw in chapter 2, donations have important implications for Buddhists in that they generate merit, a spiritual reward. This is true for offerings of any kind, even the smallest. Monastics were understood to be particularly fruitful fields for the generation of merit, though often nuns were seen as less fruitful sources of merit.[35] In contrast, the scene of Atiraï filling Manimekhalaï's bowl, which stimulates its endless supply of food, dramatically valorized the fruitfulness of donations to nuns.

Begging bowls are the site of daily exchanges between Buddhist lay women and monastics of food and merit. Indeed, stories explaining the rewards of food donations frequently appear in the text, including a past life in which Manimekhalaï's food donation to a sage earned her the help of her namesake, the sea goddess Manimekhalaï, in the present life.[36] Even though Sanskrit and Pali texts reflected a celibate male view that was threatened by women, we can see positive images of womanhood in the food offerings of young, attractive, and sexual women such as Sujātā, and the desirable courtesan Amrapāli. This is in keeping with the South Asian view that women are repositories of a sacred power connected with their sexuality and fertility. Like all sacred power, such as that of the *yakṣīs*, it can bestow blessings or it can destroy. Men control this female power in both human women and goddesses through marriage; unmarried goddesses are considered unpredictable and dangerous, while married goddesses are benevolent. Similarly, the sacred powers of virtuous married women are channeled and controlled by patriarchal systems of reproduction.[37] The new idea in the *Manimekhalaï* is that a celibate woman, a Buddhist nun, can herself control and channel her own female powers. In the Tamil literary tradition of south India as represented by the *Manimekhalaï*, women maintain their auspiciousness whether as celibates or as virtuous sexual women. Iconographically this is represented by the abundance of voluptuous female figures and loving couples found at south Indian Buddhist sites such as Nāgārjunakoṇḍa and Amarāvatī. Manimekhalaï's name itself evokes these female figures as it is the same term used for the broad, jeweled belts they wore, and that Manimekhalaï, as a renowned dancer, also wore.

THE DECEPTION OF THE BODY

Courtesans were also used to dramatize Buddhist teachings about impermanence, especially of the body. Actually, the beauty and desirability of courtesans was used to denigrate the human body, which, as we have seen in chapter 2, was an important theme in early Buddhism. Through the almost exclusive use of the female body to represent and denigrate the human body, early Buddhists attempted to strip away women's auspicious powers. According to the earliest Buddhist texts, as bad as the human body is, the female body is worse. We have already met with this view in the Buddha's description of the sleeping harem women as corpses. This idea is even expressed in the *Manimekhalaï*, when the prince, who desires Manimekhalaï, describes her beautiful body to her protective companion Sutâmati. In responding to him Sutâmati says,

> "Stripped of its ornaments, it is but evil-smelling flesh, subject to age and decline, prone to the worst ills. It is the seat of all the passions. It is simply a vessel in which all the vices are, as it were, stored, always ready to loom into view. Anger and hate hide there like a venomous cobra curled up in its hole. It is the consciousness which it also contains that causes our anguish in the present, our fears of the future, our feeble efforts to free ourselves, and, finally our despair.

"You, so proud of your rank, think of what this body contains.
Regard it as though all its viscera were in full view."[38]

Later in the text Manimekhalaï herself makes a speech to the prince, detailing the decline of the body, by pointing to a nearby old woman.[39]

A similar speech is found in the following poem attributed to Amrapālī after she had become a Buddhist nun and grown old:

Black and glossy as a bee and curled was my hair;
now in old age it is just like hemp or bark-cloth. . . .

My hair clustered with flowers was like a box of sweet perfume;
now in old age it stinks like a rabbit's pelt. . . .

Once my eyebrows were lovely, as though drawn by an artist;

Dark and long-lidded, my eyes were bright and flashing as jewels:
now in old age they are dulled and dim. . . .

My voice was as sweet as the cuckoo's, who files in the woodland thickets;
now in old age it is broken and stammering. . . .

Once my hands were smooth and soft, band bright with jewels and gold;
now in old age they twist like roots. . . .

Once my body was lovely as polished gold;
now in old age it is covered all over with tiny wrinkles. . . .

Once my two feet were soft, as though filled with down;
now in old age they are cracked and wizened. . . .

Such was my body once. Now it is wary and tottering,
the home of many ills, an old house with flaking plaster.[40]

This point is made even more strongly in the frequently illustrated legend of the courtesan Vāsavadattā, who is depicted as beautiful, vain, greedy, and ruthless—the stereotypical courtesan.[41] One day, while entertaining a customer, another, even richer man appeared. In a fit of greed, she killed the first customer so that she could entertain the second. Of course, she is found out, and her punishment was to have her nose, hands, and feet cut off. The Buddhist saint Upagupta, whom she had unsuccessfully tried to seduce, visited her while she waited for death in a cemetery. Despite her mutilated body, Vāsavadattā's powerful fertility still functioned as she became the stimulus for Upagupta's enlightenment, for it is through preaching to her, through seeing the effects of his words on her consciousness, that he himself fully realized the potency of what he said. By virtue of Upagupta's teaching, he achieved a higher understanding and Vāsavadattā was reborn in the realm of the gods.

In contrast to Vāsavadattā, who was after all a murderer, the courtesan Sirimā was a devoted follower of the Buddha and a generous donor. Nonetheless, she received the same treatment as Vāsavadattā. Somewhat as a ploy to justify the Buddha's use of her body, we are told that due to her great beauty, a monk fell in love with her. When she died a few days later, the Buddha ordered that her body should not be burned, but rather laid in the cremation grounds and protected from animals that would eat it. After four days her body began to bloat and maggots oozed from it. The Buddha then gathered all the monastics and lay people around her corpse and said that whoever would pay her regular price of one thousand pieces of money could have her. No one responded, so he kept lowering her price, even to a penny, and then offered her for free. Finally the Buddha said, "Such was her beauty who now has perished and gone. Behold, monks, this body diseased and corrupt."[42] Sirimā's virtues and Vāsavadattā's crimes are not relevant in this worldview; they are only their bodies.

What is engrossing about these two stories of dead and dying courtesans, and in other references to the decay of the female body,[43] is the shift in the equation of women and life to women and death. That and the focus on cremation grounds, which were and remain important sites for Buddhist meditation on impermanence, and in Tantric Buddhism became the preferred place to develop *siddhis* (supernatural powers). In tantric practice, some of the women who frequent cemeteries retain their beauty and auspiciousness, acting as tantric consorts and/or empowering *ḍākinīs*. Like *yakṣīs*, *ḍākinīs* have shape-shifting powers that enable them to transform themselves from great beauties to repulsive hags at will, rather than being passively transformed by time or someone else's power. They are in charge of their images, through which they assert their roles as the source of men's enlightenment, luring or repelling men as occasion demands. In this sense the *yakṣī* does not completely disappear from Buddhism—they are incorporated into the *śaktīs* and *prajñās* utilized by Hindu and Buddhist male practitioners in the quest for enlightenment.[44] This is shown in certain Hindu tantras of the Kaula school where worshipping the *yakṣī* as a wife is said to empower the male practitioner, transforming him into "the foremost among kings (*rajendraḥ sarvarājānām*).[45] There are many legends in which *yakṣīs* confer sovereignty on Indian kings, and several aspects of Hindu king-making ceremonies were incorporated into both Buddhist and Hindu tantric practice. For instance, *abhiṣeka*, the term for a royal consecration is also used for tantric initiations.

NOTES

1. See, for instance, Paula Richman, "The Portrayal of a Female Renouncer," 143–65, which is a thoughtful discussion of the *Manimekalaï*, the story of a courtesan who becomes a Buddhist nun, discussed below. The religions of the world abound with such stories. For Christian examples see "The Life of St. Pelagia the Harlot" and "The Life of St. Mary the Harlot," both of whom became Christian ascetics, in Ross S. Kraemer, ed., *Maenads, Martyrs, Matrons, Monastics: A Sourcebook on Women's Religions in the Greco-Roman World*, (Philadelphia: Fortress Press, 1988), 316–32 and 412–13; and of course the legends of the Magdalene.
2. Some sense of the power and influence of the Indian courtesan can be seen in the character of Seeda Bai in Vikram Seth's novel of India in the 1950s, *A Suitable Boy* (1993. New York; HarperCollins, 1994). See also Mirza Mohammad Ruswa's novel *The Courtesan of Lucknow*, trans. Khushwant Singh and M. A. Husaini (1961. Islamabad: Alhamra Publishing, 2000).
3. Several Pali *jātaka*s involve courtesans, see., e.g., nos. 92, 276, 318, 419, 423, 425, 481, 522, and 536; as do several of the *Theragāthā* cxxix, cxcviii, ccxxiv, and cclxiii.
4. See Richman's discussion, "The Portrayal of Female Renouncer," 156.
5. A similar story is told in the Pali *jātakas*, no. 318, but there it does not involve Yaśodharā.
6. Basham, *Wonder*, 184.
7. *Vinaya*, Horner, IV.379.
8. Three other courtesans or prostitutes who became nuns and achieved enlightenment were Vimalā, Abhaya's mother, and Aḍḍhakāsī. *Therīgathā*, Rhys Davids, respectively, Part 1, 52, 30, and 26.
9. *BC*, Part III, 7. Aśvaghoṣa uses the occasion of their meeting as an opportunity to put a very antiwoman speech into the mouth of the Buddha, one that is absent from other tellings. See, for example, the *Mahāvagga* section of the *Vinaya*, Horner, IV.315–22; and the *Mahāparinirvāṇa Sūtra*, chapter II, 30–34; in Rhys Davids, *Buddhist Suttas*, and the *Milindapañha*, ed. V. Trenckner (London: Williams and Norgate, 1880). Translated as *The Questions of King Milinda* by T. W. Rhys Davids (1894. Delhi: Motilal Banarsidass, 1965), I.30–33. She is also the subject of an Apadāna and a *Therīgathā* commentary.
10. For example, she is depicted at Sikri, Dehijia, *Discourse*, 15.
11. It continues the story of Prince Ilango Adigal's *Shilappadikaram (The Ankle Bracelet)*, trans. Alain Daniélou (New York: A New Directions Book, 1965), in which Manimekhalaï's mother, Mâdhavi, is a main character.
12. Daniélou dates it to the second century, Shattan, *Manimekhalaï*, xvi, and Richman to the sixth century. Richman also gives the author as Cāttanār, "Portrayal of a Female Renouncer," 144.
13. For more information on her, see S. N. Kandaswamy, *Buddhism as Expounded in Manimeklalai* (Tamil Nadu: Annamalai University, 1978), 268–71.
14. Shattan, *Manimekhalaï*, 42–43.
15. See also the discussion of bowls as vessels of plenty in Sutherland, *Yakṣa*, 33–35.
16. Shattan, *Manimekhalaï*, 71.

17. Possessing the magic bowl is an important indication that Manimekhalaï is beyond all this, but at one point the text goes further and has her say she knows a magic formula that can suppress hunger; ibid., 103. This is not to ignore the fact that the fear of famine underlies the entire text.
18. Ibid., 149.
19. Ibid., 62.
20. Ibid., 67.
21. Ibid., 62. Surely a metaphor for a woman's ability to satisfy/contain her husband's sexuality. The text attributes this belief to the first century poet-saint Tiruvallur and links it to women who worship their husbands as gods; ibid., 95–96, though in one instance a virgin is said to have this power; 97. Ironically, this power is supplanted by Manimekhalaï's bowl, which "replaces the seasonal rains as a means of sustaining life," 92 and 147.

    See also Kandaswamy, who briefly discusses female chastity, *Buddhism as Expounded in Manimeklalai*, 230–32.
22. When Atiraï mistakenly thought her husband was dead, she attempted *satī*, burning herself on a funeral pyre, but was saved by a divine being who said her husband was safe and would return to her. Several instances of *satī* occur in the *Manimekhalaï* as a proper recourse for a widow, e.g., 6, 25, 63, 71; and Manimekhalaï learns that she was a *satī* in a past life, 39. For instances of Buddhist *satīs* in Nepal, see Todd T. Lewis, "Newar-Tibetan Trade and the Domestication of *Siṃhalasārthabāhu Avadāna*," *History of Religions* 33.21 (November 1993): 157.
23. These events parallel the story of Manimekhalaï's mother, Mâdhavi, who destroyed the wealth of Manimekhalaï's father Kavalon and caused enormous suffering to his chaste and faithful wife Kannaki. Adigal, *Shilappadikaram*, passim. At the end of the text Manimekhalaï vows to perform good works to honor the memory of Kannaki, 112, and pays homage to her sanctuary, 122–24.
24. The *Manimekhalaï* has a whole chapter devoted to men destroyed by their sexual desire for women, 93–100.
25. See Shattan, *Manimekhalaï*, 71–75, 101–02 and 107–09. Both women are responding to stressful situations, respectfully the perceived disgrace of a granddaughter and the death of a son, and each lacks the unrelieved viciousness of someone like Aśoka's Queen Tiṣyarakṣitā.
26. Even Manimekhalaï has a husband of sorts, the prince who desires her was her husband in many past lives; ibid., 88.
27. Ibid., 106–12. The male guru Aravana Adigal shows up too, to give the basic Buddhist teachings required by all Buddhist stories.
28. Ibid., 68.
29. Though Manimekhalaï seeks out her grandfather, now a Buddhist monk, toward the end of the epic, ibid., 144–46, and Aravana Adigal says she was named for the goddess who had saved her father's ancestor, 151. This may be an attempt to privilege the patrilineal system of north India, the home of Buddhism, on the matrilineal system of the south.
30. Ibid., 107.
31. Richman discusses the text as advocating female renunciation in "Portrayal of a Female Renouncer," passim.
32. Shattan, *Manimekhalaï*, 92.
33. Ibid., 102.
34. Ibid., 125–49.
35. Falk, "The Case of the Vanishing Nuns," 207–24.

36. Shattan, *Manimekhalaï*, 92–93. Another example of her giving in a past life is on 88–89.
37. Glenn E. Yocum discusses this belief in a South Indian context, but I believe it can be extended throughout South Asia; "Comments: The Divine Consort in South India," in *The Divine Consort: Rādhā and the Goddesses of India*, ed. John Stratton Hawley and Donna Marie Wulff (1982. Boston, MA: Beacon Press, 1986), especially 280–81.
38. Shattan, *Manimekhalaï*, 17.
39. Ibid., 84–85.
40. Basham, *Wonder*, 252–70.
41. See the discussion of this story in Liz Wilson, *Charming Cadavers: Horrific Figurations of the Feminine in Indian Buddhist Hagiographic Literature* (Chicago: University of Chicago Press, 1996), 95 ff.; and Avadāna no. 72, Mrs. Sharada Rani, ed., *Buddhist Tales of Kashmir in Tibetan Woodcuts* (Narthang series of Ksemenda's *Avadāna-kalpalata*), in Śata-Pitaka Series, vol. 232 (New Delhi: Mrs. Sharada Rani, 1977). For the most part this book quotes Tucci's narration of these stories in *TPS*, which also reproduces tangkas illustrating them, plates 100–130. Another set is reproduced in Antoinette Gordon, *The Iconography of Tibetan Lamaism*, 2d. rev. ed. (Rutland, VT: Charles E. Tuttle, 1959), between 110 and 111.

    Strong briefly discusses a few other courtesans in early Buddhist literature, *Upagupta*, 83–84.
42. Burlingame, *Buddhist Legends*, II.334.
43. See also the decaying courtesans in *Theragāthā* CXCVIII and CCLXIII, and the Buddha's transformation of Māra's courtesan-like daughters into old, repulsive women on the night of his enlightenment.
44. Sutherland, *Yakṣa*, 146–47.
45. Vidya Dehejia, *Yoginī Cult and Temples: A Tantric Tradition* (New Delhi: National Museum, 1986), 36.

CHAPTER 8

TANTRIC CONSORTS: INTRODUCTION

IMAGES AND PRACTICES

The *yab/yum* couple is one of the most ubiquitous images of Tantric Buddhist art. Representing the sexual union of divine beings with their consorts, these images strive to express the oneness of the two necessary elements for the generation of enlightenment: wisdom (Skt: *prajñā*; Tib: *shes rab*), a passive female principle,[1] and skillful means (*upāya*; *thabs*), an active male principle,[2] joined together on the plane of ultimate reality. The bliss they experience arises from their apprehension of the essential emptiness (*śunyatā*; *stong nyid*) of all existent beings and objects. In Tantric Buddhism the couple is imaged either standing or seated, never lying down (Plates 6 and 7, and Fig. 8.1).[3] Importantly, these images are only created for and meant to be seen by initiates; they function as supports for meditation and as objects of worship.

The *yab/yum* image is so central to tantric doctrine that its meaning is made explicit in the opening lines of many *anuttarayoga tantras* (highest yoga *tantras*, Tib: *bla na med pa'i rnal 'byor*), such as the *Hevajra Tantra,* which states: "Thus have I heard: at one time the Lord dwelt in the vagina (*bhaga*) of Vajrayoginī—the heart of the Body, Speech and Mind of all Buddhas."[4] Hevajra is an important *yidam,* a male initiatory deity, and Vajrayoginī is a divine *yoginī* with enormous initiatory powers who is often depicted alone, as the central deity. The first lines of the *Tantra* make the point that the vagina is the place where *tantras* are preached, and imply that this is also where initiations and realizations take place,[5] thus revealing the importance of the tantric consort for spiritual development. Yet, except for very rare images of the female as the dominant partner (Plates 8 and 9),[6] in all

Fig. 8.1 Mañjuśrī in *yab/yum*. Courtesy of the Division of Anthropology, American Museum of Natural History, 70.0/7065.

other cases the females are unnaturally small compared to the male figure, indicating their subordination,[7] and are depicted with curving, voluptuous bodies that accentuate their femaleness and recall earlier Buddhist images of auspicious fertile women.

Tantra[8] refers to a wide range of religious paths that developed mainly in northern India, perhaps as early as the third century C.E., among Buddhists, Hindus, and Jains, although it took several centuries to achieve widespread influence.[9] While its earliest history is unclear, we know that tantra drew extensively on preexisting traditions such as yoga, the Vedic sacrifice, rituals of sacred union, and from tribal practices. In addition to conferring divine or magical powers (*siddhis*) on its adepts, it is described as a fast path to enlightenment (in a single lifetime), a path appropriate for the current dark age (*kaliyuga*), and one of its essential features is an abundance of female symbolism. These include divine females such as Tārā and Vajrayoginī, and various *ḍākinī*s and *yoginī*s usually depicted in their fierce forms. Additionally, there is the symbolic or actual use of menstrual blood (and semen) in rituals and the valorization of female-identified attributes such as wisdom (*prajñā*).

Tantric practice utilizes the human body, upholding it as the means to salvation, and central to tantric ritual are the "five *m*'s" (*pañcamakāra*), words that in Sanskrit all begin with the letter *m*: *madya, māṃsa, matsya, mudrā*,[10] and *maithuna* (respectively, wine, meat, fish, parched grain, and sexual union).[11] The first four are described as aphrodisiacs and lead up to the fifth, actual or symbolical sexual union. Theoretically, the right-handed path (*dakṣiṇāmārga*) uses substitutes for the first four and visualizes the fifth, sexual union, while the left-handed path (*vāmāmārga*) imbibes these and other unpleasant substances[12] and involves ritual sexual intercourse. In point of fact, though, left-handed practice also frequently uses substitutes and visualization, which raises the issue of what *tantrika*s actually did or did not do. Ambiguity about practice is inherent in the *tantra*s themselves, the primary texts of tantra, in that they purposely utilize twilight language (*sandhābhāṣa*), a secret and metaphorical language that makes it hard to pinpoint literal practice.[13] Archaeological evidence from India between the eighth and twelfth centuries indicates that the highest yoga tantras, with their emphasis on sexual union, were practiced in private shrines rather than in large-scale temples.[14] This accords with the general understanding that Indian left-handed practitioners were usually wandering yogis while right-handed practitioners were traditional brahmans. A similar situation arose in Tibet where free-wheeling tantric practices were fairly widespread among nonmonastics, both householders and wandering yogis, while a more rationalized tantra flourished in the monasteries. There were, however, exchanges between the two groups.[15]

Whether through visualization or actual practice, the *tantrika* ritually uses these forbidden and sometimes polluting substances to get beyond the concepts of good and evil, forbidden and allowed, in order to experience the negation of all dualities, including gender. In tantra reality is one, but it is understood through a process of conceptual and intuitive polarization, or duality, symbolized in terms of female and male. The goal in Tantric Buddhism is to generate the thought of enlightenment (*bodhicitta; byang sems*), often glossed as semen.[16] This is accomplished through meditation techniques and yogic control over the energy channels of the subtle body combined with visualizing or ritually enacting the sexual union of wisdom (*prajñā; shes rab*) and skillful means (*upāya; thabs*). The union of wisdom and skillful means leads to a supreme bliss (*mahāsukha*), a direct and compassionate experience of the emptiness (*śunyatā*) of all existent beings and objects, which being empty lack any duality.[17]

Toward this end, the later biographical tradition of Indo-Tibetan Buddhism introduces a new type of female practitioner, the tantric consort. Tantra needs sexually active females, real or envisioned, human or divine, to enact its rituals and appear in its iconography, and it draws upon the voluptuous imagery of the courtesan and the auspicious, fertile women of the early Buddhist tradition. Westerners have become used to the term *śaktī* (power) for the female consort, but more often this refers to the Hindu tantric tradition. The Buddhist uses *prajñā* and *shes rab*, wisdom, or *vidyā* and *rig ma*,[18] knowledge. In Hindu tantra the female energy of *śaktī* is active, even dominant, as is often shown in images of goddesses standing on the prone god, such as Kālī on Śiva (Figure 8.2).[19] In Buddhist tantra the female element of *prajñā* is passive, a point I will return to shortly.

Tantric Buddhism has a rich terminology for the female consort. When visualized she is called *jñānamudrā* (*ye shes kyi phyag rgya*), wisdom or knowledge consort.[20] When an actual woman acts as a tantric consort she is *karmamudrā* (*phyag rgya*[21] or *gZungs ma*, or *las kyi phyag rgya*), often translated as action consort. Whether visualized or actual, they are considered to be *ḍākinīs*, initiatory goddesses.[22] Yeshe Tsogyel's biography uses *gSang yum*,[23] secret consort, as does June Campbell, who claims to have been a modern *gSang yum*.[24] Yeshe Tsogyel's biography is of some interest, containing as it does a rare record of a male consort, for whom it uses terms such as hero (*dPa' bo*) and *thabs*, meaning skillful means, the male complementary attribute to female

Fig. 8.2 Kālī straddling Śiva. Rajasthan, eighteenth century. Ajit Mookerjee Collection. From *Tantra: The Indian Cult of Ecstasy* by Philip Rawson, published by Thames & Hudson, New York and London.

wisdom. Of course, the primordial terms for the male and female consort are *yab* and *yum*, the honorific terms for father and mother, respectively.

Just as meditation on an initiatory deity (*yidam*) is believed to be more efficacious when he is visualized in conjunction with his consort,[25] practice with an actual woman is believed to be more beneficial than with a visualized consort since it can lead to enlightenment in this lifetime. However, the practice of union, or sexual yoga, only begins after vigorous training in the lower yogas under the supervision of a qualified guru and at the completion stage of the highest tantras (*anuttarayoga; bla na med pa'i rnal 'byor*). These earlier practices purify the subtle body (*māyā deha; sgyu lus*), an imaginary or spiritualized bodily system believed to be quite influential on one's physical and spiritual well-being. Activation of the subtle body is the first step in sexual yoga. It consists of three primary channels (*nāḍī; rtsa*): the winds (*prāṇa; rlung*) that move along them, the generative fluids called drops (*bindu; thig le*) that are located in the heart, and the five energy centers (*cakra; 'khorlo*) where the three channels meet. The main channel runs from the *cakra* at the base of the spine up to the *cakra* at the crown of the head; parallel on its left and right run the other two channels, one white and thought of as male (skillful means), and the other red and thought of as female (wisdom). Sexual union, whether enacted or visualized, involves the belief that women inherently possess something men do not: *prajñā* (wisdom or insight). Advanced male practitioners can access and appropriate that wisdom through sexual yoga. For female practitioners, men are the source of *upaya*, skillful means, which women can access and appropriate through sexual yoga. From the male point of view, which we will see is the dominant view, during sexual union the adept, who will lose any spiritual benefit if he ejaculates,[26] absorbs his consort's red drops (uterine fluids),[27] mixing them with his white drops (semen), which he then absorbs through his penis (*vajrolī mudrā* or *maithunasya parāvṛtti; bcud len*), up into the subtle body channels to the top of the head.[28] The female's red drops are not necessarily red, as they are also referred to as the vaginal secretion a woman is believed to ejaculate during intercourse. In other words, the female equivalent of semen.[29]

The many stories about courtesans seducing ascetics remind us that from the earliest periods of South Asian religious history semen has been equated with spiritual power and ejaculation with the loss of power. Sexual yoga takes this idea a step further, and completely reverses orthodox sexuality,[30] wherein the female partner absorbs the sexual fluids of the male. This reversal, combined with the prohibition against ejaculation, makes the point that tantric sexual activity is not about normal procreation, but rather about procreating the energy that will lead to enlightenment. It does not produce life, it produces the cessation of life through enlightenment, and in this it participates fully in the tantric emphasis on practicing in cremation grounds.[31]

In this reverse sexuality the male practitioner mimics but does not assume the female position of being the receptor. *Yab/yum* iconography expresses this, first by avoiding prone images (the missionary position), although the female on top would be a more gravitationally accurate representation of reversing the flow of sexual fluids. The women on top is described in the *Kāma Sūtra*, but Paul's research among Sherpas revealed this is considered wrong and defiling to the man, although he suggests that Tibetans are more sexually sophisticated.[32] However, Gedün Chöpel's sex manual, even though influenced by the *Kāma Sūtra*, does not include the woman on top.[33] Seated images, where the woman is on top, seem to capture this idea of reversing the fluid exchange, just as standing images do to a lesser degree. Regardless, all the *yab/yum* images do allow for the female to be in the weighted if not the dominant position, with the exception of the few images that depict women in the dominant position, facing the viewer and larger than their male partners (Plates 8 and 9). It would seem that for all its forbidden aspects and despite Hindu images of Kālī lying and/or standing on Śiva's prone body (Fig. 8.2), having the woman lie on top of the man is too much of a challenge to Buddhist male dominance and authority.

Turning to the female practitioner, theoretically she can mix her partner's semen with the uterine fluids within her body, absorbing and carrying them up to the top of her head,[34] but this requires that he shed a few drops during coitus, or ejaculate, in which case he loses any spiritual benefit for himself. Alternatively, visualization practices allow a woman to visualize herself as a man, and men can visualize themselves as women, for instance as in Vajrayoginī practice.[35] There seems to be some reciprocity in this for men, as Vajrayoginī can manifest and is said to have manifested as a man or a woman in various historical contexts.[36] The reverse is not necessarily the case for women. While the possibility exists that male deities can manifest as male or female—being deities they can do/be whatever they want—I do not know of any stories in which male Buddhist deities appear as females. A possible exception is the celestial bodhisattva Avalokiteśvara, a complex figure who in East Asia is frequently depicted in the female form of Kuan Yin. The fluidity of his/her sexual characteristics, and those of other deities and human beings, is discussed in chapter 12, where it is shown that the dominant tendency in sex change stories is always toward male forms.

In unpacking the meanings of female consorts, one needs always to bear in mind that the Buddhist tantric couple represents *prajñā* and *upāya*, with *prajñā* being a passive principle, the enjoyed, not the enjoyer; the known, not the knower; the object, not the subject. The meanings and implications of this will become clearer as we now turn to the biographical evidence.

MAHĀSIDDHAS

One of the first places where we meet tantric consorts is in the biographies of the eighty-four mahāsiddhas[37] (*grub chen thob pas*), eighty male and four female wandering tantric yogis who flourished in northern India between the eighth and twelfth centuries, and who deeply influenced Tantric Buddhism. Tantra's origins were outside the great monastic institutions of the period; it began and flourished among wandering *yogis* from a wide range of social backgrounds, though eventually tantra became part of the monastic curriculum. *Mahāsiddha* biographies reveal that several male *siddhas* practiced sexual union with actual women, though their practice is not usually elaborated upon. An exception is the following instruction given to the *mahāsiddha* Babhala:

> In the lotus maṇḍala [vagina] of your partner,
> A superior, skillful consort,
> Mingle your white seed [semen]
> With her ocean of red seed [womb blood].
> Then absorb, raise and diffuse the elixir
> And your ecstacy will never end.
> Then to raise the pleasure beyond pleasure
> Visualize it inseparable from emptiness.[38]

Through meditative skill the sensation of sexual pleasure is experienced as emptiness, the profound realization that all beings and all things are essentially empty, without individuality and nonenduring. As this example shows, gender, as it is defined by one's sexual organs, is essential for these practices, engaging as they do the karmic body, which we have seen is the gendered body.[39] It is the male gender that is important, though, because the instructions are completely phallocentric and almost always directed to the male practitioner.[40] I will return to this point at the end of this chapter.

Tāranātha, writing in sixteenth-century Tibet, lists many more consorts than other collections, possibly because his own guru's guru, Śāntigupta, had an accomplished consort, Menaka.[41] *Mahāsiddhas* who had human consorts include Ḍombipa (a twelve-year-old girl), Saraha (a fifteen-year-old girl), Ghaṇṭāpa (a twelve-year-old girl), Bhusuku/Śantideva, Rāma (a disciple of *mahāsiddha* Sakara), Nāropa, Tilopa, and Marpa.[42] The tantras usually recommend that the female consort be young and attractive, between the ages of twelve and twenty,[43] with sixteen being the most popular age. This seems to have been the age preferred by the controversial twentieth-century tantric master Chogyam Trungpa, who renounced his monastic vows in order to marry a sixteen-year-old English girl who had been his student,[44] and around whom rumors swirled about his additional sexual relationships with young female disciples.[45] Ancient Indian ideas about female sexuality partially explain this preference for younger women. It is believed that younger women have more female seed than older women. In a tantric context this means the male adept will receive greater benefits from a young woman.[46] Women are also believed to be more sexual than men; indeed they are thought to be insatiable and sexually aggressive, thus mature women pose a real threat to men by taking their semen.[47] This emphasis on teenagers also maintains the male adept's dominance and promotes the idea that female tantric consorts are inexperienced, that they are vessels and aids for men's spiritual advancement and not accomplished practitioners in their own right. Janet Gyatso has made this point,[48] and speaking more generally, Wendy Doniger O'Flaherty explains that a consort "is usually implied to be a mere appendage, far inferior in power and status to his or her spouse."[49] Indeed, the age requirement suggests that women have to stop practicing when they reach twenty. The *Hevajra Tantra* says that a female tantric consort can be trained by her male partner in just one month, which markedly contrasts with his years of practice.[50] We will, however, soon meet some examples of accomplished women practitioners of various ages.

Mahāsiddhas who were involved with courtesans or prostitutes include Vyālipa, Tilopa, and Śāntigupta, which is appropriate in that prostitutes were occasionally used as female consorts in tantric rituals.[51] King Dārika, for one, was sold as a slave to a *devadāsī*, a Hindu temple dancer and courtesan, and he is called *sMad 'tshong wa ma'i g-yog* (from *sMad pa*, to lower, and *tTshong wa*, to sell), the prostitute's slave, or *sMad 'tshong can*,[52] the prostitute's man. Frequently, the tantric consort is a low-caste woman, such as a barmaid—alcohol being one of the forbidden substances utilized by *tantrikas*—and taverns often doubled as brothels.[53] A well-known example is the barmaid with whom Virupa is often depicted (Plate 10), and others can be found in the stories about Lūyipa, Ṭeṅgipa, Saraha, Kāla Virūpa and Śāntigupta, while Ḍombipa was one among many whose consort was an outcaste woman.[54] As mentioned above, important terms for a female tantric consort are *ḍombī* and *caṇḍālī*, female outcastes, though the latter term carries additional important meanings, such as the Tibetan yoga of raising mystic heat (*gtum mo*),[55] and it is also the name of a female deity corresponding to the Hindu Kuṇḍalinī.[56] These examples are connected to the so-called forbidden aspects of tantra, most obviously the five *m*'s, but may include incest—as when the *Guhyasamāja Tantra* recommends sexual union with one's mother, sister, or daughter as the best means for realization. It even suggests union with the Buddha's mother,[57] while the *Hevajra Tantra* recommends the wives of others.[58] As we saw in the discussion of early Buddhist sexual ethics, these are all forbidden women, which makes them appropriate tantric consorts. Similarly, the use of menstrual blood is considered efficacious precisely because it is thought to be so polluting.[59] At the same time, prostitutes, barmaids, and outcastes are marginal women and as such often are also powerless women, creating yet another image of female tantric consorts as vehicles for men's development and not as accomplished practitioners in their own right.[60] Sometimes tantric consorts are wives (Saraha), as in the case of many married practitioners, for instance the Newari Buddhists of Nepal.[61] In the next chapter we will see some tantric consorts who were royal women.

References to female tantric consorts as *ḍākinī*s introduce the divine and semidivine initiatory females who are so prominent in the lives of Tibetan saints, although they are sometimes actual historical women who initiate adepts, awaken their consciousness, and instill them with supernormal powers.[62] On rare occasions the term is used to describe a highly advanced, living female practitioner. *Ḍākinī* was translated into Tibetan as *mKha' 'gro ma,* which means "sky goer"—they cross over between realms, as between the divine and the mundane. Being initiatory goddesses, they have important salvational roles and they also represent wisdom (*prajñā*), which they can bestow along with *siddhi*s, the supernormal powers that lead to enlightenment. They do this through dreams, visions, or sudden appearances in various forms: as old, disgusting women, or as dogs (a despised animal in India), or as young, beautiful women, and so on. Milarepa is a well-known example of a celibate *tantrika* who constantly interacted with *ḍākinī*s, as did the *mahāsiddha*s Kāṇhapa, Bhikṣanapa, Kantalipa, Udhilipa, and Nāropa, among others. The divine *ḍākinī*s Vajravārāhī and Vajrayoginī frequently appear to *siddha*s (Plate 11), especially in Tāranātha's version of their lives.[63]

*Ḍākinī*s are comparable to *yakṣī*s in their ability to grant boons, to bestow blessings. The great alchemist and *mahāsiddha* Nāgārjuna was said to have propitiated numerous *yakṣī*s in order to obtain power over the elements, and they acted as his consorts.[64] Iconographically, *ḍākinī*s are usually depicted like the *yakṣī*s in early Buddhism, as voluptuous, mostly nude women.

According to Tāranātha, the female tantric consort was not simply a tool in the hands of the male adept, or at least not always. For example, Ḍombipa's consort, known as the *yoginī* of the Ḍombi caste, is listed as one of his most prominent and successful disciples—she became a teacher in her own right and created her own lineage of teachings.[65] In general, he mentions many women practitioners and teachers, referring to them as accomplished *yoginī*s.[66] The next chapter examines fuller biographies of female tantric consorts.

Many deities and celestial buddhas are frequently portrayed in the *yab/yum* posture of sexual union, though others are simply flanked by two female figures (Plate 12).[67] Similarly, *mahāsiddhas* are often depicted with the human or divine females who helped them, though their iconography is rather inconsistent, especially in whether or not it includes females.[68] Sometimes women stand to the side, or sit on one thigh—rarely are they shown in *yab/yum*.[69] A particularly startling exception is that of Legs smin kara (Plate 13), a Tibetan form of the name Lakṣmīnkarā, one of the four women *mahāsiddhas*. Even though Lakṣmīnkarā is the more important person in this scene, she is placed in the typical female subordinate position. Unfortunately, this image comes from an incomplete set of *mahāsiddha* banners of unknown provinance, so it is unclear if any other *siddhas* in this set are presented in *yab/yum*.

NOTES

1. Buddhist tantric metaphysics developed, in large part, from the *prajñāpāramitā sūtras*, in which a feminine noun, the abstract and quiescent concept of wisdom, is said to manifest in women. See the discussion D. L. Snellgrove, *Buddhist Himalaya: Travels and Studies in quest of the origins and nature of Tibetan Religion* (New York: Philosophical Library, 1957), 81–82.
2. See Shashibhushan Dasgupta, *Obscure Religious Cults* (1946. Calcutta: Firma K. L. Mukhopadhyay, 2d. ed., 1962), 28. These are often also referred to respectively as emptiness (Skt: *śunyata;* Tib: *stong nyid*) and compassion (*karuna; thugs rje*). See the discussion in Keith Dowman, *Masters of Mahāmudrā* (Albany, NY: State University of New York Press, 1985), 10–11, and Cabezón, "Mother Wisdom, Father Love," 181–99. Robert Thurman discusses it in terms of wisdom and compassion, in Marylin M. Rhie & Robert A. F. Thurman, *Wisdom and Compassion: The Sacred Art of Tibet*, expanded edition (New York, NY: Harry N. Abrams, Inc., 2000), 17–19.
3. In Hindu images Kālī is sometimes shown straddling the prone and dead body of Śiva (Fig. 8.2).
4. *The Hevajra Tantra*, II.2 and I.47, ed. and trans. D. L. Snellgrove (London: Oxford University Press, 1952). See also Snellgrove's brief discussion of *bhaga, Indo-Tibetan Buddhism*, 152–53, n. 671, and other examples, 160, 248, and 289. The Tibetans kept the Sanskrit word *bhaga* to signify a ritual context, ibid. II.3; and see also, for example, Yeshe Tsogyel's biography, which uses both *bhaga* and *mtshan ma*, discussed below.
5. See Janet Gyatso, *Apparitions of the Self: The Secret Autobiographies of a Tibetan Visionary* (Princeton, NJ: Princeton University Press, 1998), 250.
6. Adelheid Herrmann-Pfandt discusses some of these images in "Yab Yum Iconography and the Role of Women in Tibetan Tantric Buddhism," *Tibet Journal*, xxii.1 (spring 1997): 12–34. Gilles Béguin in Rhie and Thurman, *Wisdom and Compassion*, discusses a Kalacakra mandala in the Musée Guimet that shows some couples with the females in the dominant position, 376, pl. 156; and see also another, more recent Kalacakra mandala, 384, pl. 160.
7. See Frédérique Apffel Marglin's study of three different male/female poses in Indian iconography, which finds that size disparities indicate hierarchy

and subordination, "Types of Sexual Union and their Implicit Meanings," in Hawley & Wulff, *The Divine Consort* 298. The use of relative size to indicate status goes back to the earliest Buddhist art; see Huntington, *The Art of Ancient India*, 121, and her discussion of additional compositional means to emphasize important personages, 145–46.

8. For more on tantra see *Tantra in Practice*, ed. David Gordon White (Princeton, NJ: Princeton University Press, 2000) and Dowman, *Masters*, 1–32; for women in tantra, see Serinity Young, "Tantra," in *EOW*, vol. 2, 956–59.
9. See, for example, Dasgupta, *Obscure Religious Cults*, 17–23, for his discussion of the roots of tantra.
10. As will be seen shortly, in Buddhist tantric practice *mudrā* is also a word for the female consort. Dasgupta seems to suggest that in the context of the five *m*'s *mudrā* should be translated as women, *Obscure Religious Cults*, 23.
11. The important elements that are ingested in a tantric ritual involve forbidden, polluting substances, and these can vary in Tibetan practice, for instance, the biography of Yeshe Tsogyel has "excrement, semen, meat, blood and urine." Stag-śam Nus-ldan-rdo-rje, *The Life of Lady Ye-Śes-mtsho-rgyal Rediscovered by Stag-śam Nus-ldan-rdo-rje with two hagiographies of Padmasambhava from the terma finds and visions of Ñan-ral Ñi-ma-'od-zer and A-'dzom 'Brug-pa Gro-'dul-dpa'-bo-rdo-rje* (Tashijong: The Sungrab Nyamso Gyunphel Parkhang, 1972), f. 48. Translated by Keith Dowman, *Sky Dancer: The Secret Life and Songs of the Lady Yeshe Tsogyel* (London: Routledge & Kegan Paul, 1984), 30. Sexual intercourse is listed separately as an action, although wine or *chang*, which is ubiquitous in tantric rituals, is not listed.
12. See, for example, the story of the *mahāsiddhas* Kāṇhapa and Bhadrapa, and the brief discussion in Dowman, *Masters*, 129 and 161. See also D. L. Snellgrove, *Indo-Tibetan Buddhism: Indian Buddhists and Their Tibetan Successors* (London: Serinida, 1987), 160–61, and also 160–70 for his general discussion of tantric feasts.
13. The exact meaning of this term has been challenged, but it certainly fits the texts. Samuel has a good brief discussion of some of the issues, *Civilized Shamans*, 414–19, as does Snellgrove in his Introduction to *The Hevajra Tantra* and in *Indo-Tibetan Buddhism*, 170–76. But see also Per Kvaerne's discussion of contending views of this term and his examination of it in Buddhist songs, *An Anthology of Buddhist Tantric Songs* (Bangkok: White Orchid Press, 1977, 1986), 36–60.
14. Samuel, *Civilized Shamans*, pp. 411–13, following Nancy Hock's work.
15. See Samuel for more on these points, ibid., 432–34.
16. This can be seen in the alternate phrase that the goal is to generate the drops (*bindu; thig le*) of enlightenment, with *thig le* being a common word for semen.
17. See, for example, Dasgupta, *Obscurse Religious Cults*, xxxiv–xxxvii and 27–28.
18. Dowman adds *pho nya mo*, *Masters*, 402, n. 139 in reference to text on 145. Das adds *dPa' mo, Tibetan-English Dictionary*, 1033, the feminine of the noun for hero (Skt: *vira*), 788. Other important terms are *caṇḍālī* and *ḍombī*, female outcastes, discussed below, and *dūtī*, female messenger. Tibetans translate *śaktī* as *nus ma*.
19. See Marglin's discusses of these images, "Types of Sexual Union," 298–315.
20. Guenther discusses some of these terms in *Nāropa*, 269–70, note E, and 272, note H, as does Per Kvaerne, *An Anthology of Buddhist Tantric Songs* (Bangkok: White Orchid Press, 1977, 1986), 34–36 and 42–43.
21. See, for instance, James B. Robinson, *Grub thob brgyad*, in *Buddha's Lions: The Lives of the Eighty-Four Siddhas*, with the Tibetan text, *Grub thob brgyad cu rtsa*

bzhi'i lo rgyus (Berkeley, CA: Dharma Publishing, 1979); and by Dowman, 317, f. 21, l. 4.

22. Jérôme Edou, *Machig Labdrön and the Foundations of Chöd* (Ithaca, NY: Snow Lion Publications: 1996), 102. *Ḍākinīs* will be discussed further shortly.
23. Stag-śam, *Life*, for example, f.5, l.5.
24. Campbell focused on *Gsang yum*, spelling it *songyum*, as the primary term for actual women who act as completely secret consorts to purportedly celibate lamas in monastic settings. *Traveller in Space*, chapter 6.
25. Benoytosh Bhattacharya, *The Indian Buddhist Iconography* (Calcutta: Firma K. L. Mukhopadhyay, 1958), 124. Success in such a visualization practice is said to prepare one for enlightenment during the *bardo* state after death; Daniel Cozort, *Highest Yoga Tantra* (Ithaca, NY: Snow Lion Publications, 1986), 92.
26. There are stories about both Krișṇa and Śiva not ejactulating during sex; see Marglin, *Wives of the God-King*, 201–02 and 214.
27. Shaw's brief explanation of these drops is informative, *Passionate Enlightenment*, 157–58 and nn. 81 and 82, 249–50.
28. I have simplified this actually complex practice. For more details about Buddhist practice, see Cozort, *Highest*, 69 ff; Snellgrove, *Indo-Tibetan Buddhism*, 170–76 and 257–70; Guenther, trans., *Life and Teaching of Nāropa*, 76–78, with the Tibetan text on 262–63; and Dasgupta, *Obscure Religious Cults*, 87–107. David Gordon White, *The Alchemical Body: Siddha Traditions in Medieval India* (Chicago, IL; University of Chicago Press, 1996), 199–202, has a good discussion of practice from the Hindu perspective. See also Wendy Doniger O'Flaherty, *Women, Androgynes, and Other Mythical Beasts* (Chicago, IL: The University of Chicago Press, 1980), passim; and Marglin, "Types of Sexual Union," 298–315.
29. See Marglin, *Wives of the God-King*, 58.
30. Both O'Flaherty and Marglin note that tantric sexual union, in which the male takes in the female's sexual fluids is yet another tantric reversal in that non-tantric sex involves the female absorbing the male's sexual fluids, respectively, *Women*, 78, and "Types of Sexual Union," 310. Marglin's example describes gathering the woman's fluids on a leaf, which when mixed with other liquids, is then orally consumed by the man, "Types of Sexual Union," 309–13. This is sometimes recommended in Buddhist texts as well. See, for example, Prajñāśrī's *Abhiṣekavidhi*, translated by Snellgrove in *Indo-Tibetan Buddhism*, 254.
31. In a Hindu context, Marglin locates the "inverse sexual union" of Kālī straddling the prone body of Śiva with part of a funeral ceremony that asks the wife of the deceased to mount her husband on his funeral pyre, *Wives of the God-King*, 237.
32. Paul, *Tibetan Symbolical World*, 172.
33. Gedün Chöpel, *Tibetan Arts of Love*, trans. by Jeffrey Hopkins (Ithaca, NY: Snow Lion Publications, 1992).
34. Shaw cites the *Ḥatha-yoga-pradīpikā*, which refers to women doing this practice, *Passionate Enlightenment*, 250, n. 86. Shaw argues that women contributed to the development of tantra and were respected, active participants in it. Her frequent reading of legendary and mythical sources in creating a history of women in tantra is problematic, as is her reliance primarily on one tantra, the *Caṇḍramahāroṣaṇa*. Despite this, read carefully there is much of value in her work.
35. Cozort, *Highest Yoga Tantra*, 171, n. 1. See also Gyatso's subtle discussion of the nuances of such practice for women, *Apparitions*, 257–60.
36. See, for instance, Kelsang Gyatso, *Guide to Dakini Land* (London: Tharpa, 1992), 7–14.

37. The biographies of eighty-four mahāsiddhas were compiled by Abhayadatta, the *Caturaśīti-siddha-pravṛtti*, between the end of the eleventh century and the beginning of the twelfth. They were translated by James B. Robinson, *Buddha's Lions: The Lives of the Eighty-Four Siddhas,* with the Tibetan text, *Grub thob brgyad cu rtsa bzhi'i lo rgyus* (Berkeley, CA: Dharma Publishing, 1979) and by Dowman, *Masters,* which also compares various historical sources for each siddha. See also Jo Nang Tāranātha, *The Seven Instruction Lineages,* trans. David Templeman (Dharamsala: Library of Tibetan Works and Archives, 1983), for his account of fifty-nine siddhas and their lineages. Reginald Ray, "Mahāsiddhas," in *EOR*, vol. 9, 122–26, offers an excellent, brief overview of them, while White's, *The Alchemical Body,* a study of the Hindu siddha tradition, offers fresh insights.
38. Dowman, *Masters,* 216. See also his discussion of this song, ibid., 217–18.
39. Chapter 3 herein. See also Gyatso, *Apparitions,* 258.
40. See Gyatso on the point that the female tantric consort is generally perceived as an aid for the male practitioner rather than as an accomplished practitioner in her own right, *Apparitions,* 257 and 308–309, n. 63.
41. Tāranātha, *Seven Instruction,* 90. The consorts of *mahāsiddhas* are referred to on 11–12, 25, 26, 56, 62–63, 66, 67, 77, 78, and 86–91.
42. In general, see their individual stories in Robinson and Dowman, listed above. More particularly, see Dowman, *Masters,* 344 and 145–46; Guenther, *Life and Teaching of Nāropa,* 76–80, though this section is not included in the Tibetan text he appended, 262–63; Tāranātha, *Seven Instruction,* 45–48; and *The Life of Marpa,* trans. Nālandā Translation Committee (Boston & London: Shambhala, 1995), 104 and 153, where he recommends this practice to others. Of course, this is in addition to his wife, Dakmema. Yeshe Tsogyel predicts one of her incarnations will be as Marpa's consort; Dowman, *Sky Dancer,* 171. R. A. Stein suggests Marpa had eight additional wives for his Heruka rites, but does not cite a source; *Tibetan Civilization,* trans. J. E. Stapleton Driver, (Stanford, CA: Stanford University Press, 1972), 97.
43. See, e.g., Snellgrove, *Indo-Tibetan Buddhism,* vol. I, 260.
44. Tom Clark, *The Great Naropa Poetry Wars* (Santa Barbara, CA: Cadmus Editions, 1980), 13.
45. Trungpa never denied having sex with many women, and he was a heavy smoker and drank alcohol to such excess that he probably died of cirrhosis of the liver. Rick Fields, *How the Swans Came to the Lake: A Narrative History of Buddhism in America,* 3rd ed. (Boston & London: Shambhala, 1981, 1992), 360; and Gregory Jaynes, "A Spiritual Leader's Farewell," *Time,* June 22, 1987, available online at http://www.ramsjb.com/talamasca/avatar/trungpa.html. See also D'Arcy Jenish, "A Troubled Church: A Buddhistgroup recovers from controversy," *Maclean's,* October 29, 1990, and online at http://www.ramsjb.com/talamasca/avatar/vajradhatu.html.

    His sexual legacy continued with his successor, Osel Tendzin, who died prematurely from AIDS-related pneumonia, and never denied that he had infected several disciples through sexual encounters. Jenish, "A Troubled Church"; and Fields, *Swans,* 362–67. The sexually inappropriate behavior of Buddhist gurus in America is discussed in *Swans,* 362–67.
46. O'Flaherty, *Women,* 56–57, 110, and 112.
47. See further discussion in chapter 11 herein.
48. Gyatso, *Apparitions,* 257 and 308–309, n. 63.
49. O'Flaherty, *Women,* 78. In general, this book should be consulted for its presentation of complex South Asian ideas about what it is to be female, male, and sexual.

50. *Hevajra Tantra* I.90 and II.46.
51. See, respectively, *The Life of the Mahasiddha Tilopa*, trans. Fabrizio Torricelli and Sangye T. Naga (Dharamsala: Library of Tibetan Works and Archives, 1995), 32; Shaw, *Passionate Enlightenment*, 136; and Tāranātha, *Seven Instruction*, 84. See also the discussion of the rich assortment of Indic terms for prostitutes in chapter 6 herein. Additional Tibetan terms for prostitutes are: *tshogs pa can* and *tshongs can ma*, both connected to the word for a tantric ritual feast, *tshogs 'khor*, Skt: *gaṇacakra*. Das glosses the first term to the Sanskrit *veśya* and the second to *gaṇika*, *Tibetan-English Dictionary*, 1033.
52. Dowman, *Masters of Mahāmudrā*, p. 358. Geshe Kelsang Gyatso glosses this story by saying the prostitute was an emanation of Vajrayoginī, *Guide to Dakini Land*, 12.
53. Dowman, *Masters of Mahāmudrā*, 35. See also the story of Yid thog ma, discussed in chapter 9.
54. See, respectively, Robinson, *Buddha's Lions*, 122; and Tāranātha, *Seven Instruction*, 2, 17, 84, which contains many examples of low-caste consorts, 26–28, 56, 62. These stories call to mind the *caṇḍalī* who attempted to seduce Ānanda, the Buddha's favorite disciple, *Śārdūlakarṇa* in the *Divyavadāna*, ed. Cowell & Neil, appendix A, 611–55.
55. See some discussion in Cozort, *Highest Yoga Tantra*, who translates this as Fierce Woman, 71–72 and passim.
56. See, for instance, *The Hevajra Tantra*, I.31.
57. Quoted by Snellgrove, *Indo-Tibetan Buddhism*, 171.
58. *The Hevajra Tantra*, I.97 and n. 2.
59. See chapter 11 herein, which contains a discussion of South Asian beliefs about female pollution.
60. This is discussed further in chapter 10 herein.
61. See David N. Gellner's rich study of Tantric Buddhism in Nepal, *Monk, Householder and Tantric Priest: Newar Buddhism and Its Hierarchy of Ritual* (Cambridge: Cambridge University Press, 1992, 1993), especially 273–81 for a detailed outline of the initiation ceremony of female and male lay tantric practitioners led by a guru and his wife.
62. See, Gyatso, *Apparitions*, 243–64, and Hildegard Diemberger, "Lhakama [*lha-bka'-ma*] and Khandroma [*mkha'-'gro-ma*]: The Sacred Ladies of Beyul Khenbalung [*sbas-yul mKhan-pa-lung*]" in Ernst Steinkellner, ed., *Tibetan History and Language: Studies Dedicated to Uray Géza on his Seventieth Birthday* (Wien: Arbeitskreis für Tibetische und Buddhistische Studien Universität Wien, 1991), 137–53. See also Herrmann-Pfandt, *Ḍākiṇīs*.
63. Examples of their appearances occur in *Seven Instruction* on 2, 11, 15, 18, 23, 67, 69, 70–72, 84, 93, and 100.
64. Dowman, *Masters*, 114–17. The Tibetan text in Robinson, *Buddha's Lions*, has *'byung mo*, 331, f. 78, l. 4, female elementals, which he translates as demonesses, 76. Tāranātha's version of his life says he practiced the *sādhanas* of the nine *yakṣīs*, among others, 4, and in the life of Mahāpadmavajra, he adds that power over the *yakṣīs* is one of the ordinary or mundane *siddhis*, 26.
65. Tāranātha, *Seven Instruction*, 21–22. See also 76, 77, 87, and 90, for additional examples of accomplished female consorts.
66. For examples, see Tāranātha, *Seven Instruction*, 25–26, 30–31, 54–55, 87, 90, 98–100.
67. Stein makes the point that Indian and Nepalese iconography depicted the tantric relationship by seating the female consort on the male's hip, "thus contenting themselves with a vague allusion, [while] the Tibetans made a very real and visible representation of [the] male organ penetrating the fe-

male organ." *Tibetan Civilization*, 282. However, there are many Indian examples of *yab/yum* images.

68. For example, compare any set of *mahāsiddha* paintings with the eighty-four drawings in Lokesh Chandra, *Buddhist Iconography: Compact Edition* (New Delhi: International Academy of Indian Culture & Aditya Prakashan, 1991, 1999), 404–26 and even with some additional drawings on 688–91. As Dowman mentions, greater iconographic liberties were taken with historical figures, *Masters*, xvi.
69. In Chandra, *Buddhist Iconography*, see Kaṅkaṇa, Ghaṇṭāpāda, Tsapari, Siṁhapada, and Ka la da ge, between 404–26.

CHAPTER 9

TANTRIC CONSORTS: TIBET

PADMASAMBHAVA

The great eighth century C.E. Indian *mahāsiddha, tantrika,* and missionary to Tibet, Padmasambhava, is a figure of unparalleled significance in Tibetan Buddhism. In iconography he is often depicted flanked by his two most highly accomplished tantric consorts: the Indian Princess Mandāravā and the Tibetan Queen Yeshe Tsogyel (Plate 14). Like the historical Buddha, Padmasambhava was a prince who married and lived surrounded by beautiful women,[1] all of whom he, too, abandoned, but not for long. He went to practice asceticism in cemeteries, a favorite haunt of *tantrika*s, where he gave and received teachings from *ḍākinī*s, somewhat imitating the Buddha, who also entered a cemetery, put on the shroud of a dead woman, and began his slow reconciliation with women before achieving enlightenment.[2] For non-tantric Buddhists a significant difference between them is that Padmasambhava returned to the world and practiced sexual yoga with several different consorts. For tantric Buddhists, however, other traditions exist, such as the *Caṇḍasamhāroṣaṇa Tantra,* which describes the Buddha in his tantric form. Also, according to Tsongkhapa's student Khadubje (mKhas Grub rJe, 1385–1438), the Buddha practiced with an actual consort just before incarnating as Śakyamuni. He had reached the tenth stage of a bodhisattva, but in order to achieve enlightenment he needed the initiation of wisdom (*prajñā*), which required practice with a consort. The celestial buddhas summoned the divine courtesan (*divyavesyā*) Tillottamā (Tib: *Thig le mchog ma*) and then gave him initiation.[3] This meant that the Buddha was already enlightened when he took birth as Śakyamuni—his enlightenment under the Bo tree in India was a display for the sake of others.

Padmsambhava's consorts were often royal women, such as the Indian Princess Mandāravā and the Tibetan Queen Yeshe Tsogyel. Padmsambhava met Mandāravā, who had refused to marry, while she was living apart from society in order to pursue Buddhist practice. It caused a huge scandal when Padmasambhava took her as his consort and led to their repeated persecution and eventual imprisonment, but they were always saved by miracles or their magical powers. He and Mandāravā later traveled widely, and she developed into a powerful practitioner,[4] as did Yeshe Tsogyel,[5] whom Padmasambhava met when he went to Tibet.

Yeshe Tsogyel is said to have written Padmasambhava's biography, though she herself played a very small part in it. One needs to look at her biography, and indeed that of Mandāravā,[6] to round out the picture of their relationship to Padmasambhava. Importantly, all three biographies are *terma*s, revealed texts, traditionally said to have been hidden to await discovery at an appropriate time. Based on their discovery dates, they are all considerably later than the eighth century,[7] and whether Yeshe Tsogyel and Mandāravā were actual historical women is questioned by Western scholars. For example, even though Yeshe Tsogyel is said to be one of King Trisong Detsan's (Khri srong lde brtsan) wives in Padmsambhava's and her biographies, she is not thus listed in any of the ancient chronicles. For Tibetans, however, these three, Padmsambhava, Yeshe Tsogyel, and King Trisong Detsan are at the center of their most important historical event, Tibet's conversion to Buddhism.

YESHE TSOGYEL AND MANDĀRAVĀ

The biographies of Mandāravā and Yeshe Tsogyel are similar in several ways. Both were royal women whose conception and birth were surrounded by miracles, and they had many suitors so eager to marry them that they threatened war as a way of winning them.[8] This, of course, was one way to stress how special they were.

Both women were, however, determined to pursue their religious practice to the exclusion of everything else, and they refused to marry. Yeshe Tsogyel suffered the most, as she was brutally beaten into submission.[9] (In chapter 10 we shall see that to this day Tibetan women are often beaten when they want to pursue religious lives.) King Trisong Detsan had to intervene by taking her as one of his wives in order to prevent her contending suitors going to war over her. Once married to the king, she learned to read and write, and had the freedom to study and practice Buddhism because King Trisong Detsan was also a Buddhist. The king particularly desired to receive tantric teachings from Padmasambhava, teachings that can lead to the attainment of buddhahood in one lifetime. When Padmasambhava came to court the king demonstrated his eagerness by offering Padmasambhava everything he owned, including Yeshe Tsogyel, who is said to have been either twelve or sixteen years old at the time.[10] Padmasambhava accepted her as his tantric consort, and explained the nature, if not the details, of what their relationship will be:

> This Great Being is free of any germ of desire,
> The aberrations of lust are absent;
> But woman [*mi mo*] is a sacred ingredient of the Tantra,
> A qualified Awareness Dakini [*Ye shes mKha' 'gro*] is necessary; . . .
> Without her the factors of maturity and release are incomplete,
> And the goal of tantric practice is lost from sight.[11]

He installed her as his lady (*jo mo*) and consort (*rGyal ma,* which actually means queen), and gave her initiation. As mystic partners (*yab/yum*) they practiced secret yoga (*gSang sPyod*), and later "mystic sexual yoga."[12]

Mandāravā and Yeshe Tsogyel were both serious practitioners of Buddhism before they met Padmasambhava, and after receiving teachings from him they continued their practice alone in wild, isolated places.[13] Both became powerful teachers in their own right and were sought after by disciples; they performed miracles, achieved enlightenment, and are said to have vanished directly into the sky without leaving a corpse. Further, they are considered to be *yeshe*s, or *prajñā*s, female wisdom beings.[14] Like Padmasambhava they are divinities who can manifest at will.

In one of the rare recorded instances of a male consort,[15] Yeshe Tsogyel purchased a young brahman slave boy, Atsara Sale, whom she trained and initiated. Earlier in her biography, Padmasambhava explained the necessity of a male consort to her in the following words: "Now, girl, without a consort [*dPa' bo,* hero], a partner of skillful means, there is no way that you can experience the mysteries of tantra,"[16] which is equally true for male practitioners. He then tells her to go to Nepal where she will meet her future consort. Yeshe needed a male consort to balance her female wisdom and insight with male skillful means, just as male practitioners require female wisdom. In the following song she explained why this is a particular necessity in the present dark age:

> Whenever a perfected Buddha appears
> There is no need of a consort (*thabs*);
> when the Buddha has gone depend upon a consort (*thabs*),
> For thereafter Means and Insight should united.

> When my goal has been reached
> I will no longer have need of Sale,
> but now I need a partner to illuminate the path.[17]

Her consort is described as follows:

> He was handsome and attractive and a red mole[18] on his chest threw out brilliant luster. His front teeth were like evenly matched slates of conch and his four incisors were like white conches that spiraled clockwise. His intelligent eyes were haloed with a red tint, his nose was pointed and his eyes azure. His thick hair curled to the right and his fingers were webbed like a duck's feet.[19]

Some of these attributes, like webbed fingers, are among the thirty-two marks of the Buddha. More important, he is described in the same terms as a female consort in a male saint's biography; the text lingers over his appealing physical attributes.

Jérôme Edou makes the point that the male consort should be called a *ḍāka*, the masculine equivalent of *ḍākinī*, but more often he finds the term *dPa' bo*, hero or warrior, the term used in Yeshe Tsogyel's biography. He says "their roles do not cover as wide a range of activity, status and powers as those of a *ḍākinī*."[20] This may, in part, be due to the small number of female practitioners who have recorded their practice. *dPa' bo* is the Tibetan translation of the Sanskrit *vīra*, which comes from the root *vīr*, as does one word for semen, *vīrya*. Of course, this suggests the important idea that the hero is a virile man, and alludes to the ritual emphasis on semen. O'Flaherty adds some additional terms developed from the root *vṛṣ*, to rain or pour forth, rain obviously being connected with semen in the word *vṛsha*,[21] which Monier-Williams glosses as a man and as semen,[22] though she lists *retas* as the most important word for semen[23] from the root *ri*, a flow of rain, water, or semen.[24] These are all synonyms for the Tibetan word for semen, *khu ba*, though in a ritual context the word *thig le* is used for semen and for the drops (Skt: *bindu*) of enlightenment, which reminds us that semen is often used to gloss *bodhicitta* (the thought of enlightenment).

The opening chapters of Yeshe Tsogyel's biography present vivid tantric images through the dreams that predicted her birth. Her mother dreamed that she received a rosary made of coral and conch shell beads; the coral beads poured forth blood and the conch shell beads poured forth milk.[25] As is by now obvious, in tantric symbolism the color red (coral) signifies blood and women, while white signifies semen and men. Yeshe Tsogyel's biography is an endless succession of male/female imagery symbolizing the union of wisdom and skillful means. This is the case whether Yeshe Tsogyel pursues her practice with various male consorts or on her own. For example, she practiced such fierce austerities in the harsh climate of Tibet that she was often on the point of death. On one such occasion Padmasambhava appeared to her in a vision, offering a "skull cup of *chang*"[26] that sustains her. The skull cup symbolizes a vagina and the white *chang* (barley beer) represents semen, thus demonstrating her experience of the union of opposites.

Sometimes the sexual imagery is more explicit, and it can play with expectations about sexual orientations, as when she has a vision of a naked red-skinned woman who puts her vagina (*bhaga*) against Yeshe's mouth. Being a true *tantrika*, Yeshe drinks the blood that flows from it and is restored in her practice.[27] At another point she is tormented by visions of sexy young men who are the equal of any male ascetic's dancing girls:

> [T]hese demons projected themselves as charming youths, handsome, with fine complexions, smelling sweetly, glowing with desire, strong and capable, young men at whom a girl need only glance to feel excited. They would begin by addressing me respectfully, but they soon became familiar, relating obscene stories and making lewd suggestions. Sometimes they would play games with me: gradually they would expose their sexual organs, whispering, "Would you like this, sweetheart?" and "Would you like to milk me, darling?" and other such importunities, all the time embracing me, rubbing my breasts, fondling my vagina (*mtshan ma*), kissing me, and trying all kinds of seductive foreplay.[28]

Yeshe Tsogyel is portrayed as an extraordinary, determined woman of great power,[29] but her biography can be chilling. Her story highlights the particular suffering of women, a point she herself makes to Padmasambhava,[30] especially the sexual utilization of women at and for the pleasure of others, mainly in unwanted marriages. In this sense the biography continually contrasts the exploitation of mundane sexuality with the liberating sexuality of tantra. It goes so far, that in addition to all she went through in her early life, she is later gang raped by seven bandits while pursuing her Buddhist practice in an isolated area[31]—a very real threat for women seeking solitude. Mandāravā, too, was almost raped by demons, but she manifested a fierce form and intimidated them.[32] Yeshe's rape inspires her to compose a song about the empowering experience of tantric sexuality as spiritual initiation and source of enlightenment, prompting one to wonder if such practices really do free women from the patriarchal pattern of co-opted female sexuality. This text certainly wants us to think so.

Yeshe Tsogyel's biography powerfully, indeed brutally, depicts the lack of autonomy in women's lives, autonomy being a necessary prerequisite for the tantric path. Female saints who resisted marriage in order to pursue spiritual lives is a common theme in world religions.[33] Most cultures deny women the freedom to choose how they want to live, forcing them to resist society's norms if they want to pursue the religious life. Certainly, for a woman to follow the tantric path was extraordinary. Yeshe Tsogyel's biography purposely gains a great deal of its power from stressing her willful resistance to societal pressure and the sexual constraints she experienced as a woman. In this, the text's clear-eyed sympathy for the plight of women is quite moving, but that plight is never challenged.

Yeshe Tsogyel sometimes also pursued her practice within society. In addition to her long sojourns at the royal court, she performed many services for suffering humanity: "I gave my body to ravenous carnivores, I fed the hungry, I clothed the destitute and cold, I gave medicine to the sick, I gave wealth to the poverty-stricken, I gave refuge to the forlorn, and I gave my sexual parts to the lustful [*chags se mas can la smad sbyin pa*]."[34] All but the last are traditional acts of a male bodhisattva. Giving oneself sexually seems to be the special provenance of female bodhisattvas.[35] In Yeshe Tsogyel's case this was a leper whose wife had left him and whose place Yeshe agreed to take.[36] Elsewhere in the biography she variously emanates as a woman or as a man in order to sexually satisfy both men and women.[37] Similarly, Mandāravā manifested many emanations in order to practice sexual union with anyone who was present.[38]

As a great bodhisattva, a spiritual being available to one and all, Yeshe Tsogyel manifests whatever is needed. This is also a subtle allusion to the fact that people see what they want in her, a point she made in her final song before vanishing into the cosmos:

> Tell them [the people] that this incorrigible woman, this wanton uninhibited woman,
> This woman has achieved the impossible nine times over.
> Tell them that this Daughter of Tibet, this unlovable spinster,
> Now is Queen of Kunzang's absolute, empty being.
> Tell them this woman, over-extended in vanity and deceit,
> Successful in her final deceit, has gone to the South-West.
> Tell them this passionate woman, repeatedly fallen in her maze of intrigue,
> Through intrigue has vanished into the sphere of inner space.
> Tell them that this widow of Tibet, rejected by Tibetan males,
> Has captured the state of Buddhahood.[39]

Wanton, spinster, daughter, queen, and widow—she is all women and this song claims that her spiritual victory was achieved through negative aspects that society attributes to women: their vanity and deceit, their tendency to intrigue. Yeshe Tsogyel's biography takes society's views of women and spins them into a cosmic dance of liberation.

TERTONS

Given Padmasambhava's own practice with tantric consorts, it is no surprise that tantric consorts are extremely important to *tertons* (*gter ton*), the discoverers of texts and other artifacts believed to have been hidden by Padmasambhava centuries before. Generally, before receiving their main revelations, *tertons* practice sexual yoga with a consort as a means of accelerating and enhancing their visionary powers. A contemporary *terton*'s refusal to practice sexual yoga with a consort is said to have delayed his ability to find *termas* (treasures).[40] "When he subsequently began to uncover treasures once again, his lack of a consort resulted in his excavated statues of Padmasambhava lacking their traditional hand-held tridents, which are symbolically understood as signifying the consort."[41] Another *terton*, Karma Glingpa, the fourteenth-century discoverer of the *Bardo Thos grol* (*Tibetan Book of the Dead*), is believed to have died early because he was unable to find the wife who had been prophesied for him.[42] In this regard, the fact that the female *terton* Jomo Manmo (1248–1283) discovered texts before taking a consort[43] raises the question of whether female *tertons* actually need a male consort, or if their inherent female powers, enhanced by spiritual practice, are sufficient to the task.

YID THOGMA

A very self-actualized female tantric consort is the culture heroine Yid Thogma (Yid 'phrog ma), who had several tantric consorts of varying species during her search for wisdom and medicines. When we first meet her in the biography of Yuthog, the semilegendary first Tibetan doctor, she is a barmaid who, after being caught having sex with a monk, was put in a covered box and set adrift on the ocean.[44] She arrived at the island of a great *rishi*, Bamiba, and through her brewing skills got him drunk and seduced him. He regretted this, but realized the importance of sexual practices, called the skillful path or the male consort path (*thabs lam*), and he continued to practice with her for another seven days, after which he gave her many teachings and charms that helped her on the rest of her journey.[45]

Yid Thogma continued her travels, made offerings of skulls filled with beer to various beings, human and semidivine, and, depending on one's point of view, took them for her consorts or became their consort. In any event, they gave her charms and medicines, which is actually similar to the gift-exchange practices of courtesans that establish relationships of patronage and friendship.[46] As we have seen in the discussion of sexual yoga, apparently only one partner gains spiritual benefits, though the partners could take turns. Yig Thogma's assertiveness strongly suggests that she was the teacher of sexual yoga and that her guru fee was her consorts' medical knowledge. All gurus command fees or gifts, especially tantric gurus, and relationships between gurus and disciples endure even after the guru's death.

MILAREPA

Some examples of such tantric practices from Milarepa's lineage, a yogi known for his celibacy, show the complexity of the historical record on this topic. Tsang Myon Heruka (gTsang sMyon Heruka, 1452–1507), the author of a well-known Milarepa biography and compiler of his songs, is known to have had a tantric consort,[47] and he included a song/story in which Milarepa practices sexual yoga (*las kyi phyag rgya; karma mudrā*) with the goddesses of long life, Tseringma and her four sisters. As it summarizes a great deal about this practice, I have quoted it at length. The goddesses greet him as follows:

> We five girls . . . represent the four known types of womanhood
> Called Lotus, Conch, Mark and the Elephant.[48]
> Pray practice Karma Mudrā with us.
> Will you grant our prayer?
> Do you know well
> The four techniques of Karma Mudrā
> Called falling, holding, turning back, and spreading—
> If so, you may apply them now,
> For your servants are prepared.
>
> It is said in the Supreme Tantra,
> (That the qualified yogi) should attract the maids of Heaven,
> Of Nāgas, of Asuras, or of human kind.
> It also says that of all services
> The best is Karma Mudrā.
> Thus we come here this evening. . . .

Milarepa answers them:

> It is true that of all offerings
> A qualified Mudrā [consort] is the best.
> Most wondrous indeed are the four perfected Mudrās. . . .

When Wisdom and Skill together join
The Bliss of Two-in-One is offered best.

The Four Blisses and Four Moments are
The essence of the Four Bodies of Buddha.
Like the crawling of a tortoise
(Slowly Tig Le) should drip down.
Then hold it in the Central Channel,
And like a coursing beast,
Reverse it (to the head). . . .

This is a path of bliss—of emptiness, of no thoughts, and of two-in-one,
A path of quick assistance by a goddess.
Following this inspiring way
You, fair ladies, will reach Liberation,
and, in the Realm of No-arising will remain.
Oh gifted fairies, you are indeed well qualified!

> The Karma Mudrā was then performed, during which the five goddesses offered Milarepa their bodies, words, and minds—also many foods and drinks to please him.[49]

Milarepa's biographer Tsang Myon Heruka claimed to be in the lineage of Milarepa that passed through his disciple Rechungpa,[50] who also had a tantric consort, the noblewoman Dembu. Milarepa disapproved of this practice and worked hard to get Rechungpa to give her up. Rather than condemning such practices, though, he explained to his disciples that they have to be done at the right time and under the right conditions.[51]

MACHIG LAPDRON

A historically grounded example of a woman who was a tantric consort and wandering *yoginī* is the great Tibetan teacher and codifier of the *chod* (*gCod*) lineage, Machig Lapdron (Ma gcig la phyi sgron ma, 1055–1153),[52] said to be an emanation of Tārā and an incarnation of Yeshe Tsogyel.[53] Machig was an integral part of the eleventh-century Tibetan renaissance of Buddhism and also founded a community of disciples at Zangri, the Copper Mountain, on the right bank of the Tsangpo River, about thirty kilometers downstream from Tsetang.[54] Her *chod* practice is the only Tibetan lineage to have been taken up by Indian as well as Tibetan Buddhists.[55] *Chod* literally means to cut, and refers to visualizing one's body as being cut up and then offered to demons, ghouls, and gods.[56] This practice is said to facilitate the realization that there is no enduring self and it has its roots in *jātaka* stories that tell of the Buddha offering his body to save other beings.[57]

Practitioners are called *chodpas* and they live as wandering yogis who frequent cemeteries. As part of their practice these fearless yogis remove dead bodies during epidemics.[58] Illness in general, but especially plague and epidemics, are believed to be caused by low spiritual beings and demons who can be appeased by accomplished *chodpas*.

Machig's birth into the family of a regional ruler was surrounded by signs, wonders, and auspicious dreams, and even as a child she showed many signs of spiritual accomplishment. She was a particularly gifted reader of sacred texts, especially the *Prajñāpāramitā sūtras*. Reading sacred texts aloud had great value in a preliterate society like medieval Tibet and people acquired merit when they hired readers for special celebrations.[59] Machig's *chod* practice is grounded in the Prajñāparamitā texts, and she was most influenced by the chapter on the four *māras* (demons), which led to her profound realization that there is no enduring self.[60] Her mother taught her to read, and together with her sister, a nun who was sixteen years older, all three studied Prajñāparamitā. Women remained important in Machig's lineage both as patrons and disciples, including her own daughter, and to this day many nuns follow her practices.[61] Her main male guru, Phadampa Sangye, also had several other women disciples.[62]

According to one biography, Machig refused to marry,[63] and some sources say she became a nun. By the time she was twenty she amazed one and all with her erudition and her spiritual accomplishments, but her visionary experiences were directing her toward becoming a wandering *yoginī*. In one such vision, Tārā predicted by name the arrival of Thodpa Bhadra, her future consort, adding that "her teaching will become like the sun rising in the sky and you will reach the level of no return."[64] In other words, she will become a buddha. Later, through dreams and visions, *ḍākinī*s predicted there would be good spiritual results for her and for others from her union with Thodpa Bhadra.[65] Some sources, however, say she broke her monastic vows when she took him as her tantric consort, and all the sources agree that they were subject to slander.[66] I will return shortly to the inconsistencies in her biographies.

Machig met Thodpa Bhadra and began to practice with him while staying with a rich lay woman who had hired her to recite Prajñāparamitā texts. One night her benefactress noticed light pervading the entire house and fearing a fire, went to find out what was causing it. She saw "a five-colored light, similar to a rainbow, which pervaded the entire house and within this, all ablaze, two lights like moons were joined, one white, one red."[67] Machig defined their practice as follows: "The yogi who has reached the level of utilizing emptiness on the path (*lam du 'khyer*) and who has mastered the yogic techniques of channels, winds and drops with the assistance of great joy, may immensely increase his physical power. This is called the great seal of action, karmamahāmudra."[68]

Machig and Thodpa Bhadra moved to Central Tibet where she gave birth to a son the next year and later another son and a daughter. This means that she and Thodpa Bhadra lived both as husband and wife and as tantric consorts. Sixteen years later Machig left her family and returned to her gurus for further instruction, and they advised her to establish a community at Zangri in Central Tibet. She later switched to visualization practices of sexual yoga after Tārā appeared to her in a vision. Tārā told her instead to perform the secret practice of holding the *khaṭvāṅga* (a long staff topped by a trident; see Plate 11) to join with the hidden consort, in her case, Heruka.[69] The *khaṭvāṅga* symbolizes the tantric consort, which can indicate that the practitioner visualizes union rather than practices sexual yoga, and it frequently appears in tantric Buddhist iconography.[70] About six years later, before departing for India, Thodpa Bhadra brought their two youngest children to her, a girl and a boy, then about fifteen and ten years old. Machig became the guru of her children, both of whom became proficient practitioners and continued her lineage.

Despite the power and enduring influence of the foregoing women, the female tantric consort was and remains suspect. As with Machig, both Mandāravā's[71] and Padmasambhava's biographies[72] report that people were critical of him for having a female companion. This suggests that there was an enduring tension between the Buddhist emphasis on monastic celibacy and the tantric emphasis on ritual sexuality, real or envisioned. More prosaically, venereal disease seems to have been a rather grim by-product of tantric sexual yoga. Machig Zhanen (1062–1150), who has been confused with Machig Lapdron, developed an incurable venereal disease from practicing with different yogis.[73] In fairly recent times, a prominent American tantric teacher, Osel Tendzin, died of AIDS-related pneumonia after having infected some disciples through sexual encounters.[74]

Tibetan biographical literature is dominated by monastics, and unlike the biographies I have been quoting, monastic biographies do not discuss tantric consorts. In part, this is because of the emphasis on celibacy, or perhaps, as suggested by a contemporary Western woman who claims to have been a tantric consort,[75] this is such a totally secret practice that it is not even mentioned in the so-called secret biographies that emphasize the dreams, visions, and other spiritual experiences and practices of the biographical subject.[76] In American Buddhism, though, this has become entangled in what has been called a conspiracy of silence about the inappropriate and damaging sexual behavior of some gurus, which a few practitioners find similar to the secrecy practiced by the families of alcoholics.[77]

The beginnings of the Tibetan Buddhist problem with the tantric consort go back to the reforms of Atiśa[78] and Tsongkhapa that emphasized monastic celibacy, respectively in the eleventh and fourteenth centuries, as well as the enduring dominance of the Gelugpa (dGe lugs pa) order, the order of the Dalai Lama and therefore well known and highly regarded by Tibetans and westerners. Those in the Nyingma (rNying ma pa) order who marry, and practitioners who openly take consorts, continue to present problems for some Tibetans and for many westerners whose financial support has a growing influence on the development of Tibetan Buddhism in exile.

By comparing three biographies of Machig from different time periods, Edou deduced that the status of female practitioners changed over time, making Machig "more acceptable to the stronger patriarchal ideology" that later developed in Tibet.[79] Campbell also believes that the status of female consorts has declined to a very low position in the present.[80]

As mentioned, some of the texts surveyed here are *termas*, texts believed to have been discovered centuries after being hidden, and traditionally, the *tertons*, finders of these texts, have worked in conjunction with a female consort. The recent breaking of this tradition in eastern Tibet by a highly respected *terton* seems to be another step in the ongoing direction of limiting the involvement of women. At the same time, also in eastern Tibet, Charlene Makley has documented what Tibetan women perceive as their subversive role when they maintain restrictions on women within monastic compounds that the Chinese flaunt.[81] Elsewhere I have discussed the active role of Buddhist nuns in resisting the Chinese occupation because they consider themselves less valuable than monks; they believe that their imprisonment is not as much of a loss to Buddhism as a monk's would be.[82] These fragmentary bits of information suggest that in Tibet today both lay and monastic women not only accept but may actually be contributing to a further lowering of their religious status. One has to ask, given the purposeful inclusion of women and female imagery in Tantric Buddhism, exactly who is served by this inclusion and who performs the services. I propose some answers in the following chapter.

NOTES

1. For Padmasambhava I have mainly used the biography entiled *Padma bka' thang shel brag ma*, discovered by Terchen Urgyan Lingpa (Leh, India: 1968),

and translated into English from Gustave-Charles Toussaint's French translation by Kenneth Douglas and Gwendolyn Bays, entitled *The Life and Liberation of Padmasambhava* (Berkeley, CA: Dharma Publishing, 1978), hereinafter respectively *Padma* and Douglas and Bays, *Life*. In general, see A. M. Blondeau, "Analysis of the Biographies of Padmasambhava," in *Tibetan Studies in Honour of Hugh Richardson*, ed. Michael Aris and Aung San Suu Kyi (Warminister, UK: Aris and Phillips, 1979), 45–52. *Padma*, Canto 21; Douglas and Bays, *Life*, 128.
2. Discussed in chapter 1 herein.
3. mKhas grub rje, *Introduction to the Buddhist Tantric Systems*, trans., F. D. Lessing and A. Wayman (1968. New York, NY: Samuel Weiser, Inc., 1980), 336, n. 3 and 37. See also Cozort, *Highest Yoga Tantra*, 92.
4. *Padma*, Cantos 99–100. See also her biography, Lama Chonam and Sangye Khandro, trans., *The Lives and Liberation of Princess Mandarava* (Boston: Wisdom Publications, 1998).
5. Cantos 107–08 and 747, and see her biography, Stag-śam, *Life of Lady Ye-Śes*, and Dowman, *Sky Dancer*, discussed below.
6. Mandārava also has a short biography contained within the *Padma kha' thang*.
7. For example, Padmasambhava's biography is said to have been composed by Yeshe Tsogyel and was discovered in the fourteenth century. Mandāravā's biography, translated in Chonam and Khandro, *Lives*, was discovered around the turn of the twentieth century. Yeshe Tsogyel's biography was revealed by Taksham Nuden Dorje of Kham in the eighteenth century, who is believed to have been the reincarnation of Yeshe Tsogyel's consort, Atsara Sale, and thus to have had access to her intimate and highly subjective experiences. More specifically, this text is a mind treasure in the sense that the discoverer retrieved it through meditation practices and it is believed that Yeshe Tsogyel guided his hand as he wrote it down or even that she dictated it. Dowman, *Sky Dancer*, xxv–xvi.
8. Mandāravā's biography opens with several past lives in which she is pursued by many suitors, Chonam and Khandro, *Lives*, e.g., 34–37.
9. Dowman, *Sky Dancer*, 116; Stag-śam, *Life of Lady Ye-Śes*, f. 22–23.
10. Stag-śam has sixteen, f. 39, l. 4. Dowman has twelve, 26.
11. Dowman, *Sky Dancer*, 24; Stag-śam, *Life of Lady Ye-Śes*, f. 36, ll. 4–5 and f. 58, l. 4.
12. Dowman, *Sky Dancer*, 24 and 35; Stag-śam, *Life of Lady Ye-Śes*, f. 35, l. 5-f. 36, l. 1.
13. Chonam and Khandro, *Mandarava*, chaps. 25–29; Dowman, *Sky Dancer*, chapter 4 ff; Stag-śam, *Life of Lady Ye-Śes*, ff. 36 ff.
14. For more on this aspect of Yeshe Tsogyel, see Anne Carolyn Klein, *Meeting the Great Bliss Queen: Buddhists, Feminists and the Art of the Self* (Boston, MA, Beacon Press, 1995), passim.
15. A *dPa' bo*, *virā* or *ḍāka*, Dowman, *Sky Dancer*, 197, n. 40. For example, none of the four female *mahāsiddhās* in the eighty-four siddha tradition are said to have had consorts. See their biographies in Robinson and Dowman.
16. Dowman, *Sky Dancer*, 44; Stag-śam, *Life of Lady Ye-Śes*, f. 76, l. 4.
17. Dowman, *Sky Dancer*, 51; Stag-śam, *Life of Lady Ye-Śes*, f. 88, ll. 2–3.
18. Chöpel's love manual has a section on the meaning of moles, but those on women's bodies. Moles on the chest refer to the children she will have. Hopkins, *Tibetan Arts of Love*, 175–177.
19. Dowman, *Sky Dancer*, 48; Stag-śam, *Life of Lady Ye-Śes*, f. 84, ll. 2–5.
20. Edou, *Machig*, 102. See also Gyatso, *Apparitions*, who cites some *tantras* that feature the *ḍāka*, 306, n. 23.

21. O'Flaherty, *Women*, 20.
22. Monier-Willliams, *Sanskrit-English Dictionary*, 1011–12.
23. O'Flaherty, *Women*, 20.
24. Monier-Willliams, *Sanskrit-English Dictionary*, 887, col. c.
25. Dowman, *Sky Dancer*, 11.
26. Ibid., 70; Stag-śam, *Life of Lady Ye-Śes*, f. 125, ll. 2–3.
27. Dowman, *Sky Dancer*, 71; Stag-śam, *Life of Lady Ye-Śes*, f. 127, l. 3.
28. Dowman, *Sky Dancer*, 78; Stag-śam, *Life of Lady Ye-Śes*, f. 141, l.3-f. 142, l. 2.
29. I briefly discuss the pitfalls of the "extraordinary woman" as a model for women in Young, *Sacred Texts*, xxv.
30. Dowman, *Sky Dancer*, 89; Stag-śam, *Life of Lady Ye-Śes*, f. 161, ll. 3–5.
31. Dowman, *Sky Dancer*, 118; Stag-śam, *Life of Lady Ye-Śes*, f. 222, ll. 1–2.
32. Chonam and Khandro, *Mandarava*, 164.
33. This seems to be a particularly Buddhist issue, as in the many legends about Kuan Yin in which either she escapes marriage or helps another woman to do so. Reed, "Gender Symbolism," 166.
34. Dowman, *Sky Dancer*, 135; Stag-śam, *Life of Lady Ye-Śes*, f. 256, ll. 2–4.
35. Faure, *The Red Thread*, 118. See some stories about Kuan Yin in Allan L. Miller, "Spiritual Accomplishment by Misdirection: Some *Upāya* Folktales from East Asia," *History of Religions* 40.1 (August 2000): 93–94. Faure also discusses some examples of male bodhisattvas, especially the sexually ambiguous Avalokiteśvara/Kuan Yin, *The Red Thread*, 118–24, though more often than not male bodhisattvas are enticing in order to convert beings rather than actually being sexual. See, e.g., the story of Avalokiteśvara taking the form of Kāma, the god of love, in John Clifford Holt, *Buddha in the Crown: Avalokiteśvara in the Buddhist Traditions of Sri Lanka* (New York: Oxford University Press, 1991), 48. See also Faure's discussion of Asaṅga's ambiguous views, *Red Thread*, 40–41. It would seem that the belief in the polluting nature of women extends even to the divine realm so that males do not risk becoming female while females are not under any such risk. Of course, it may also refer to the belief that females, human or divine, are more sexual than males.

    See also the story of Vasumitra, an enlightened courtesan who liberates beings through their sexual desires, in Thomas Cleary, *The Flower Ornament Scripture: A Translation of the Avatamsaka Sutra* (Boston & London: Shambhala, 1993), 1270–73. Faure discusses her briefly, *Red Thread*, 121.
36. Dowman, *Sky Dancer*, 136; Stag-śam, *Life of Lady Ye-Śes*, f. 259.
37. Dowman, *Sky Dancer*, 146; Stag-śam, *Life of Lady Ye-Śes*, f. 280, ll. 4–5.
38. Chonam and Khandro, *Mandarava*, 184.
39. Dowman, *Sky Dancer*, 179; Stag-śam, *Life of Lady Ye-Śes*, f. 340, ll. 2–4. Significantly, the text uses *jo mo*, lady, rather than *bu med* or other lower terms for women.
40. David Germano, "Re-membering the Dismembered Body of Tibet: Contemporary Tibetan Visionary Movements in the People's Republic of China," in *Buddhism in Contemporary Tibet: Religious Revival and Cultural Identity*, ed. Melvyn C. Goldstein and Matthew T. Kapstein (Berkeley, CA: University of California Press, 1998), 68–69 and 168–69, n. 7. See also Gyatso, *Apparitions*, 255–56, for more on the reasons for this requirement.
41. Germano, "Re-membering," 169.
42. Eva M. Dargyay, *The Rise of Esoteric Buddhism in Tibet* (Delhi: Motilal Banarsidass, 1977), 152.
43. Dargyay, *Rise of Esoteric Buddhism*, 119–23. Another short biography of her is in Tsultrim Allione, *Women of Wisdom* (London: Routledge & Kegan Paul, 1984).

44. Rechungpa, *Tibetan Medicine*, 154. This biography is of uncertain date, but it was printed in the early seventeenth century, see ibid., 326.
45. Ibid., 156–57.
46. Davidson, *Courtesans and Fishcakes*, 109–36.
47. Samuels, *Civilized Shamans*, 519. Other Milarepa biographies, however, have him practicing sexual yoga. See the forthcoming study of Milarepa biographies by Francis Tiso.
48. See the discussion of a similar list of female types in Guenther, *Nāropa*, 77. Snellgrove has equivalents for men, *Hevajra Tanra*, II.118–19. These are elaborated upon in the *Kāma Sūtra*, II.1.1–4, and picked up by Chöpel in his love manual, *Tibetan Arts of Love*, 173–75.
49. Garma C. C. Chang, *The Hundred Thousand Songs of Milarepa*, vol. 2 (Boulder, CO: Shambhala, 1977), 358–60.
50. Samuels, *Civilized Shamans*, 520.
51. Chang, *100,000 Songs*, vol. 2, 640. For their story, see Song no. 57. Interestingly, Milarepa's lineage through Rechungpa is less monastic than the lineage through Gampopa. Allione, *Women of Wisdom*, 131, n. 23.
52. Janet Gyatso, "The Development of the Gcod Tradition," in Barbara Aziz & Matthew Kapstein, eds., *Soundings in Tibetan Civilization* (New Delhi: Manohar, 1985), briefly discusses her problematic dating, 330 and n. 38.
53. Yeshe Tsogyel 's biography contains the prediction that she would be reborn as Machig and her male consort Atsara Sale would become Thodpa Bhadra, Machig's consort, while Padmasambhava would emanate as Machig's main guru, Phadampa Sangye. Dowman, *Sky Dancer*, 86–87. Gyatso cites additional sources for Yeshe's rebirth as Machig, "Development of the Gcod," 338, n. 91. She is often also connected to Vajrayoginī.
54. Edou, *Machig*, 116. Another important woman practitioner of tantra is Niguma, sometimes said to be the sister of Nāropa, sometimes his consort. She, too, established a teaching lineage of her Six Yogas. The history of this lineage is contained in Book Nine of *The Blue Annals*, 728–52, which says she was a disciple of Virūpa and one of Khyungpo Naljor's teachers. See also Matthew Kapstein, "The Illusion of Spiritual Progress: Remarks on Indo-Tibetan Buddhist Soteriology," in *Paths to Liberation: The Mārga and Its Transformation in Buddhist Thought*, ed. Robert E. Buswell, Jr. and Robert M. Gimello (Honolulu, HI: University of Hawai'i Press, 1992), 193–224, and Shaw, *Passionate Enlightenment*, 107–10; and Dge 'dun rgya mtsho, Dalai Lama II, *Selected Works of the Dalai Lama II*, trans. Glenn H. Mullin (Ithaca, NY: Snow Lion, 1985), 99–151, for more on Niguma. The biography of another female *chodpa* is that of A-Yu Kadro in Allione, *Women of Wisdom*, 233–64. Anne Carolyn Klein also discusses this biography, "Primordial Purity and Everyday Life: Exalted Female Symbols and the Women of Tibet," in *Immaculate & Powerful: The Female in Sacred Image and Social Reality*, ed. Clarissa W. Atkinson, et al. (Boston, MA: Beacon Press, 1985), 111–38.
55. Edou, *Machig*, 162. Janet Gyatso discusses the development and history of *gCod* in "The Development of the Gcod Tradition," 320–41.
56. A *gCod* manuscript is translated in W. Y. Evans-Wentz, *Tibetan Yoga and Secret Doctrines* (London & New York: Oxford University Press, 1935, 1967), 277–334.
57. See, for instance "The Story of the Tigress," in Āryaśūra, *The Jātakamālā*, trans. J. S. Speyer (1895. Delhi: Motilal Banarsidass, 1971, 1982), 1–8.
58. Allione, *Women of Wisdom*, 149. See also 246–47 where *chodpa*s took care of a dead body, and 253 where one cures an epidemic among livestock.
59. Ibid., 144–45.

60. Edou, *Machig*, 132; *Phung po gzan skyur gyi rnam bsad* in *Gcod kyi chos skor* (New Delhi: Tibet House, 1974), f. 33, l. 5-f. 34, l. 1.
61. Heather Stoddard, lecture, Tibet House, New York City, April 2, 2001.
62. Edou, *Machig*, 137; *Phung po gzan skyur*, f. 40, l. 6. See also the biography of A-Yu Khandro, who initially studied with her aunt, practiced with other female *chodpas*, and had many female disciples, Allione, *Women of Wisdom*, 233–64.
63. Edou, *Machig*, 112.
64. Ibid., 135; *Phung po gzan skyur*, f. 37, ll. 4–6.
65. Edou, *Machig*, 141–42; *Phung po gzan skyur*, f. 45, l. 3-f. 46, l. 1.
66. Edou, *Machig*, 113 and 145; *Phung po gzan skyur*, f. 51, l. 2.
67. *Phung po gzan skyur*, f. 49, ll. 3–4; Edou, *Machig*, 144.
68. Edou, *Machig*, 113; *Phung po gzan skyur*, f. 106, ll. 5–6-f. 107, ll.1–2.
69. *Khyod kyi yab he ru ka sbas pa'i tshid gyis kha tvan ga la brten nas gsang ba'i brtul zugs* (emended from shugs) *bskyed la*, *Phung po gzan skyur*, f. 60, l. 4; Allione, *Women of Wisdom*, translates this passage (176) as the *khaṭvāṅga* being the secret consort, and elaborates upon its meaning, 35–36; Edou has "use the khatvanga," *Machig*, 151.
70. The *Hevajra Tantra* also glosses it as representing emptiness, I.75.
71. Chonam and Khandro, *Mandarava*, 156–8.
72. *Padma*, Canto 49.
73. Edou, *Machig*, 111.
74. Jenish, "A Troubled Church"; and Fields, *Swans*, 365.
75. Campbell, *Traveller in Space*, see especially 97–123. Oddly enough, although she began her study of Buddhism with Trungpa, she never mentions his sexual activities.
76. See Janice D. Willis, *Enlightened Beings: Life Stories from the Ganden Oral Tradition* (Boston, MA: Wisdom Publications, 1995); on the three types of Tibetan Buddhist biographies, 5–29.
77. Fields, *Swans*, 363.
78. See Samuel, *Civilized Shamans*, 471.
79. Edou, *Machig*, 102.
80. Campbell, *Traveller*, 97–105 and 109–10.
81. Charlene E. Makley, "Gendered Practices and the Inner Sanctum: The Reconstruction of Tibetan Sacred Space in 'China's Tibet,' " *The Tibet Journal* xix.2 (summer 1994): 61–94.
82. Serinity Young, "Women Changing Tibet, Activism Changing Women," in *Women's Buddhism, Buddhism's Women: Tradition, Revision, Renewal*, ed. Ellison Banks Findly (Boston, MA: Wisdom Publications, 2000), 229–42.

CHAPTER 10

THE TRAFFIC IN WOMEN

At the beginning of this book I suggested that some Buddhist practitioners have remained in the Buddha's harem, where they continue to focus on his initial rejection of women. This rejection has served as a convenient symbol for the limited roles available to women in Buddhism, and the more or less strict separation of women from male monastics. Equally, the Buddha's reconciliation with women and the feminine *before* he achieved enlightenment symbolizes the necessity of including woman's auspicious powers in order to achieve enlightenment, an inclusion paralleled in the Buddha's past life as Sumati when he initially rejected and then accepted the woman who was to be his wife in all future lives before making his vow to become a Buddha. We have also seen the inclusion of women richly displayed in sculptures and carvings at the earliest Buddhist archaeological sites spread across South Asia, and centuries later rearticulated in tantric texts and iconography. These are indications that male practitioners must personally, either through visualization or practice with a woman, experience the absence of duality in order to achieve enlightenment. Toward this end, actual women were sometimes involved or utilized in tantric practice and female imagery permeates tantric art.

It is clear from tantric biographies and iconography, as well as the *tantras* themselves, that aspects of women were purposely articulated and incorporated into Buddhist practice. I have argued that this was not a new idea, not a complete turnaround in Buddhist thinking, but rather the development or elaboration of an important theme in early Buddhism, female auspiciousness. In both periods, the incorporation of female imagery did not translate into a new social reality for actual women, although, as we have seen, some of the first women converts to Buddhism are said to have achieved enlightenment, and we have met with strong-willed women who successfully opted for the vigorous tantric path. Many modern women, especially Western converts, see a great potential for women in Tantric Buddhism, and they are trying to make that a reality, despite what appears to be the purposeful acceptance of their secondary religious status by Tibetan women in Chinese-occupied Tibet.[1]

In this chapter I am arguing that historically the tantric valorization of women did not translate into a social reality for several reasons, perhaps most significantly because tantra is an esoteric movement, and not a path for the many. Few women, or even men, follow in the footsteps of Milarepa or Machig Lapdron. And, as we have seen, the institutionalization or routinization of Tantric Buddhism into huge, predominantly male monastic establishments has led to embracing symbolic representations of women and marginalizing, when not actually excluding, real women. More insidiously, in surveying tantric literature and art it became increasingly clear that I was witnessing the familiar scenario of the traffic in women.

Claude Lévi-Strauss observed the almost universal practice of the exchange of women by men, primarily through marriage, in a study that included India and Tibet, as well as China.[2] In a groundbreaking essay, Gayle Rubin applied Lévi-Strauss's observations to the oppression of women by elaborating two of his ideas about this exchange. The first is that women are gifts; senior men give women to other, mostly junior, men as wives. The second is incest, which Lévi-Strauss saw less as a prohibition against marrying one's mother, sister, or daughter than as an obligation to give these women away.[3] The exchange of women is an important part of meeting any group's or family's need to form alliances beyond their own group. Women are exchanged in order to establish enduring kinship relationships and to create affinities between families, communities, and even nations. For instance, by giving away his daughter, a father gains a son-in-law and establishes kinship ties and mutual obligations with the son-in-law's family. In India this part of the traditional marriage rite is specifically referred to as a gift (Bengali: *sampradān*), meaning the gift of a virgin girl (Hindi: *kanyadan*).[4] In nomadic Tibet, the bride's family is called "the givers of the bride" (*bag ma gtong mkhan*).[5] Through marriage the groom is transformed into a son-in-law of the bride's house and the bride into the vessel or field of the groom's family line.[6] She moves into his family's house and assumes their social status.

Irrespective of its rich variety of marital forms—monogamy, polygamy, and polyandry—Tibetans and northern Indians, among others, believe it is male blood that passes through the generations, making women's contribution secondary.[7] As in China, Tibetan ancestors are included in the word for paternal fathers/grandfathers, *yab mes*, and descendants by the word for sons/grandsons, *bu tsha* or *sras dbon*.[8] Through these male terms, language itself reveals families to be primarily male institutions dedicated to the continuation of patrilineal descent with women acting as conduits of male fertility. Women are transacted to be the glue for relationships between families, theirs and their husbands', and between the generations within families. Paul summarizes the foregoing as part of the patrilineal ideology that pervades Tibetan culture:

> Underlying this ideology is the theory, widely distributed in Asia, that agnatic descent is passed through and expressed in the bone (Tibetan *rus*), while uterine descent is passed through and manifested in the flesh (Tibetan *sha*). Implicit in this formulation is the idea that patrilineal inheritance, like bone, is enduring and solid, while matrilineal relationship, like flesh, is ephemeral and obedient to the eternal round of growth and decay which characterizes the natural world. The fact that the words for "bone" and "clan" are the same obviously expresses the same notion.
>
> Bone and flesh can be symbolized by the colors white and red respectively, and may be conceived of as the solid form of substances which, in liquid form, would be semen and blood, specifically menstrual blood. It is thought that these latter two substances are responsible for conception. Each is filled with countless "bodyless souls," and when the two fluids mingle during intercourse, a struggle ensues as to which bodyless soul will animate the new child [a female or a male].
>
> The symbolism of semen and blood, bone and flesh, and white and red, is rife throughout the religious symbolism, almost always representing the forces of male and female in sexual and/or magical creation.[9]

As we have seen, blood and semen are also the basic materials, actual or symbolized, that lend power to tantric rituals.

Lévi-Strauss also made some pertinent observations about the universal sexual division of labor, which Rubin took further when she said it is really "a taboo against the sameness of men and women, a taboo dividing the sexes into two mutually exclusive categories, a taboo which exacerbates the biological differences between the sexes and thereby creates gender."[10] In tantric rituals we can recognize the division of spiritual powers along sexual lines, wisdom (*prajñā*) to women and skillful means (*upāya*) to men, and its exacerbation of biological difference by its utilization of menstrual blood and semen. Tantra further exacerbates biological difference by embracing cultural views about women's pollution in their rituals. Rubin makes the point that "from the standpoint of nature, men and women are closer to each other than either is to anything else—for instance, mountains, kangaroos. . . . Far from being an expression of natural differences, exclusive gender identity is the suppression of natural similarities. It requires repression: in men of . . . the feminine; in women of the . . . masculine."[11] In its utilization of prevailing gender ideologies tantra locates a necessary component of enlightenment in the opposite sex, and as we have seen in the discussion of tantric consorts, this is as male driven and male defined a practice as is South Asian family life.

The exchange of women and the sexual division of labor are also involved in maintaining a compulsory heterosexuality,[12] and tantra is all about heterosexuality because tantra is specifically about the biological difference of gender. When tantra emphasizes that the human body is the means to enlightenment it is specifically referring to the karmic body, which is the gendered body,[13] and its practices require heterosexual activity.

Sexual difference and the low status of women are universals that tantra extols. Like the proverbial finger pointing at the moon, tantric practices and practitioners often focus on the finger rather than the goal, the realization that all forms are essentially empty and the cessation of dualistic thinking, including the notion of gender.

Tantra is a practice in which men sexually utilize women for their own spiritual benefit. It is not a straightforward economic exchange, as it can be when a practitioner purchases the services of a prostitute; more often it is a distinctly unbalanced exchange of sexual, religious, and social power. The male practitioner requires a female, any female, to complete his spiritual training or to speed it up. He takes her bodily fluids and the powers attributed to them into himself, for his own benefit, not hers. Now, whether or not this is possible, and if so no matter how small the number of men that can do this,[14] the concept pervades tantric literature. Most important, the emphasis on using the penis to extract women's sexual fluids makes men the primary subjects and presents women as objects for their utilization. We see this in the vast majority of texts that are directed toward men, not women, in the huge predominance of male biographies compared to the scarcity of female biographies, and in the vast number of *yab/yum* artworks that focus on a male central figure, making the female unnaturally small in proportion to him and placing her back to the viewer (Plates 6 and 7).

Women's status as a commodity is further highlighted when they are shared, as in the example of Tilopa sharing Nāropa's tantric consort,[15] the instructions of Prajñāśrī's *Abhiṣekavidhi*,[16] the *Candamaharosanatantra*,[17] and mKhas grub rje,[18] that the disciple take the guru's tantric consort, or when they are prostitutes. The widespread Tibetan practice of polyandry, in which several men, usually brothers, share one woman as their wife, is a socially accepted example of this.[19]

The preferred female tantric consort is a young and marginal woman without social power. When they were not, either by virtue of being royal women (Yeshe Tsogyel and Mandāravā) or when they had the support of their family (Machig Labdron), they became important teachers—it is their male tantric consorts who are insignificant. These exceptional women are the exceptions that prove the rule: tantra is not and was never about gender equality.

NANGSA'S STORY

The story of another Tibetan woman, Nangsa (sNang sa, said to have lived in the eleventh century),[20] contains many of the foregoing elements and others from earlier chapters. Several biographies have been written about Nangsa, including very popular folk dramas.[21] Quite often the biographies of Tibetan women say they were punished or severely beaten to deter them from rejecting marriage and pursuing a religious life—most notably in the case of Yeshe Tsogyel—and this was also part of Nangsa's story. I used to think these scenes were a dramatic device to display the women's determination, but recent research on Buddhist nuns in Zangskar, a Tibetan-speaking region of northwest India, brought out the reality of these stories when several nuns reported that they had been brutally beaten to prevent them from becoming nuns.[22] That Nangsa's story speaks deeply to Tibetan women, both lay and monastic, about their limited choices in life was demonstrated when an all-female cast put on a performance of a traditional play about Nangsa. Kim Gutschow recorded that the actresses

> appeared to take up the play as an allegory for the difficult choice between the religious and the married life. At rehearsal parties which lasted far into the night, the young actresses confided their own deepest fears of marriage and dashed dreams for the celibate life. Palkyid admitted that as an oldest daughter, she was destined to marry; thereby destined for joy in this life but suffering in the

next. Kesang said she had wanted to join the nunnery rather than be sent off as a slave to an unknown husband, but had cared for her sick and aging parents instead of studying religion (*chos*). Lobsang recounted that when she divorced her husband after just a week of marriage, she had tried to become a nun but had been unable to master the archaic scriptures. While other actresses had not sought out the celibate life, most identified with the play, a Tibetan *Bildungsroman* of a woman who seeks to renounce worldly life in spite of nearly insurmountable obstacles.[23]

Whether they are specifically resisting marriage[24] or stating a preference for a life devoted to religion, these women are asserting their subjectivity, they are voicing a definition of self that precludes being a commodity. This has been a constant theme in the all too few biographies of women in Buddhism. Certainly, it is significant that even Buddhist biographies of men never portray the happy exchange of a woman from her natal family to her husband, not even with minor characters. The refusal of men to marry in these texts, for example Milarepa, is less dramatic because no one tries to force him. Biographies that contain scenes of women resisting marriage do more than simply show women being treated badly; they raise questions about the meaning of gender and subjectivity by depicting women's resistance to being commodities and by framing them in an act of self-definition, one that defines the spiritual self as the doer, not the done-to. The biographies represent that in order to pursue the religious path, women must be self-actualizing agents. Unlike male saints, usually women are initially unsuccessful and are forced to marry and to delay their spiritual hopes, which only serves to underscore that married women cannot pursue the spiritual life.

Through beatings, their female bodies are ruthlessly shown to be at the disposal of others, and beatings are the price they pay for so radically repositioning their identity. And as we shall see shortly, when they finally escape the patriarchal exchange system of family life, this does not necessarily mean that they have escaped the patriarchal exchange system of religious life.[25] For while the biographies truthfully represent women's condition as a commodity, and subtly subvert the exchange of women through their sympathetic heroines, they also reproduce it by tacitly admitting that this is the nature of the social world. In effect, the biographies encourage the men in their audience to reflect on what it means to be a gendered being, specifically what it means to be a woman, not in order to change or improve women's situation, but to recognize and act on their male advantage for spiritual progress. Using women as commodities of exchange between men both in literature and in real life goes hand in hand with female pollution to delimit a social and psychological space of purity and freedom that is exclusively male. As will be seen in the next chapter, which discusses female pollution, it is a space that requires constant surveillance and maintenance. The biographies are part of that maintenance.

In actual life, Tibetans put a high value on getting along with others and in sacrificing personal desires and goals for the good of their families. As mentioned in chapter 3, Tibetans experience an extended sense of self that includes relationships with various spirit beings, past and future lives, and family members. For Tibetans, as for many traditional people, that which benefits the family benefits its individual members. Yet it appears that Tibetan men can be almost as reluctant as Tibetan women to marry, but for different reasons. The men shirk from the heavy responsibility of supporting a family, even though wives are an important part of the domestic economy. Sherry Ortner found that both men and women are anxious about being stuck in an unhappy relationship, but women have additional fears about having to move into a new community, living among a family of strangers, and having an unpleasant husband.[26] Because of their perceived higher status, men have the advantage over their wives when it comes to behaving badly.

Returning to the biographies, Nangsa's story has all the elements of a traditional biography, such as beginning with the auspicious signs and dreams that surrounded her conception and birth. By the time she was fifteen she had many suitors, but preferred to practice religion. Unfortunately for her, a local king decided he wanted her to marry his son. The father's passionate desire for her and the fact that he is easily confused with his son because they shared the same title, Lord Drachenpa, suggests that it was to be a polyandrous marriage, with the father and son sharing Nangsa.[27] The text says it is the father who first sees Nangsa and cannot take his eyes off her,[28] but in a speech he uses his son's personal name and says he is eighteen years old.[29] Later the text says, "In consequence of the marvelous fruits of her body, Lords Drachenpa both father and son did not dare to be separated as much as an hour from Nangsa, yearning (for her) from every viewpoint."[30] Though she opposed any marriage, not just this one, Nangsa was forced to comply. Her parents told her that if she did not marry the king he would kill them and that would not lead to her enlightenment.[31] Further, the text continually says that it must be her karma to marry the prince.

The prince loved her deeply and after seven years Nangsa gave birth to a son, but the king's sister, Nyemo, who acts like the world's worst mother-in-law in this tale, was jealous and made trouble between the couple. At several points Nangsa expressed a full understanding of her situation, that she was prevented from practicing religion out of love for her son and because the demands of her husband's family obstructed her time and energy. In traditional South Asian patrilineal families the wife is often under the control of almost everyone in her husband's family and must please them all at all times. Matters came to a head when Nangsa gave alms to some yogis. Nyemo flew into a rage, beat Nangsa, and pulled out some of her hair. Since Nangsa's husband loved her so much, Nyemo decided to protect herself by telling him that Nangsa had beat her and yanked out her hair, and that Nangsa had slept with the yogis. Nangsa is constrained from defending herself because to say Nyemo lied would spread dissent in the family, something to be avoided at all costs. So, she remained silent. Her husband then jerked her around by her hair, kicked her, and beat her with the blunt side of his sword. The servants pleaded for her and eventually managed to separate them.

The next day her father-in-law, who had heard all about the yogis, caught her giving alms to a beggar. He in turn beat her and took away her son. Nangsa died that night from a combination of severe physical injuries and a broken heart at losing her son.

So far the story dramatizes the helplessness and marginal position of a wife in her husband's family. She is at everyone's mercy, or in this case, their lack of it. Even her son is not her own, but is under the control of her husband's family. Her beatings ring true when compared to those described by Gutschow's informants,[32] and are similar to the beatings Yeshe Tsogyel received because she refused to marry.

After Nangsa's funeral her husband's family asked for a divination and they were told to leave her body alone for seven days because she would come back to life. For Nangsa will become a *delog* (*'das log*)—yogis, most often women, who have shamanic death experiences, journey to hell, and return to report on how sins are punished there.[33] This death experience will eventually free her from worldly life, though not necessarily from patriarchy. When Nangsa's corpse woke up, her husband's family all pleaded with her to return with them, but she adamantly refused, even in the face of long, moving speeches by her small son. For all that, when Nyemo vowed never to be wicked again, Nangsa relented and returned with them.

Once home Nangsa was unhappy, and only wanted to practice religion, and she also wanted to visit her parents, whom she had not seen in the seven years of her marriage. With her husband's permission, she set off to their house with her son and a maid.

Once at her parents' house Nangsa took up her weaving, but also sang songs to the women who visited her, calling upon them to practice religion. Her singing and her longing to practice religion angered her mother so much that she threw Nangsa out of the house. Nangsa then went to the well-known guru Śakya Gyaltsan. He put her through several tests, refusing to take her as a disciple until she threatened to kill herself.

Now her productivity and fertility are completely outside the patrilineal family, neither her parents nor her husband's royal family have access to them, so the king sent an army after her. The king and his son captured and berated her guru, saying:

> You are an old dog that has seduced our snow lion.
> Why did you attack our snow lion?
> You are a horrid cock,
> Why did you try to rape this pheasant?
> Why did you pull out her feathers and wings?
> You are an old donkey,
> Why did you rape our beautiful wild horse?
> Why did you cut off her mane?
> You nasty old bull why did you have sex with our beautiful young yak and shave off her mane?
> You dirty old cat.
> Why did you rape our pure tigress and cut off her fur?
> You, the obscene Sakya Gyaltsan, have acted insolently.
> You have made love to our Queen Nangsa.[34]

The alternation of sexual accusations with those of shaving Nangsa's hair indicate that Nangsa took vows and also practiced sexual yoga with her guru, especially since later, when everyone repented and apologized, they refer to them as the *yab/yum*, the tantric couple. More specifically, they are understood to be emanations of Cakrasamvara (Tib: 'Khor lo sdom pa bde mchog) and Vajaravarāhī (Tib: rDo rje phag mo), a widely known divine *yab/yum* pair.

The story ends with a performance of Nangsa's miraculous powers, her son is made king, and her husband, his father, and Nyemo are shown to be so repentant of their past injuries to her that they all decide to stay with Nangsa and her guru.

While the patrilineal family is assured through her son, the physical move of her husband and his family to her retreat area only redefined the patrilocal pattern, it did not abrogate it. Through marriage she passed from her natal family to her husband's family. As a tantric yogi her product is now spiritual advancement and they are there to get it. They continue to be important to her life in ways her natal family did not. Of course, for Tibetan women it must indicate Nangsa is free of the burdens of domestic life and the controls of the patriarchal family—a dream achieved. Śakya Gyaltsan is, however, another form of patriarchy, that of the male-only lineages discussed in chapter 4, and that of the male *tantrika*'s sexual use of a consort discussed in chapters 8 and 9.

We saw that Yeshe Tsogyel was also a frequent object of exchange among men. Her refusal to be married, to be trafficked by her father, was punished by beatings and led to her marriage to King Trisong Detsen. He, in turn, gave her to Padmasambhava in exchange for tantric teachings. Being gang raped makes a final important point about the traffic in women: if you are a woman alone you are perceived as belonging to no one man and are therefore available for use by any man. To this day in South Asia a woman traveling alone is often taken to be sexually available, and as a rule women do not travel without a companion. The biographies tell us that on the one hand, if women refused to marry they were beaten, and on the other hand, if they tried to go it alone they were subject to the physical and psychic violence of rape.

Some tantric women, such as Mandāravā, Machig Lapdron, Yid Thogma, and Nangsa, break out of the male exchange system by exchanging themselves for teachings. This does not seem to be a completely satisfying solution, especially since male disciples do not exchange sex for teachings. And the few examples we have seen of gurus and male disciples sharing the same female consort or utilizing prostitutes reify rather than subvert the traffic in women.

Stories of women rejecting marriage in order to pursue the spiritual path parallel Manimekhalaï's rejection of prostitution for the same reason. It is difficult to see being a courtesan as a personal choice, given that they usually inherited the occupation from their mothers. Also, let us not forget the courtesan's close cousins, the concubines and harem women in the Buddha's biography. The Buddha's father directs them to seduce the Buddha in exactly the same manner that the god Indra directed the celestial courtesans (*apsaras*) to seduce celibate sages who challenged his power. The women are never consulted; they are commanded. They are trafficked. The same is true of the god Māra's daughters, whom he instructed to seduce the Buddha. There are both human and divine models for the traffic in women, as well as secular and sacred models in the form of female tantric consorts and Hindu temple courtesans (*devadasīs*).

Then there is the symbolic traffic in women, such as the utilization of female imagery for its auspicious powers in Buddhist art, while actual women are marginalized. Existing, as they do, alongside the many negative textual images of women, this cooptation of female auspiciousness is revealed not to be an inclusion of women as much as an abduction. In tantra it is not women who are wanted, but their bodily products. In the secular world men exchange women's fertility for social advancement. In the sacred world men exchange women's fertility for spiritual advancement. In all cases, symbolic and actual women are never valued in and of themselves, but rather for what they can confer on men.

Returning to the discussion of contemporary nuns in Zangskar and their reactions to Nangsa's story, Gutschow makes the point that nuns, too, enter a new form of exchange controlled by men, albeit in their case a nonsexual exchange. As we know, making offerings to monastics confers merit. Even though traditionally nuns have been seen as "lesser fields of merit than monks," giving to a nun does accrue some merit. Once a woman has the permission of her family, she needs to be approved by monks before she can become a nun, before she can confer merit. In other words, a man, although a monk, now controls a woman's, a nun's, exchange value of merit for offerings. On another level, among Zangskar monastics monks also profit from the physical labor of nuns, who despite *Vinaya* rules to the contrary, perform wifely domestic tasks for the monks.[35] This is often the case in other parts of the Buddhist world wherever nuns and monks have frequent contact. At the same time, nuns do not receive the full support of their families as monks do; nuns are required to work on the farms of their families in exchange for their support.[36] Further, in the vast majority of cases, the most advanced training is only given to monks—not that nuns really have the time to pursue such studies. (This situation appears to be changing for nuns in exile, in large part due to the influence and financial support of westerners.) As if this is not enough, despite their shaven heads and monastic robes, nuns are not freed from unwanted sexual advances. And when there are sexual lapses, nuns seem to take them more seriously than monks.[37] The saddest example of this has to be Tibetan nuns who returned to lay life because they were raped in Chinese prisons.

A final form of the nonsexual exchange of women connected to monasticism has been documented in the D'ing-ri sections of Tibet and Nepal. These Tibetan Buddhists tend to follow the rule of having just one daughter-in-law per household, regardless of the number of sons, which can be accomplished through polyandry, in order to keep the land and the household together. One consequence of this is to reduce the available female labor in a household. Parents get around this by not marrying one of their daughters into another household, and instead, they keep her at home. Since this is frowned upon, such families tell their neighbors the girls eventually want to become nuns. At around age thirty-five she is sent to a nunnery, which gives her most productive years to her natal family.[38]

In either case, monasticism does not override gender roles, it incorporates them, as do tantric sexual practices, whether visionary or actual.

NOTES

1. See Shaw, *Passionate Enlightenment*, and Rita M. Gross, *Buddhism after Patriarchy: A Feminist History, Analysis, and Reconstruction of Buddhism* (Albany, NY: State University of New York Press, 1993), both passim. The modern Tibetan movement is briefly discussed in chapter 9 herein.
2. Lévi-Strauss, *Elementary Structures of Kinship*, passim. Ivan Strenski has argued that "Lévi-Strauss's theory may be applied to the formation of Buddhist society," "On Generalized Exchange and the Domestication of the Sangha," *Man* 18.3 (September 1983): 470.
3. Gayle Rubin, "The Traffic in Women: Notes on the 'Political Economy' of Sex," in *Toward an Anthropology of Women*, ed. Rayna R. Reiter (New York: Monthly Review Press, 1975), 173.
4. According to the Hindu lawmaker Manu this is the highest form of marriage, with the lowest two being abduction and rape, III.27–34.
5. Klein, "Primordial Purity," 122.
6. "The most common reference to marriage is in terms of a field and the seed in the field." Lina M. Fruzzetti, *The Gift of a Virgin: Women, Marriage, and Ritual in a Bengali Society* (1982. Delhi: Oxford University Press, 1990), 24. On the gift of the virgin, see ibid., especially 17–18; Lynn Bennett, *Dangerous Wives and Sacred Sisters: Social and Symbolic Roles of High-Caste Women in Nepal* (Columbia University Press, 1983), 71–72 and 80–87; and Freed, *Rites of Passage*, 479–81; Marglin, *Wives of the God-King*, 55. The exception that proves the rule were the marriages of *devadāsīs's* brothers, whose daughters became *devadāsīs*. In these marriages the father of the bride does not give his daughter and thus receives no merit, and there are no relations with the bride's parental house. These brides came from very poor families; Marglin, *Wives of the God-King*, 80. See also the fertility rituals of *hijrās* and *devadāsīs* discussed in chapter 6 herein.
7. Nancy E. Levine, *The Dynamics of Polyandry: Kinship, Domesticity, and Population on the Tibetan Border* (Chicago, IL: University of Chicago Press, 1988), 37–40 and 53; Fruzzetti, *Gift of a Virgin*, 25. See also the discussion of fetal formation in chapter 3 herein. Even Aziz, whose field work challenges the emphasis on patrilineality at all levels of Tibetan society, acknowledges that a child's social status is transmitted through the father, not the mother. See *Tibetan Frontier Families*, especially 51–75
8. Stein, *Tibetan Civilization*, 95.
9. Paul, *Tibetan Symbolic World*, 21.
10. Rubin, "Traffic," 178.
11. Ibid., 179.
12. See Adrienne Rich's classic article on this term, "Compulsory Heterosexuality and Lesbian Existence," *Signs* 5 (1980): 631–60.
13. See the discussion on karma in chapter 11 herein.
14. Campbell quotes the Dalai Lama, who when asked how many qualified tantric masters currently exist replied, "As far as I know—zero." *Traveller*, 204, n. 15. Similarly, mKhas grub rje, writing early in the fifteenth century, says fully accomplished practitioners no longer exist; Wayman and Lessing, *Introduction*, 323.

15. Dowman, *Masters*, 145; Guenther, *Life and Teaching of Nāropa*, 76–80, though this section is not included in the Tibetan text he appended, 262–63; and Tāranātha, *Seven Instruction*, 47–48.
16. Translated by Snellgrove, *Indo-Tibetan Buddhism*, 259.
17. Quoted by Paul, *Tibetan Symbolic World*, 36.
18. mKhas grub rje, Lessing and Wayman, *Introduction*, 321.
19. See Stein for this and other forms of woman sharing, *Tibetan Civilization*, 97–99. See also Aziz, *Tibetan Frontier Families*, 134–56.
20. Allione, *Women of Wisdom*, 64.
21. I have used *Rigs bzang gi mkha' 'gro ma snang sa 'od 'bum gyi rnam thar* from the collection of the American Museum of Natural History, No. 70.2/2502, purchased in 1958 from Marion H. Duncan. This appears to be the manuscript Duncan collected in Batang sometime before 1932 and which he translated in *Harvest Festival Dramas of Tibet*. Another biography is translated in Allione, *Women of Wisdom*, 61–140.
22. Kim Gutschow, "The Women Who Refuse to Be Exchanged: Nuns in Zangskar, Northwest India," in *Celibacy, Culture, and Society: The Anthropology of Sexual Abstinence*, ed. Elisa Sobo and Sandra Bell (Madison, WI: University of Wisconsin Press: 2001), 47–64, and online at http://www.gadenrelief.org/chu-celibacy.html
23. Gutschow, "The Women Who Refuse," website, 3.
24. See also Sherry Ortner, who found the avoidance of marriage to be a stated motivation for becoming a nun, *Making Gender: The Politics and Erotics of Culture* (Boston, MA: Beacon Press, 1996), 130, and explained that the source for a popular ritual called Nyungne, which leads to a better (no doubt male) rebirth, was brought into the world by a female bodhisattva, Gelungma Palma, who in a past life ran way from home to avoid marriage, ibid., 201.
25. My thinking in this paragraph has been influenced by Victoria Wohl, *Intimate Commerce: Exchange, Gender, and Subjectivity in Greek Tragedy* (Austin, TX: University of Texas Press, 1998), especially the Introduction.
26. Ortner, *Making Gender*, 132.
27. Paul also reads the text in this sense, *Tibetan Symbolic World*, 209; and Aziz documents cases of such marriages, *Tibetan Frontier Families*, 153–56.
28. *Rigs bzang gi mkha' 'gro ma snang sa*, f. 9a, l. 3.
29. Ibid., f. 9a, l. 3.
30. Ibid., f. 17a, ll. 1–2.
31. Ibid., f. 15a, l. 3.
32. See examples, Gutschow, "The Women Who Refuse," website, 5–7.
33. See Françoise Pommaret, "Returning from Hell," in Lopez, *Religions of Tibet*, 499–510.
34. Translation modified from Allione, *Women of* Wisdom. Rigs *bzang gi mkha' 'gro ma snang sa*, f. 80a–b.
35. Gutschow, "The Women Who Refuse," website, 2.
36. This is not universally the case in Tibetan Buddhism. In the one Sherpa nunnery Ortner studied in Nepal, families do support nuns. However, she notes that the nuns generally came from well-to-do families. In fact, Ortner specifically mentions that nuns are not supposed to do agricultural work because it involves killing insects and worms; *Making Gender*, 128. The pattern of male dominance holds among Ortner's nuns, though, as the head of the nearby monastery is also the head of the nunnery, ibid., 119–21.
37. Gutschow, "The Women Who Refuse," 7 has several examples.
38. Aziz, *Tibetan Frontier Families*, 106.

CHAPTER 11

WOMEN, MEN, AND IMPURITY

FEMALE SEXUALITY AND POLLUTION

To be in a state of impurity means that one has been exposed to pollution or has been involved in sexual activity. Culturally and religiously, South Asian women are represented as excelling at both, which allows men to claim purity for themselves. The very nature of this discourse endows men with purity in that it focuses on women, not men, or if men are the subject it is as victims of women's sexuality or pollution. In contrast to the exploration of women's auspiciousness in previous chapters, what follows are these two very different but equally important themes in the lives of South Asian women. As we shall see, fantasies about women's voracious sexual appetites and perceptions of female pollution are the reverse side of the female coin.

Asian ideas about pollution involve many features of everyday life, such as death and contact with other castes.[1] My interest here is on female pollution, which in many cultures focus on menstruation and childbirth.[2] Having arisen in South Asia, Buddhism accepted the widely held belief that a menstruating woman, through the most casual physical contact, can pollute men, especially monks or high-caste males, as well as temples or other sacred places. According to the law book of Manu:

> Even if he is out of his mind (with desire) he should not have sex with a woman who is menstruating; he should not even lie down in the same bed with her. A man who has sex with a woman awash in menstrual blood loses his wisdom, brilliant energy, strength, eyesight, and long life. By shunning her when she is awash in menstrual blood, he increases his wisdom, brilliant energy, strength, eyesight, and long life.[3]

It was also believed that giving birth is polluting to the mother, the child, and the household in general. The consequences of contact with a woman in a state of pollution are believed to render a man incapable of communicating with the sacred and may even lead to illness.[4]

The power of these ideas finds further expression in black magic, which prizes the commanding power of menstrual blood, even the ashes of towels used by women to absorb menstrual blood, and which finds the menstrual blood of widows and prostitutes to be particularly efficacious.[5] And, of course, it is used in tantric rituals for initiations and for commanding deities. Tibetan love magic is most expressive of its power:

> the easiest way in which a woman may gain the love of a man she desires is to burn one of her used monthly towels and to mix some of the ashes surreptitiously with the man's food or drink. Instead of the ashes she may also use a drop of menstruation blood. Or the woman may try to smear a little of her menstruation blood on the man's head. The resulting pollution (*grib*) will cause the man to loose his will-power so that he will readily comply with the wishes of the woman who charmed him.[6]

Such ideas are found all over the world, and they express belief in the power of women, accidentally or on purpose, to control men, a power that is turned against them to justify men's actual control of women.

In her study of purity and pollution, Mary Douglas has shown that these are fundamentally conceptions of order and disorder; that which causes pollution is matter out of place. Thus, a menstruating woman is out of place within the sacred and contact with her can render men equally out of place.[7] While unpolluted women, like men, can be polluted by contact with menstruating women, men have to go through more elaborate procedures than women to regain their pure state, because it is a purer state than that of women. In order to recover from contact with a menstruating woman men need to bathe while reciting mantras, put on fresh clothes, and ingest certain pure foods. Women need only change their clothes and sprinkle water on their heads.[8] Women have less purity to recover and therefore do not need to do as much as men.

In India the belief in women's pollution goes back at least to the Vedic period and the myth that the god Indra, in order to purify himself from the pollution of murder, transferred one-third of his pollution to women and thus caused them to menstruate. This myth of the origin of menstruation equates it with the sin of murder and defines it as polluting. Interestingly, Indra transferred the other two-thirds to the earth and trees; the earth being an important female deity, and trees, as we have seen, having a profound connection with female fecundity.[9] This is an important reminder that in ancient India women were, and can still be, perceived in two contradictory ways, as sexually threatening and polluted as well as being the bearers of manifold blessings through their auspicious powers as fertile women. This contradiction is expressed in another Indian myth that negatively connects women and trees. It explains that women began to menstruate because of their sexual passion. Prior to this time, wish-fulfilling trees existed, but they died off after women started menstruating.[10] It is easy to see the wish-fulfilling trees as *yakṣī* tree spirits bestowing blessings in the premenstrual period of the myth and belief in the destructive force of women's pollution and sexuality in the postmenstrual period.

The Buddhists also have a negative myth about the origins of sexuality. After the earth was formed, heavenly beings whose merit had run out were reborn there and began to eat pieces of it. Due to these primal meals they developed orifices to discard their waste, and hence sexual characteristics, along with desire and greed.[11] This text connects sexuality with entrapment in the world, and it presupposes a primordial sexless state, one that the sex-change stories in the next chapter will show means the absence of femaleness and the presence of maleness.

A Tibetan creation story says that human beings came from the union of a monkey and a rock demoness (*brag srin no*).[12] The monkey was actually an emanation of the celestial bodhisattva Avalokiteśvara, and *srinmos* are particularly fierce demons that continue to function in Tibetan Buddhism.[13] It is a female *srinmo* who delays the spread of Buddhism into Tibet until she is violently subdued.[14] Based on this legend Tibetans divide themselves into those who are influenced by their male monkey ancestor and are reliable, intelligent, and compassionate, and those influenced by their demonic female ancestor who loved killing, and are jealous and very passionate. In other words, they are more sexual,[15] and sexuality is perceived to be female and demonic. The excessiveness of the sexuality attributed to the female is dramatized by its implied comparison to the male monkey, since throughout South Asia it is monkeys that are perceived as highly sexual, which will be shown shortly.

Popular Indian ideas about sexuality say that women are sexually eleven times stronger than men, a belief, in part, connected to the notion that the loss of semen debilitates men because one hundred drops of blood are the equivalent of one drop of semen.[16] A great deal of ink has been spilled about Indian men's sexual anxieties and actual impotence, particularly in relation to their wives, who are described as sexually voracious.[17] A typical story is that of the bride who, during their wedding journey to the groom's home, left her unresponsive husband for a well-endowed monkey.[18] In reality, men fear female sexuality because of its unboundedness, not because of possible pollution through the female body. As in the story of the bride and the monkey, women are believed to be so unbridled in their lust that they will leave civilization behind, ignore caste restrictions, and even resort to monkeys. In contrast, female pollution can be contained by isolating women, and it is also cyclical and thus predictable, unlike women's sexual urges, which can erupt at any time. In the story of the bride and the monkey sight is an important element. The bride is aroused by seeing the monkey's erect penis and thus approaches him. Later in the story, the husband goes looking for his bride and sees her not only having sex with the monkey, but he sees her in the dominant position with the monkey lying supine beneath her. As discussed above, this is an unacceptable sexual position and in this story depicts the sexual aggressiveness of the woman.

Other stories that reveal deep-seated male fears about the sexual powers of women as well as male fears about loosing masculinity are the many folktales based on the motif of the *vagina dentata* in which women seduce men in order to cut off their penises, thereby rendering men into women.[19] These stories describe men who fear their own sexual desires, and who demonize its object, women. At the same time, the women in these stories are inevitably tamed by the loss of their vaginal teeth. In other words, they become sexually powerless and are thus deemed safe for heterosexual intercourse.

Returning to female pollution, Buddhism not only accepted this idea, it helped promulgate it. One need only recall that the Buddha's biography strikingly proclaims the pollution of women when it explained that while in his mother's womb he was protected from such pollution by being enclosed in a jeweled box (*ratnavyūha . . . paribhoga*,[20] Plate 2). And, despite the positive female connotations carried by images of Queen Māyā giving birth, some texts gloss the miraculous birth from her side as a means of avoiding contamination through the birth canal.[21] As already mentioned, the Tibetan saint Tsongkhapa is similarly described as being encased in a box within his mother's womb to avoid pollution,[22] while Padmasambhava completely avoided the contamination of a womb by being born from a lotus, and the Tibetan epic hero Gesar emerged from his mother's head contained in an egg.[23] Oddly enough, protection from female pollution through birth was extended to a highly revered woman like Yeshe Tsogyel, whose biography begins by saying she was "born without being smeared [polluted] by the womb."[24]

Bernard Faure summarizes these and similar ideas as follows:

> Death is not the only event that reveals the horrible reality of the female body; another such "moment of truth" is menstruation. Because its outflow threatens the self-enclosure of the body, menstruation became a convenient emblem of defilement, and its cyclical nature served as a reminder of change and decline. Corporeality renders women particularly vulnerable: they can be—and are often—penetrated, and cannot help overflowing their bodily limits, spilling an impure blood. Their body is therefore open, passive, and expansive. Thus, despite the Buddhist advocacy of nonduality, it seems practically impossible for them to transcend sexual difference.[25]

Some of the clearest articulations of Buddhist gender ideologies occur in discussions about the advantages of being born male rather than female, advantages that are described in terms of worldly and spiritual benefits. In large part, the Buddhist discourse on gender, whether from the elite perspective of the biographies or the blunter ideas expressed in folk beliefs, was fundamentally flawed because it did not distinguish between sexual characteristics (biology) and gender (social roles), but rather conflated them. In the same way that biological sexual characteristics identified the male or female gender, it identified female and male social roles; biology was destiny, and as we shall see, a product of one's karma. At root, the Buddhist discourse on gender was based on observations of prevailing gender inequality, which were then interpreted in terms that not only left the status quo intact, but actually served both to support it and to blame women for it. For instance, in Tibet women, not men, performed work that is perceived as polluting, such as cleaning out latrines and handling fertilizer, work that increased their perceived state of pollution.[26] Miraculous stories of sex transformation, as in the *Vimalakīrti* and *Lotus Sūtras*, which will be discussed in chapter 12, seemingly subvert the whole notion of gender. However, the existence of ritual means to protect male babies from being transformed into female babies (such as putting a gold ring on the baby's penis),[27] the preference for male children shown by rituals surrounding their birth and early childhood,[28] and practices meant to assure the transformation of females into males in the next life,[29] confirm a deep commitment to gender ideology.[30] Indeed, some Buddhist heavens are said to be so pure that no women are allowed in them.[31]

The spiritual disadvantages of being born female are inculcated into both women and men in such obvious ways as the wide spread Tibetan practice of announcing the birth of a son by placing a white stone outside the house and the birth of a daughter with a black stone; white being auspicious and black unfavorable.[32] Other ways include listing one of the eight good qualities of a woman as "always having male children,"[33] while commonly used words for women are *bu med*, not a boy, and *skye dman*, low born.[34] Additionally, women are denied access to certain spiritually charged sites, from particular sections of monasteries, and so on.[35] Toni Huber has discussed the double-sided nature of denying women access to the highest sections of Crystal Mountain in Tibet, yet allowing, indeed encouraging, them to perform a ritual during this pilgrimage that will assure their rebirth as males. Huber quotes an informant who explained that women are denied access because they are polluting and they are lower than men (*skye dman*, low born). When they reach the point beyond which only males can go, the women "walk just seven steps down to the other side. On these seven steps they pray that in their next life they will be reborn as a man so they can complete the pilgrimage."[36] This future event is assured by the power of the place, a power that women can weaken by offending the presiding deities through pollution. This testament of women's negative power is subsumed within a paternalistic discourse that explains the restrictions as being protection for women who would become ill or die if they transgressed them,[37] and that defines the feminine character "as disrespectful, irreverent and arrogant, impetuous, and envious ... [while male character is presented as] reverent, considerate, and cautious."[38] Significantly, at several mountain sites the exclusion of women is connected with "intense celebrations of masculinity and the symbols of male power, usually including public displays of male prowess in handling weapons and horses and in oratory."[39] When some Tibetan nuns and other women attempted to defy the ban on women in parts of Crystal Mountain, physical violence was used against them "to enforce ritual exclusion."[40] What we can see in all this is that at the same time they are asserting restrictions on women and celebrating their own maleness, men are expressing a degree of anxiety about the stability of masculinity. I will return to this point shortly.

In addition to not distinguishing between biology and social roles, in supporting biology as destiny, Buddhist thinkers extended their ideology of gender into the psychological realm. The Chinese *Sūtra on Changing the Female Sex* makes this explicit in its conflation of women's negative mental characteristics with their physical pollution:

> The female's defects—greed, hate, and delusion and other defilements—are greater than the male's. . . . You (women) should have such an intention. . . . "Because I wish to be freed from the impuri-

> ties of the woman's body, I will acquire the beautiful and fresh body of a man."[41]

This *sūtra* also brings us back to the important point that women are required to internalize these negative representations of the female state by praying to be reborn as men.[42]

Tibetan folk beliefs are typical in creating lists of negative female characteristics, such as the eight mental deficiencies of women: "persistent suffering from delusions; fickle-mindedness; unreliability; dullness, hypocrisy; attachment to sensual objects; possess low intelligence; and lacks confidence."[43] Similar lists appear in the biographies of the Buddha.[44] The fact that the Tibetans do not have equivalent lists of male characteristics suggests not only that men do not possess mental deficiencies, but further, that men can be characterized by the antonyms of women's deficiencies—they are reliable and possess high intelligence just by virtue of having not been born female. Such ideas about gender pervade most cultures, and they are rarely questioned. For example, the biographers of even the most highly revered Tibetan women have them unquestionably voice these views.[45] Additionally, Tibetan Buddhist women are believed to accumulate more sins than men because as mothers they acquire the sins of their young children—something fathers somehow avoid—as well as their own.[46]

THE INSTABILITY OF MASCULINITY

Shifting the focus to men for a moment, Buddhist masculinity also encompasses a complex space, much of which clusters around two related but contending poles. Most obviously, Buddhist masculinity is hegemonic—central Buddhist concepts privilege men with particular forms of power. This can be observed in hierarchies of religious and secular power. At this end of the pole masculinity is stable. The other pole is less obvious, encapsulating as it does male fears that masculinity is fluid, that it can be diminished, even worse, that a man can be transformed into a woman. In two Buddhist stories from Japan, monks are changed into women, one by a dream and the other when his genitals fall off. Subsequently, both monks marry men and give birth to children.[47] Seen in this light, denying women access to sacred places and positions of spiritual power goes beyond fears of female pollution or avoiding sexually distracting and possibly voracious women. If women can weaken men's power, spiritual or otherwise, by seducing them and/or by polluting them, then they can also weaken their masculinity, causing them to drift toward femininity.[48]

This view is enhanced by stories based on the motif of the *vagina dentata* that bespeak male fears of literal castration by women. Male restrictions on women are about the fear of losing masculinity, of being infected by femaleness—either through female sexual aggression or pollution.

In what follows, it will be useful to remember that particular versions of masculinity emerge in tandem with particular perceptions of equality and inequality. Basing male power on the subjugation of women is predicated on the male belief that women have the power to undermine it, and indeed to undermine masculinity. This establishes a highly anxious social system that requires constant surveillance. Depictions of women as sly and underhanded only intensify the need for male vigilance and weaken confidence in their masculinity. For example, cultures that locate male honor among a man's female relatives require men to maintain constant surveillance and/or restriction over their female relatives and to inflict instant punishment for any transgressions. This system places a man's honor outside of himself, makes it public, somewhat mobile, and thoroughly unpredictable. Male honor is inevitably exaggerated when it is so overextended that it is difficult to control and very vulnerable to attack.[49]

NOTES

1. See, for example, Sherry B. Ortner's discussion of a range of polluting factors, "Sherpa Purity," *Journal of the American Anthropological Association* 75.1 (February 1973): 49–63.
2. For a general overview, see Carol S. Anderson, "Purity and Pollution," in *EOW*, vol. 2, 819–21.
3. Doniger and Smith, *The Laws of Manu*, IV.40–42.
4. In India, these ideas go back at least to the Vedic period; see Frederick M. Smith, "Indra's Curse, Varuṇa's Noose, and the Suppression of the Woman in the Vedic *Śrauta* Ritual," in Leslie, *Roles and Rituals for Hindu Women*, 17–45; and Bennett, *Dangerous Wives*, 214–46, who provides details on menstrual taboos and ritual practices among Nepalese Hindus. For Tibet, see Chophel, *Folk Culture*, 5 and 12; Aziz, "Women in Tibetan Society and Tibetology," 28; Ortner, *Making Gender*, 24; and Toni Huber, *The Cult of Pure Crystal Mountain: Popular Pilgrimage and Visionary Landscape in Southeast Tibet* (New York: Oxford University Press, 1999), 16–17. Chapter 12 herein will explore specific Buddhist practices in East Asia. For Chinese beliefs, see Furth, *A Flourishing Yin*, 94–116. See also, Yalman on menstrual pollution beliefs among Sinhalese Buddhists and South Indian Hindus, "On the Purity of Women," passim.
5. René de Nebesky-Wojkowitz, *Oracles and Demons of Tibet: The Cult and Iconography of the Tibetan Protective Deities* (1956. Graz: Akademische Druck-u. Verlagsanstalt, 1975), respectively, 347 and 343.
6. Ibid., 500.

7. Mary Douglas, *Purity and Danger: An analysis of the concepts of pollution and taboo* (London: Routledge and Kegan Paul, 1966), passim.
8. Marglin, *Wives of the God-King*, 62. Ortner discusses other means of purification; "Sherpa Purity," 57–60.
9. Smith discusses this curse and its enactment in Vedic ritual in "Indra's Curse," 17–45. He also demonstrates the ritualized ways that women's fecundity is celebrated while women's religious roles are diminished. Bennett discusses a Nepalese variant of this myth, *Dangerous Wives*, 215–18.
10. Wendy Doniger O'Flaherty, *The Origins of Evil in Hindu Mythology Evil* (Berkeley, CA: University of California Press, 1976), 27.
11. From chapter 13 of the fifth century C.E. *Visuddhimagga*, trans. Warren, *Buddhism in Translation*, 324–27.
12. Tarthang Tulku, *Ancient Tibet* (Berkeley, CA: Dharma Publishing, 1986), is following the *Mani bKa' 'bum*, 102–03. Stein also briefly discusses this legend, *Tibetan Civilization*, 46.
13. See Gyatso, "Down with the Demoness," passim.
14. Ibid., passim.
15. Ibid., 44; and Tulku, *Ancient Tibet*, 104.
16. I am grateful to Stan Freed for describing these ideas. Conversation, February 27, 2003.
17. Sudhir Kakar tells several other stories, *Intimate Relations: Exploring Indian Sexuality* (New Delhi: Penguin Books, 1989), especially 43–63. See also O'Flaherty, *Women*, 50–51 and 109–12.
18. Herman W. Tull, "The Tale of 'The Bride and the Monkey': Female Insatiability, Male Impotence, and Simian Virility in Indian Literature," *Journal of the History of Sexuality* 3.4 (April 1993): 574–89, passim.
19. See, for example, Verrier Ellwin, *Myths of Middle India* (1949. Delhi: Oxford University Press, 1991), 373–87; O'Flaherty, *Women*, 93 and 267.
20. *LV*, 74.15; Bays, *Voice*, 103ff.
21. See the discussion in chapter 2 herein.
22. Thurman, *Tsong Khapa*, 5 and Blo bzaṅ 'phrin las rnam gyal, *'Jam mgon*, 88–89.
23. David-Neel and Yongden, *Gesar*, 76–77.
24. *Mngal gyis ma gos pa skye ba*, Gyelwa Jangchup's introduction, Stag-śam, *Life of Lady Yeshe Tsogyel*, f. 4, 1.5; Dowman, *Sky Dancer*, 4.
25. Faure, *Red Thread*, 57.
26. Aziz discusses this and other gender-specific terms in "Moving toward a Sociology of Tibet," especially 79–80.
27. It is believed that such a sex change is caused by the curses of midwives who dislike the mother or by witches. Constraints on the mother are that she avoid quarrelling with other women and "not visit other women's houses or eat anything given by another woman"; Chophel, *Folk Culture*, 4. Beliefs of this sort encourage women to distrust other women and increase their dependence on men. See Aziz's discussion of these and other Tibetan birth practices in "Women in Tibetan Society," 28–29. She notes there are no rituals to assure that a female infant retains her sexual distinction. See also Huber, *The Cult of Pure Crystal Mountain*, 253, n. 62.
28. Some of these have been discussed in chapter 3 herein. Allione reports evidence for the Tibetan preference for male children in a story about a Tibetan woman who advised a pregnant woman to say 100,000 prayers to Padmasambhava to ensure the birth of a boy; *Women of Wisdom*, 47. One wonders which idea dominates here, Padmasambhava's miraculous powers or

his legendary nonwomb birth from a lotus, the ultimate example of a pure male birth.

29. For instance, prayers recited by professional readers during death rites that specify, if one must reincarnate, that it be in male form, which is said to be better than female form. W. Y. Evans-Wentz, ed., *The Tibetan Book of the Dead* (London & New York: Oxford University Press, 1927), 207, and the encouragement of women from early childhood to pray to be reborn as men, Karma Lekshe Tsomo, "Tibetan Nuns," in Willis, *Feminine Ground*, 122–23.
30. On a more elevated level, an early Buddhist notion is that upon mastering the practices of meditation one acquires certain supernormal powers (Pali: *iddhis*). Buddhaghosa devotes a chapter to this in his *Visuddhimagga*. Among these powers are the ability to transform one's own body and the ability to create bodies made of mind. Either power could enable a change of sex, for oneself or for others. See, for example, the story of the nun Utpalavarṇā discussed in chapter 12.
31. See chapter 13 herein.
32. Aziz, "Women in Tibetan Society," 28.
33. Allione, *Women of Wisdom*, 131.
34. Aziz discusses this and other gender-specific terms in "Moving toward a Sociology," especially 79–80.
35. Huber, *Crystal Mountain*, 123–26 and passim. The restriction of women from Hindu mountain cults is discussed in William Sax, *Mountain Goddess: Gender and Politics in a Himalayan Pilgrimage* (New York: Oxford University Press, 1991), 94–97, and passim. See also Makely, "Gendered Practices and the Inner Sanctum," 61–94, for her discussion of Tibetan women maintaining gender restrictions in the face of Chinese attempts to dismantle them. In contrast, Huber cites reports of Tibetan nuns attempting to defy the ban on women in parts of Crystal Mountain, Huber, *Crystal Mountain*, 253, n 58, discussed below.
36. Huber, *Crystal Mountain*, 123. Taking seven steps is a ceremonial way of performing a pilgrimage that might not be directly undertaken, 251, n. 35.
37. Ibid., 124.
38. Ibid., 123.
39. Ibid., 253, n. 60.
40. Ibid., 253, nn. 58 & 60.
41. Paul, *Women in Buddhism*, 308.
42. This is the same situation women are put in the Hell of the Bloody Pond—their salvation lies only in accepting their inferior and polluting state. See the discussion in chapters 2 and 13 herein. An additional example comes from the story of Princess Pure Faith in the *Mahāratnakūṭa Sūtra*, which women can use as a ritual recitation that will lead them to rebirth as a man. Cited by Nancy Schuster, "Changing the Female Body: Wise Women and the Bodhisattva Career in Some *Mahāratnakūṭasūtras*," *JIABS* 4.1 (1981): 37.
43. Norbu Chophel, *Folk Culture of Tibet* (Dharamsala: Library of Tibetan Works and Archives 1983), 86. He also lists eight physical deficiencies and five unworthy qualities of women, 86 and 83, but none for men. Allione offers a slightly different list of five unworthy qualities and a rather sexist list of eight good qualities, *Women of Wisdom*, 131, nn. 17, 18. Variations such as these suggest how wide spread these ideas were.
44. See chapter 1 herein.
45. See, for example, Dowman, *Sky Dancer*, 89; Edou, *Machig Labdrön*, 151; Rechung, *Tibetan Medicine*, 160; and the song of Bardarbom discussed herein in chapter 12.

46. Ortner, *Making Gender*, 124.
47. Faure, *Red Thread*, 77–78, fn. 39.
48. My thinking in this paragraph has been influenced by A. Corwell and N. Lindisfarne, "Introduction" to their edited volume, *Dislocating Masculinity*.
49. My thinking in this paragraph is influenced by Marshall G. S. Hodgson's discussion of male honor in Irano-Mediterranean culture, *The Venture of Islam: Conscience and History in a World Civilization*, vol. II (Chicago, IL: The University of Chicago Press, 1974), 140–46; but see also Yalman, for South Indian and Sri Lanka, "On the Purity of Women," especially 43–45.

CHAPTER 12

SEX CHANGE

A primary Buddhist belief is that sexual characteristics are fluid; genitals can change in the next lifetime or even in this one.[1] That the belief in sex change was enduring and widespread is shown by the surprising number of sex-change stories that exist and by their incorporation not only into prominent Buddhist texts, but their presence within discussions of central Buddhist concepts such as karma, emptiness, and illusion. The Buddhist creation myth that describes sexual characteristics as a decline from a primordial nonsexual state lends support to the belief that sexual characteristics, being secondary, can drift.

Most of the stories that follow are more expressive of male fears about losing masculinity than of female hopes of gaining it. In researching Afghan stories about women changing into or disguising themselves as men, Margaret Mills found that they are usually told by men, not women.[2] In other words, even though the stories feature women, they reveal male concerns. This is equally true of the stories that follow, which were told by men and preserved in texts controlled by men. These stories represent male views, anxieties, and fantasies. Although a few stories subvert the wholesale negation of women and challenge the basic notion of gender, overall they privilege maleness. Most tellingly, the vast majority of stories are about women becoming men. An important genre of stories that for the most part indicate gender is fixed, that an individual's sexual characteristics remain constant from life to life, are those of the Buddha's past lives. Yet they, too, privilege maleness. As will be shown, gender is understood to be a reward or a punishment, and many texts argue that achieving an advanced stage of awareness precludes one from being reborn as a female.

FEMALE TO MALE STORIES

Two sex-change stories take place around the Buddha's visit to Trāyastriṃśa heaven where he went to preach to his mother and his descent back to earth at Sāṃkāśya. Sculptures of his descent from this heaven often show a single bowed figure at the base (Figure 2.12) that could be either a monk or a nun, given the similar robes and shorn heads of all Buddhist monastics and the worn condition of these sculptures. As alluded to briefly in chapter 2, the ambiguous gender of this lone figure lent itself to various stories about who exactly was the first person to greet the Buddha upon his descent. The fifth-century Chinese pilgrim-monk Fahien preserved a story about a nun called Utpalavarṇā that was related to him when he visited Sāṃkāśya. He was told that there was such a huge press of people waiting to see the Buddha come down from heaven that Utpalavarṇā could not make her way forward. The Buddha, out of compassion and because of the merit she had acquired, transformed her into a *cakravartin*, a male king or buddha with all the accompanying auspicious bodily marks, including a sheathed penis. In this guise she was able to get to the very front of the crowd, where the Buddha then changed her back into a woman and predicted her future enlightenment.[3] Fahien adds that a *stūpa* was erected on the spot where she was the first to do reverence to the Buddha.[4] Several elements in this story are of interest. To begin with, it shows that gender was believed to be fluid. It also indicates that nuns were not particularly deferred to, for which we have other evidence.[5] Further, due to the merit she had acquired through acts of generosity in her past lives, Utpalavarṇā was deemed capable of enlightenment and thus favored by the Buddha. She was the unique woman, the token woman, and not at all representative of her sex. As will be shown, uniqueness is at the heart of sex-change stories, the unique potential for enlightenment. At the same time they raise the broader question of whether or not women can become buddhas, whether or not women can liberate.[6] In Utpalavarṇā's case the answer seems to be yes because she does not remain in a male form.

Several centuries later the Japanese Zen master Dōgen (1200–1253) told a story about Utpalavarṇā that presents a very different woman. While teaching his disciples that even a completely superficial acceptance of the precepts can, in the fullness of time, lead to salvation, he used Utpalavarṇā as an example. He said that in one of her past lives, before she met the Buddha Śakyamuni, she was a prostitute who put on a nun's robe as a joke. Even though she put it on as a joke, it eventually led to her meeting Śakyamuni.[7]

Dōgen's story is probably based on the *Therīgāthā* commentary that created an absurdly elaborate tale claiming that Utpalavarṇā had been a courtesan who committed incest. A version of this story is included in the Tibetan *Kangyur*.[8] Obviously, Utpalavarṇā presented problems to latter Buddhists. Before looking at other stories about her, there is an even stranger sex-change story told about the Buddha's visit to Trāyastriṃśa heaven. The *Pujawaliya*, a biography of the Buddha composed in Sri Lanka in the thirteenth century,[9] says the Buddha's mother changed sex when she was reborn as the male god Mātru, the chief of the gods in Trāyastriṃśa heaven.[10] A clearer example of Buddhist misogyny is hard to find; even the Buddha's mother has to become male. Further, Utpalavarṇā does not appear in this text at all; instead it is a man who first greets the Buddha upon his descent, the monk Śariputra.[11]

Another Chinese version of Utpalavarṇā's tale reveals some of the discomfort felt about her prominence as it manages to diminish her and to put her in a woman's proper place. It says that when the Buddha descended from Trāyastriṃśa heaven, Utpalavarṇā was present, but she *disguised* herself as a *cakravartin*, greeted the Buddha, and then returned to her normal form, which cuts out the Buddha's acknowledgment of her merit and his transformation of her sexual characteristics. The Buddha praised her, but the text comments that everyone else was upset by seeing a woman assume such an honored position.[12]

James Legge, in his translation of Fahien, the original Chinese source on Utpalavarṇā, states that the text is ambiguous in defining who transformed Utpalavarṇā, the Buddha or she herself,[13] which is one of several elements that have conspired to allow people to take liberties with her story.

In the *Vinaya* and *Therīgāthā*, Utpalavarṇā (called Uppalavaṇṇā) is said to be particularly gifted in the power (Pali: *iddhi*) of transformation or shape-shifting, and that she did attain enlightenment, all elements of Fahien's story. The *Therīgāthā* preserves four poems attributed to her. One is a response to the demon Māra's attempt to distract her from meditating by reminding her that solitary women in lonely places could easily be raped. Part of her reply to him refers to her powers of shape-shifting:

> What can you do?
> Here though I stand, I can vanish and enter into your body.
> See! I stand between your eyebrows, stand where you cannot see me.[14]

A second poem attributed to her refers to her transformation into a *cakravartin* at the time of the Buddha's descent:

> With a chariot and four horses I came,
> Made visible by supernormal power,
> And worshiped, wonder-working, at his feet,
> The wondrous Buddha, sovereign of the world.[15]

So the Pali texts support the original story that traveled back to China with Fahien, and again later with another pilgrim-monk Xuanzang, who also told it, but the ambiguity of Fahien's text, the uncertain gender in the iconography, and her absence in Pali versions of the Buddha's descent, conspired to allow her story to be modified in ways that reveal a Buddhist discourse on gender that relentlessly diminishes and disempowers women.

Another tale of sex change within the biographies of the Buddha is of particular interest because it is a rare past-life story in which the Buddha was born as a woman, the beautiful Rūpavatī. It is certainly one of the most graphic and goriest of sex-change stories. While out for a walk one day Rūpavatī saw a woman who had just given birth to a son. The woman was so hungry that she tried to eat her infant. Rūpavatī pleaded with her not to do this, but the woman could not be dissuaded. Rūpavatī then picked up a knife, and perhaps in anticipation of her sex change, cut off both her breasts, which she gave the woman to eat.[16] Later she stood among the gods and performed an act of truth (*satyavacana*), a formal verbal statement that, if true, gives miraculous powers to the speaker. Rūpavatī's states that she had only acted out of the desire for enlightenment and she asked that by the power of that truth she be turned into a man.[17] This happens at once, and s/he becomes a man called Rūpavata and is made king. Later s/he is reborn as a brahman who sacrifices her/himself to a hungry tigress. This story is also contained in Ksemendra's story collection, where she is called Rukmavati, and it is depicted in a standardized set of wood blocks, which represent the gift of her breasts by two women sitting with a child, and includes images of the Buddha telling this story to his disciples, of her/his next life as a man sacrificing his body to birds, and of Rukmavan on the throne.[18]

In Mahāyāna Buddhism, which developed around the first century C.E., sex change is a particularly prolific genre of storytelling. Most of these stories involve bodhisattvas, heroic beings of infinite compassion, who can be divine or human, female or male. Two well-known stories focus on the celestial bodhisattva associated with wisdom, Mañjuśrī, and differentiate themselves from earlier Buddhist tales by having Śariputra, an important disciple of the Buddha who is highly regarded in the Theravāda traditions, plays the dupe.

The first comes from the *Vimalakīrti Sūtra,* which was composed in Sanskrit between the first century B.C.E. and second century C.E., and later translated into Tibetan, Chinese, Japanese, and other Asian languages. It was an extremely popular text throughout the Mahāyāna world, where it was recited at temple festivals, copied as a means of generating merit, and its hero, the lay bodhisattva Vimalakīrti, was often the subject of painting and sculpture.[19] In chapter 7 a dialogue occurs between Mañjuśrī and Vimalakīrti about the illusory nature of all beings, human and otherwise, and the attitude a bodhisattva should take toward these illusory beings. The discussion is interrupted by an unnamed goddess who expresses her delight at their discourse by causing a rain of flowers to fall. The flowers fall off the robes of the bodhisattvas but stick to the robes of those who are still mired in illusion. Śariputra, who has also been listening to the discourse, cannot get the flowers off his robe, and he enters into an argument with the goddess, culminating with his challenging her to change her female form. The goddess complies with his request, but with a twist; she simultaneously changes herself into Śariputra's male form and changes Śariputra into her female form. In one stroke she neatly dramatizes both the chapter's theme of the illusory nature of all beings and negates any idea that the female gender precludes spiritual achievement. After she restores their original forms, Vimalakīrti explains to the disgruntled Śariputra that the goddess has attained irreversibility; in other words she will achieve buddhahood.[20]

A different view of female spiritual potential is upheld in the *Lotus Sūtra,* one of the best known and earliest works of Mahāyāna. In chapter 11 Mañjuśrī is asked if there is anyone capable of achieving perfect enlightenment, and he answers yes, the eight-year-old daughter of Sāgara, king of the Nāgas.[21] Śariputra challenges the spiritual accomplishments of Sāgara's daugther, arguing that no woman has reached buddhahood because no woman can achieve the five exclusively male states: that of the gods Brahma and Indra, a guardian of the four quarters, a *cakravartin,* and an irreversible bodhisattva. These five are states of power defined by maleness, which comes down to having a penis. When Sāgara's daughter magically transforms herself into a male, she silences Śariputra, yet also confirms his views. Her vagina vanishes to be replaced by a penis and she is seen by all as a male bodhisattva preaching in a Buddhist heaven, specifically as one who possesses the thirty-two marks of a Buddha, including a sheathed penis.[22] Unlike the *Vimalakīrti Sūtra*, this *sūtra* suggests one must be male to become a Buddha.

Both these stories are curious entries into Buddhist gender battles in that neither heroine is actually a woman. The first is a goddess and the second a *nāginī*. Further, Sāgara's daughter is only eight years old; she has not reached puberty and the polluting female processes associated with it. Understandably, having a child represent the high accomplishment of enlightenment powerfully suggests that the realization of wisdom (*prajñāpāramitā*) is not a matter of age, a point made by the frequent references to Mañjuśrī, the bodhisattva of wisdom, as a sixteen-year-old prince. Further, it evokes her past lives, during which she followed the bodhisattva path, achieving *prajñāpāramitā* and its subsequent magical powers. She is a bodhisattva who has chosen this form for rebirth. Also, like the goddess of the *Vimalakīrti*, she is nameless. While in most parts of Asia women are frequently identified through their relationships to men, as so and so's daughter or wife, or the mother of so and so (always a son even if daughters have been born first), South Asian women are frequently identified by their personal names. Diana Paul makes the point that Mahāyāna texts, which raise this issue of whether women can be buddhas, "are silent in explicitly naming any."[23] Being nameless contributes to anonymity and indeed, to nonexistence.

These stories are not just about sex change, they are also about spiritual power and they are meant to demonstrate the doctrine of emptiness, that all beings, all objects, are empty of any enduring reality, including sexual characteristics. Still, their cumulative effect makes the point that being male is so much better than being female. Another story involves yet another goddess, the great Indian river goddess Gangā. It appears in one of the earliest and most important Mahāyāna *sūtras*, the *Aṣṭasāhasrikāprajñāpāramitā* (*The Perfection of Wisdom in Eight Thousand Verses*), and it focuses on the heroic aspects of bodhisattva nature. As Miriam Levering has pointed out, in deploying specifically male heroic epithets to describe bodhisattva nature, texts such as this ignore the "rhetoric of gender equality" promoted in texts like the *Vimalakīrti Sūtra*.[24] The *Aṣṭasāhasrikāprajñāpāramitā* describes the bodhisattva as fearless, undaunted by dangers, and independent, attributes exclusively associated with men, not women. The goddess, however, asserts that she is without fear, causing the Buddha to smile. When questioned about his smile the Buddha predicts her future buddhahood will occur when she is reborn as a man in Akṣobhya's Pure Land, Abhirati.[25]

Yet another story involves Vimalakīrti's daughter, Candrottarā, who is told by a bodhisattva that one cannot become a Buddha while in a female body. The eloquent Candrottarā uses the doctrine of emptiness to argue against this view. She is so successful that the Buddha himself predicts her future buddhahood.[26] In celebration of this Candrottarā leaps into the air and for no apparent reason transforms herself into a male. In her reading of this text Paul suggests Candrottarā, who had many aggressive suitors, changed sex to avoid marriage.[27] However, even though she received the prediction of her future enlightenment while in a female body, she immediately changed into a male body, further suggesting that one must be male to become a Buddha.

A similar example comes from the *Sutra of the Buddha Teaching the Seven Daughters*, which is the story of seven sisters who, upon hearing they will become buddhas, leap into the air and without reason change into boys. It also contains a short description of their Pure Land, the heaven they will occupy when they become buddhas. The text does not specify that women will not be allowed in this Pure Land, but we will see innumerable examples of male-only Pure Lands in the next chapter, which, when combined with the unexplained transformation of the girls into boys, strongly suggests that this will be the case.[28]

In these and most of the Buddhist stories that follow, sex change is always female to male.[29] Texts like the *Pure Land, Aṣṭasāharikāprajñāpāramitā, Lotus sūtras*, and several others, insist one must become a man before achieving enlightenment because one of the marks of an enlightened being is a sheathed penis, one of the thirty-two marks of the historical Buddha.[30] Even with an unusual penis, the male remains the normative human, and when a woman becomes a man she achieves higher status.[31]

The story of Sumati from the *Mahāratnakūṭa* is about the eight-year-old daughter of the mayor of Rājagṛha. It seems to have been particularly popular in East Asia since by the early eighth century it had been translated into Chinese three different times. Sumati, too, is asked why she does not change into male form in order to complete the highest stages of bodhisattvahood that lead to buddhahood. As did the goddess in the *Vimalakīrti Sūtra*, she also argued against this from the point of view of the emptiness or illusory nature of all phenomena, including sexual characteristics. Yet she had already announced that when she became a Buddha her Pure Land would not admit women.[32] She then performed an act of truth, saying that if her words are true her body will change into the male body of a thirty-year-old monk, which it did.[33] After this, Mañjuśrī predicted her future buddhahood. So, in the end, her story, too, suggests one must be male to become a Buddha.

Another such story is that of the twelve-year-old daughter of King Prasenajit, called Pure Gift, who also performed an act of truth and after successfully debating the illusory nature of all forms turned into an eight-year-old boy. She then received the prophecy of her future buddhahood from the Buddha.[34]

Additionally, important shapers of the Buddhist tradition such as the fourth-century Indian philosopher Asaṅga insisted that women could not be buddhas. In his influential *Bodhisattvabhūmi* (*The Stages of the Bodhisattva*) he wrote:

> Completely perfected Buddhas are not women. And why? Precisely because a bodhisattva . . . , from the time he has passed beyond the first incalculable age (of his career) has completely abandoned the woman's estate. . . . Ascending (thereafter) to the most excellent throne of enlightenment, he is never again reborn as a woman. All women are by nature full of defilement and of weak intelligence. And not by one who is by nature full of defilement and of weak intelligence, is completely perfected Buddhahood attained.[35]

This hardly reads as a casual statement. Rather, it is further evidence that whether or not women could become buddhas was an important point that was frequently argued.

Contrasting two Mahāyāna texts from South India that were fairly contemporary, the *Manimekhalaï* and the *Śrīmālā Sūtra,* sheds some light on the thinking behind all these discussions of women's potential for enlightenment. The latter text contains no sex-change story and in it Queen Śrīmālā achieved enlightenment. In the *Manimekhalaï,* the heroine Manimekhalaï did not achieve enlightenment. Instead, she is given a prophecy that she will in a future life, but as a man.[36] Additionally, she is given and utilizes the power to shape-shift into a man. One can see these two texts as representative of two different schools of thought in Buddhism: one advocating enlightenment for both women and men and the other denying women access to the highest experience of the tradition. The different resolution in these two texts from a similar region and period suggests that Buddhists could be supportive of women, though not all Buddhists were willing to go all the way when it came to the ultimate achievement of buddhahood. Padmanabh Jaini has been able to outline a similar but much more clearly drawn argument between the two major schools of Jainism, indicating that such arguments were in the air for centuries.[37] See, for instance, the *Śrīmālā*'s reception among Chinese Buddhists, which is discussed in chapter 13.

A Chinese Buddhist folktale returns us to the issue of female pollution when it specifies that women are required to become men because of their gender-specific pollution. Interestingly, it also shows that being postmenopausal does not improve women's status, presumably because of their prior menstrual trail of pollution. It is the story of the woman Huang, married to a butcher who says they are equally polluted, he through shedding the blood of animals, and she through the blood of childbirth. Woman Huang then studied the *Diamond Sūtra* so well that Yama, the god of the underworld, questioned her about it. Later she was reborn as a man, and through a dream recalled her past life, found her former husband and converted him, and helped her former children.[38] Being male, she does not commit the sin of pollution, and could advance to buddhahood.

An important factor in this ideology was and remains the enormous popularity of the Buddha Amitābha cult throughout Asia. This cult encodes perfection as male through its requirement that upon hearing Amitābha's name women should come to despise the female state, which will lead them to be reborn in his paradise of Sukhāvatī and never again be born as females.[39] This widespread belief holds out to women the promise of permanent rebirth in a Buddha Land where they will inevitably become buddhas, but in male form.

All these tales about women changing into men, whether as magical displays of spiritual power or in fulfillment of the requirement that one must be male in order to become a Buddha, need to be compared to stories that do not require such a change.[40] For instance, the goddess in the *Vimalakīrti Sūtra* changes sex more in play, to undermine Śariputra's attachment to outer forms. Having accomplished this goal, she returns to and remains in her female form, and then receives the prediction of her future buddhahood from Vimalakīrti.

Another such story comes from Tibet and is about the much loved celestial bodhisattva Tārā. In a past life she incarnated as a woman called Princess Moon of Wisdom and so rapidly advanced in spiritual understanding that her gurus encouraged her to transform her body into a man's. She declined, instead vowing *always* to incarnate in female forms.[41] Comparing the two stories we see that the *Vimalakīrti* plays fast and loose with the sex-change story, acknowledging that it is possible through the advanced spiritual power (*siddhi*) of shape-shifting but undercutting the tendency of these tales to describe only female to male change and also underlining that the *siddhi*s are displays of spiritual power, and do not necessarily lead to permanent change. Tārā's story also undercuts the genre by completely rejecting it—it is not a sex-change story. But it is a powerful story because it is so specifically not about a sex change.

As Paul ably demonstrates in her discussion of the commentarial literature, in theory a female can achieve enlightenment, can become a buddha. Sadly, then as now, the theoretical rarely impacts social reality, and for reasons the foregoing stories make clear, the cult of a female buddha was never developed as were the cults of various male buddhas. Though often characterized as female buddhas or goddesses, both Tārā and Kuan Yin actually are celestial bodhisattvas. According to the strict rules of Tibetan iconometry, the precise proportions of the buddhas, bodhisattvas and deities, buddhas are the largest figures, bodhisattvas smaller, the detities still smaller. This system prescribes that Tārā is the size of a goddess, not a buddha or a bodhisattva. Kuan Yin is depicted textually and iconographically in both male and female forms. Indeed, Ortner was told that a popular ritual called *Nyungne*, which leads to a better (no doubt male) rebirth, was brought into the world by a female bodhisattva, Gelungma Palma.[42]

On a more mundane level, sex-change stories most often reflect culturally perceived notions of prestige associated with gender.[43] In stories where women change into or disguise themselves as men they become heroic, but stories about men becoming women often lead to their powerlessness and humiliation. To say in patriarchal cultures that a woman is like a man is to say that she is more than or better than a woman. When religious women are told that in order to achieve success in religious terms they must become men, they are being asked to abandon their female sexuality. Interestingly, both men and women abandon their sexuality when they take vows of celibacy, but with different consequences for women than for men. Few men are then perceived as women,[44] but often celibate women are perceived as men, or encouraged to actually become men, or perceive themselves through this more prestigious term. In other words, religious women are asked to repudiate their gender, their womanhood, in ways that religious men are not. According to the Chinese text, *The Sūtra on Changing the Female Sex*:

> If women can accomplish one thing (Dharma), they will be freed of the female body and become sons. What is that one thing? The profound state of mind which seeks enlightenment. Why? If women awaken to the thought of enlightenment, then they will have the great and good person's state of mind, a man's state of mind, a sage's state of mind. . . . then they will not be bound to the limitations of a woman's state of mind. Because they will not be limited, they will forever separate from the female sex and become sons.[45]

An historical example of a spiritually advanced Tibetan woman making the vow to reincarnate as a man in her/his next birth is Jetsun Rigdzin Chönyi Zangmo (1852–1953), abbess of Shukseb Nunnery (near Lhasa) and a recognized incarnation of the great female teacher, Machig Lapdron (1055–1153).[46] Edou reports her story, adding that many Tibetan Buddhist nuns and lay women make this vow. Zangmo's male incarnation ended up leaving the religious life for study in Beijing. This is a particularly telling example of the pervasive influence of negative ideas about Buddhist women in that the original incarnation, Machig Lapdron, is one of the few examples of a man said to have chosen rebirth as a woman in order to continue a spiritual career.[47] It is to this rare genre of Buddhist stories that we now turn.

MALE TO FEMALE STORIES

Buddhist stories about sex changes from male to female are much rarer than those about female to male changes. Two such exceptional stories occur in the biography of Upagupta, the Buddhist monk and master of *siddhi*s (spiritual power), who was Aśoka's guru. Upagupta's biography is filled with examples of his skillful means as a teacher of Buddhism, examples that frequently involve *siddhi*s. In two of these he shape-shifts into a woman. The first time he becomes a woman to help a monk who kept thinking of his former wife while trying to meditate. Upagupta appeared before him in the form of his wife, shocking the monk into realizing his attachment to her. Upagupta then resumed his normal male form and preached to the monk to help him overcome his attachment.[48] The second time was to undo a monk's false sense of detachment, which Upagupta did by taking on the form of a drowning woman. The monk grabbed hold and pulled her/him out of the river, but then he felt desire for her and took her to an isolated spot, only to discover she was Upagupta.[49] These two instances of sex change are meant to demonstrate Upagupta's advanced spiritual powers and because of their short duration in no way undercut his masculine authority. In fact, the whole purpose of these incidents is to point out how threatening women are to monks in order to help monks maintain their celibacy by maintaining their distance from women. The stories also remind the errant monks of the fluidity of sexual characteristics; they could lose their masculinity and be reborn as women.

The most fascinating and far-reaching sex change in Buddhist history has to be that of the Indian male celestial bodhisattva Avalokiteśvara into the Chinese female celestial bodhisattva Kuan Yin. In either form this is one of the most important and most widely worshipped deities in Buddhism. In part, this transformation occurred through an early fifth-century mistranslation of the Sanskrit *Lotus Sūutra* into Chinese, in which the male Avalokiteśvara, meaning all-seeing, became the female Kuan Yin, all-hearing.[50] Once feminized,

Kuan Yin's iconography began incorporating *yin* (female) symbolism such as the moon, water, and a vase.[51]

A Chinese text, *The Sutra of the Bodhisattva Kuan Yin (Who Explains) the Conditions to be Born in Pure Land,* for which there seems to be no Indian original, describes a past life in which Kuan Yin was male, indicating that s/he changed sex through rebirth as well. This is a particularly interesting example in that a male birth is one of the rewards of good karma, especially since this is the past life in which s/he made the vow to become a future buddha, yet s/he was reborn as a female.[52] Actually, this *sūtra* is as interesting in its sexual fluidity as it is in its sexual politics. In this life Kuan Yin is a dutiful son, and the celestial buddha Amitābha, who also changes sex in this *sūtra,* is the mother, the ideal Buddhist mother who, on her death bed, encourages her two young sons to pursue buddhahood. This is a neat co-optation of the primary female role in traditional societies, that of motherhood. While the fluidity of the sexual characteristics seems to undercut the whole notion of gender, in fact we see that no gender really means the absence of females and the presence of males. In this story it is obvious that males make better mothers, just as they make better children and better buddhas.

Female celestial beings such as Kuan Yin are commonly believed capable of manifesting as either female or male, as are the earthly women Yeshe Tsogyel and Mandāravā in their *ḍākinī* forms.[53] This is in keeping with the predominant stories of female to male sex changes and the perceived liability in changing from male to female. The dominant notion seems to be that if a woman or a goddess has enough spiritual power to change into a man, why wouldn't she? On the other hand, although men and male deities may momentarily transform into females to help someone, they have no reason to change permanently into females because it would be a loss of power and status.

Kuan Yin's gender may also have been an issue of class perception. It seems poor, less educated people saw Kuan Yin as the goddess of mercy, a sort of all-powerful and giving mother, while priests and wealthier, educated lay people worshipped Kuan Yin as a male deity connected with Amitābha's Western Paradise, where women are not allow to be born. Yet others saw Kuan Yin as nonsexual, unless s/he chooses to manifest in either female or male form.[54] The ideas of the latter group were popularized in *pao-chüan,* texts written for popular distribution and for reading aloud in small groups that might include illiterates. They are pointedly addressed to "pious men and women," and women responded by joining popular sects of Buddhism in large numbers where they achieved equal status with men.[55] This indicates that people make of religion whatever they need, and demonstrates that religion functions as an ideology, but one that is endlessly open to interpretation and reinvention. We will see some of this flexibility in the next section, which deals with the seemingly inflexible ideology of karma.

KARMA

Sex change through rebirth is connected to the notion of karma,[56] the belief that all actions have consequences, either in the present life or in the next, and include the determination of one's sex.[57] This view of sexual characteristics as the inevitable outcome of karmic retribution or reward highlights additional dimensions of Buddhist gender ideology, especially when compared to Hindu stories of rebirth in which a change of sex is quite rare.[58] In a Buddhist context, though, being born male is the fruit of good karma while being born female is the fruit of evil karma.

Bardarbom, one of Milarepa's leading female disciples and one of his dharma heirs, sang a song to Milarepa about the difficulties of being born female:

> Because of my sinful Karma I was given
> this inferior [female] body. . . .
>
> Great is our ambition, but our perseverance small.
> We are experts in slander, ingenious to blame,
> The source of news and gossip. . . .
> Seldom do we think of impermanence and death.
> The sinful hindrances always follow us like shadows.[59]

In general, though, Buddhism tends to emphasize the karma of gender as something for women to aspire to rather than as a punishment; because women are generally not believed able to achieve enlightenment, the best they can do is to pray to be reborn as men.[60] But, it also maintains the loss of masculinity as a potential karmic punishment for men.

The *Ṣaḍgatikārikā* presents a simple karmic formula:

> The man who does not restrain his thoughts and unites with the wives of others, or who finds delight in illicit parts of the body, will be reborn as a woman.
>
> But the woman who is of good morals and little passion, who abhors her femaleness and constantly aspires to masculinity will be reborn as a man.[61]

A more detailed vision is contained in *The Meritorious Virtue of Making Images*.[62] As the title suggests, merit can be acquired by making or maintaining buddha images, and such merit can mitigate karma. This text emphasizes that the actual Buddhist position toward karma is not all that rigid. One's karma can be altered by intense tantric practice, including directing the consciousness at the time of death; by good deeds, such as making donations; building and repairing *stūpa*s and images; sponsoring the reading or printing of scripture; and religious acts such as pilgrimage.[63] More specifically, in this text the Buddha explains that whatever sins a man has committed, all that evil karma can be exhausted by building a Buddha image.

After listening to the Buddha's speech, the celestial bodhisattva Maitreya raises a question:

> Blessed One, there are women whose will is narrow; many of them cherish envy in their hearts, and hatred and spite, and sycophancy and falsehood; they show no awareness of kindness and do not repay it. Not one of them is able to be firm and diligent in the search for enlightenment; they are always seeking to deceive.
>
> Blessed One, if a woman such as this should build an image of the Buddha, will her karma too be exhausted and annulled? Will she become a man in the future, steadfast and unwearied in seeking the reward of Buddhahood? Will she gain insight and compassion, and learn to weary of the world?
>
> And the Buddha said to the bodhisattva Maitreya:
>
> Maitreya, if a woman is able to build a Buddha image, then she will never be born as a woman again.[64]

The Buddha then elaborates on why people are reborn as women:

> Maitreya, there are eight causes whereby a woman is reborn as a woman. And what are these eight? (1) Love for the body of a woman; (2) attachment to the passions of a woman; (3) constant delight in the beauties of a woman; (4) insincerity of heart to hide her wicked deeds; (5) weariness and contempt for her husband; (6) constant thoughts of other men; (7) perverse ingratitude for the kindness of others; and (8) wicked adornment of her body for the sake of deception.
>
> But if she can build a Buddha image and renounce these things forever, then until she herself gains Buddhahood she will always be a man, and she will never be born as a woman again.
>
> Maitreya, there are four causes whereby a man is reborn as a woman. And what are these four? (1) Disrespectfully laughing and shouting at the Buddha, or bodhisattvas, or Worthy Ones; (2) slan-

> dering one who is pure in keeping the precepts, saying he does not keep them; (3) flattering and fawning in order to deceive; and (4) envying the happiness of other men.
>
> If a man has done these things, then when his life is over he will surely be reborn as a woman, and experience the measureless suffering of his evil ways. But if he repents what he has done, awakens his faith, and builds a Buddha image, then these sins are all annulled, and he will not experience the retribution of becoming a woman.[65]

Obviously, enjoying womanhood dooms one to repeat it, but no such injunction is put on men and their enjoyment of masculinity. Men become women for insulting or slandering other men, buddhas, and monks (this text was obviously written by monks), or for rejecting masculinity and acting like a woman by being deceptive or envious.

Of particular interest, the Buddha goes on to explain why men are reborn as eunuchs or hermaphrodites—suggesting women do not receive these rebirths—and why men are born with female (read homosexual) desires:

> Maitreya, there are four causes whereby a man is reborn as a eunuch. And what are these four? (1) Castrating another man; (2) laughingly scorning and slandering a recluse who keeps the precepts; (3) transgressing the precepts himself because of his lustful desires; and (4) not only transgressing the precepts himself but also encouraging others to do the same. . . .
>
> Maitreya, there are four causes whereby a man is reborn as a hermaphrodite, which is the lowest possible state among men. And what are these four? (1) Uncleanness where there should be reverence and respect; (2) lust for the bodies of other men; (3) the practice of lustful things upon his own body; and (4) the exposure and sale of himself in the guise of a woman to other men. . . .
>
> Maitreya, there are four causes whereby a man is born with the lusts and desires of a woman, and enjoys being treated as a woman by other men. And what are these four? (1) despising other men, or slandering and defaming them even in jest; (2) taking pleasures in dressing and adorning himself as a woman; (3) doing lewd uncleanness with his own clanswoman; and (4) falsely accepting reverence while lacking the true virtue worthy of it.[66]

In addition to its homophobic orientation, these causes reveal the fragility of masculinity. It can be weakened not only by female pollution, but by men who despise and slander other men, or harm masculinity more directly by castration, or undo their own masculinity by masturbation, homosexual desire and acts, or dressing and behaving as a woman.

An interesting karmic case history comes from the biography of Padmasambhava. When King Trisong Detsan's eight-year-old daughter dies, Padmasambhava explained her past lives that led to this short-lived life. Of particular interest in the context of sex change through karma, seven births earlier she had been born as a brahman's son who became a monk, but committed several sins. When he observed two dogs having sex his desire was aroused and he had sex with another man's wife. He then blamed the male dog and killed it through a blow to its penis, and then in despair he jumped to his death. So, he broke his vow of celibacy through adultery, killed a living creature, and then killed himself. Of course, at the very least, he had to lose his male status and so was reborn five hundred times as different female animals, then five hundred times in hell and so on until the present incarnation. Still, the princess's karma was so bad Padmasambhava predicted that she will continue to be reborn ten more times as a beggar woman, then as vermin, and so on, then as an ugly woman who is attracted to religion, then as a woman with wisdom, and finally once again as a man, which will begin a series of male incarnations that lead to one as a famous *terton* (treasure finder).[67] In Padmasambhava's biography, and many other texts, being female is clearly the result of previous negative acts and being male the result of previous meritorious acts, which plays right into social justifications for male superiority. Teaching women to accept suffering specifically related to being female as karmic retribution for past sins[68] reveals karma's role in reifying the social status quo.

Shorter karmic case histories appear in a very popular Tibetan drama based on the *Vessantara Jātaka*. At its conclusion, predictions are made about the next lives of the leading characters with Vessantara's wife and daughter both incarnating as men.[69] This is particularly odd since the *Vessantara Jātaka* is about the penultimate life of the Buddha, so Vessantara and his wife reincarnate as the Buddha and his wife. Making such a change from the original story reveals the weight of the Tibetan belief that a woman's great virtue could only result in rebirth as a male.

The point was made earlier that karma can be mitigated by merit. In practice this can be done by oneself or by others, even after death, which directs our attention to Buddhist funeral practices. While each Buddhist culture has its own variants, Tibetan practices involve seven weeks of ceremonies, a sure indication of their importance. The purpose of a Buddhist funeral is to direct the deceased toward enlightenment or, more commonly, to shape their rebirth. This is the primary ritual role of Buddhist monks in relation to the laity, being funeral experts. Factoring in (1) the emphasis on women being reborn as men; (2) the popular wish to be reborn in a heaven, some of which exclude women; and (3) the time, expense, and effort expended on funerals in order to shape rebirth, leads to the inevitable conclusion that funerals are meant to absolutely kill womanhood while at the same time adding to the stock of manhood. As has been discussed above and will be elaborated upon in the next chapter, there is a driving force in Buddhism that co-opts feminine powers, characteristics, and subjectivity combined with what can only be seen as an ultimate goal to exterminate all actual women.

NOTES

1. Wendy Doniger explores this genre of stories, including those of sexual disguise and transvestism, in *The Bedtrick: Tales of Sex and Masquerade* (Chicago, IL: The University of Chicago Press, 2000), passim; and in *Splitting the Difference: Gender and Myth in Ancient Greece and India* (Chicago, IL: The University of Chicago Press, 1999), 260–302. See also Priscilla Rachun Linn, "Gender Roles," in *EOR*, vol. 5, 495–502.
2. See Margaret Mills, "Sex Role Reversals, Sex Changes, and Transvestite Disguise in the Oral Tradition of a Conservative Muslim Community in Afghanistan," in *Women's Folklore, Women's Culture*, ed. Rosan A. Jordan and Susan J. Kalčik (Philadelphia, PA: University of Pennsylvania Press, 1985), 187–213.
3. Fahien, *Record of Buddhistic Kingdoms*, 49.
4. Ibid., 51.
5. Falk, "The Case of the Vanishing Nuns."
6. Over the years, when I have questioned Tibetans on this topic their answers have been evasive, focusing instead on the difficulty of women's lives, which do not allow time for religious practice. According to Sherry Ortner's work among Sherpas, a Nepalese people whose culture is applicable to traditional Tibetan society, "women . . . have no direct chance for salvation; they can only hope to be reborn as men and from that position aim for higher things." *Sherpas Through Their Rituals* (Cambridge: Cambridge University Press, 1978), 182, n. 21. In general, see her discussion of reincarnation among Sherpas, 110–13.

   Marglin briefly discusses the Hindu view that women must be reborn as men in order to liberate, *Wives*, 20.
7. Quoted by Faure, *Red Thread*, 158.
8. Trans. by W. R. S. Ralston, *Tibetan Tales: Derived from Indian Sources*, 2d ed. (1882. Delhi: Sri Satguru Publications, 1988), 206–15. Her poems are in *Therīgāthā* lxiv.
9. Hardy, *Manual of Buddhism*, 518.
10. Ibid., 306–07.
11. Ibid., 301.
12. Stephen F. Teiser, *The Ghost Festival in Medieval China* (Princeton, NJ: Princeton University Press, 1988), 136–39.
13. Legge, *Record of Buddhistic Kingdoms*, 49, n. 2.
14. I have adapted the translation of Mrs. Rhys Davids, *Psalms of the Early Buddhists*, 114.

15. Ibid., 113.
16. Cowell and Neil, *Divyāvadāna*, 470.28–472.17.
17. Ibid., 473.27–28.
18. Rani, *Kashmiri Wood Blocks, avadana* no. 51, and Giuseppe Tucci, *Tibetan Pained Scrolls* (Roma: Liberia dello Stato, 1949), plate 115.
19. Paul, *Women in Buddhism*, 222. See also the frontispiece to Robert A. F. Thurman, trans, *The Holy Teaching of Vimalakīrti: A Mahāyāna Scripture* (University Park, PA: The Pennsylvania State University Press, 1976).
20. Thurman, *The Holy Teaching of Vimalakīrti*, 56–63.
21. These are semidivine half-serpent half-human beings said to posses great wealth. These aquatic beings are similar to the forest-dwelling *yakṣas* in their ambivalent powers to withhold or bestow blessings, and the females are similarly depicted in iconography as voluptuous women, though the lower bodies of the *nāginīs* are often shown as legless serpents or as equally legless mermaids.
22. H. Kern, trans., *Saddharmapuṇḍarīka or the Lotus of the True Law* (1884. New York: Dover Publications, Inc., 1963), 250–54.
23. Paul, *Women in Buddhism*, 285. She goes on to problematize Kuan Yin as a "female" bodhisattava, 285. See also her chapter on Kuan Yin.
24. See Miriam Levering's discussion of these phrases, "Lin-chi (Rinzai) Ch'an and Gender: The Rhetoric of Equality and the Rhetoric of Heroism," in Cabezón, *Buddhism, Sexuality, and Gender*, 137–56.
25. Paul, *Women in Buddhism*, 182–84.
26. Ibid., 197.
27. Ibid., 193.
28. Ibid., 22–23.
29. Doniger discusses several Hindu myths in which males become female: Viṣṇu into Mohinī, Krishna into a beautiful woman, and Śiva's forest in which all males are transformed into females, *Splitting*, 260–302.
30. Paul, *Women in Buddhism*, 169–71. See also Kajiyama Yuichi, "Women in Buddhism," *The Eastern Buddhist* xv.2 (Autumn 1982): 53–70. In response to Paul's work, Yuichi discusses these and other relevant texts that deny women can become a buddha. The sheathed or hidden penis was considered a divine attribute; see La Vallée Poussin, "Cosmogony and Cosmology (Buddhist)," *Encyclopaedia of Religion and Ethics*, ed. James Hastings (New York: Charles Scribner's Sons, 1914), vol. 4, 135, col. b.
31. Despite the number of male to female Hindu stories that Doniger discusses, she comes to the same conclusion, *Splitting*, 281.
32. Paul, *Women in Buddhism*, 207, 209. In other words, women need to change sex before being born in this Pure Land. Barnes finds the language ambiguous as to whether there will be no women or no idea of gender differences; "Changing the Female Body," 62, n. 29. I think, however, the absence of gender means the absence of the female—maleness prevails.
33. Paul, *Women in Buddhism*, 178–80.
34. Barnes presents this story from Chinese sources, "Changing the Female Body," 32–35.
35. Translated and cited by Janice D. Willis, "Nuns and Benefactresses: The Role of Women in the Development of Buddhism," in *Women, Religion and Social Change*, ed. Yvonne Yazbeck Haddad and Ellison Banks Findly (Albany, NY: State University of New York Press, 1985), 69.
36. Shattan, *Manimekhalaï*, 92.
37. Jaini, *Gender and Salvlation*, passim.

38. Beata Grant, "The Spiritual Saga of Woman Huang: From Pollution to Purification," in Johnson, *Ritual Opera*, 225–26.
39. Cowell, *Buddhist Mahāyāna Texts*, Part II, 19. See also, Paul, *Women in Buddhism*, 169–70. This heaven is discussed further in chapter 13 herein.
40. Paul, *Women in Buddhism*, has a chapter about such stories, and Barnes, "Changing the Female Body," discusses the *Gangottara-sūtra* and the *Śrīmala Sūtra*, 37–39.
41. Jo-Nang Taranatha, *The Origin of the Tārā Tantra*, trans. and ed. David Templeman (Dharamsala: Library of Tibetan Works and Archives, 1983), 11–12.
42. Ortner, *Making Gender*, 201.
43. For more on this point see Ortner and Whitehead, eds., Introduction, to *Sexual Meanings*, 13–24.
44. Notable exceptions appear among male worshippers of Dionysus and the male *bhakta* saints of India. The point, of course, is the converse: for a man to become a woman is to lose prestige, which is exactly what these god-drenched male mystics seek to do. An extreme example of sex change for men is found among the self-emasculated priests of the goddess Cybelle and the *hijirās* of India. The latter are discussed in chapter 6 herein.
45. Paul, *Women in Buddhism*, 175–76.
46. Machig Lapdron is discussed at length in chapter 9 herein. Janet Gyatso says she is believed to incarnate mainly in female forms, "Machig Labdron," in *EOW*, vol. II, 609.
47. Edou, *Machig*, 5, 122–23. Ortner also reports that many Buddhist nuns hope that by leading religious lives they will be reborn as men, *Making Gender*, 129.
48. Strong, *Upagupta*, 127.
49. Ibid., 132. This story was very popular in East Asia, where it had several variants; ibid., 321, n. 32.
50. Reed, "The Gender Symbolism," 160.
51. Ibid., 159; and Paul, *Women in Buddhism*, 252. Reed's article discusses the role of women artists in Kuan Yin's iconography and women's devotional relationship to Kuan Yin, passim.
52. Paul, *Women in Buddhism*, 264–80.
53. See, respectively, e.g., Gyatso, *Guide to Dakini Land*, 7; Dowman, *Sky Dancer*, 147; and Chonam and Khandro, *Mandarava*, 184.
54. Reed, "The Gender Symbolism," 159–77.
55. Daniel. L. Overmyer, "Values in Chinese Sectarian Literature: Ming and Ch'ing *Pao-chüan*," in *Popular Culture in Late Imperial China*, ed. David Johnson, et al. (Berkeley, CA: University of California Press, 1985), 228.
56. For brief but good general discussions of karma along with excellent bibliographies, see Nancy Auer Falk, "Karma," in *EOW*, vol. I, 560–61; and Mizuno Kōgen, "Karman: Buddhist Concepts," in *EOR*, vol. 8, 266–68. Warren, *Buddhism in Translation*, chapter III, has excerpts from Buddhist texts on karma, 209–79. Two Pali texts, the *Vimānavatthu* and the *Petavatthus*, contain brief stories about the acts that earned individuals an extended stay in heaven or hell. B. C. Law has translated some of these in *The Buddhist Conception of Spirits*, 2d ed. (1923. 1936. Delhi: Pilgrims Book Pvt. Ltd: 1997). See also the *Mahākarmavibhaṅga* and J. Gonda's discussion of its representation at Borobodur, "Karman and Retributive Justice in Ancient Java," in J. Gonda, *Selected Studies*, vol. iv (Leiden: E. J. Brill, 1975), 337–49.
57. See the discussion in chapter 3 herein.
58. Doniger, *Splitting*, 298.
59. Chang, *The 100,000 Songs*, vol. I, 143.

60. Ortner, *Sherpas*, 192, n. 21. Karma Lekshe Tsomo has discussed with Tibetan women the negative effect of praying for a male rebirth when they were children, "Tibetan Nuns and Nunneries," 122–23. See also twentieth-century biographies by Tibetan women, such as Rin-chen Lha-mo, *We Tibetans* (London: Seeley Service & Co., 1926), 130.
61. Cited by Strong, *The Experience of Buddhism*, 31.
62. Stephan Beyer suggests this was composed in the seventh century either in China or Central Asia, though it was probably based on an earlier Indian text, *The Buddhist Experience: Sources and Interpretations* (Belmont, CA: Wadsworth Publishing Company, 1974), 46.
63. Anthropological discussions of karma are in Samuel, *Civilized Shamans*, 199–222; Ortner, *Sherpas*, especially 111; and Paul, *Tibetan Symbolic World*, 102ff.
64. Beyer, *The Buddhist Experience*, 52.
65. Ibid., 53.
66. Ibid., 53.
67. Douglas and Bays, *Life and Liberation*, 606–08.
68. Fruzzetti, *Gift of a Virgin*, xx–xxi.; Bennett, *Dangerous Wives*, 283. We will see other Buddhist methods for getting women to accept their low status as their own fault in the discussion of the Hell of the Bloody Pond in chapter 13.
69. Duncan, *More Harvest Festival Dramas*, 120.

CHAPTER 13

OTHER LANDS/OTHER REALITIES

THE BUDDHIST UNIVERSE

For early Buddhists the defining feature of the universe is its impermanence. This view was enlarged by adding two pervasive South Asian notions about the nature of the universe and its construction. First, after a vast period of time (a *mahākalpa*) the universe dies and then slowly arises again. This process is repeated endlessly. Second, Mt. Meru is at the center of the world surrounded by a great ocean and large islands. The earth is a mysterious and magical place populated or visited by many kinds of mythic beings, such as *yakṣīs*, *nāgas*, *apśaras*, ghosts, ghouls, demons, deities, and so on. Such a worldview allows for the existence of mythic lands hidden in the mountains or on islands in uncharted seas. Additionally, Buddhists developed an elaborate cosmology that has a threefold division between the realms (*dhātus*) of desire (*kāma*), form (*rūpa*), and formlessness (*arūpa*).[1]

The desire realm (*kāmadhātu*) is encapsulated in the Wheel of Becoming or Rebirth (*bhavacakra; Srid pa'i 'khor lo*) and is characterized by *duḥkha* (suffering). The Wheel of Becoming is a frequent subject of Buddhist art that depicts the five or six realms or destinies (*gatis*) of the gods, humans, asuras, hungry ghosts, hell beings, and animals, all held in the grasp of Impermanence or the wrathful deity Yama (the god of Death), or Māra (Lord of the Realm of Desire and archenemy of enlightenment). It includes heavens and hells, as well as the earth. All sentient beings transmigrate through these six realms according to their karma. The only way to get off this wheel is to achieve enlightenment. To remind all beings of their situation, they were painted in the entrance halls of monasteries from the earliest times.[2] The boundaries of these realms are quite porous, as is suggested by the ability of all beings to transmigrate between regions, and by the appearance of divine beings on earth and of highly advanced human beings in the heavens or hells.

Early Buddhists texts defined sixteen hells: eight hot and eight cold, where the damned are horribly tortured, while various heavens were divided among the three realms of desire, form and formlessness. Both Tuṣita, where the future Buddha Maitreya reigns, and Trāyastriṃśa, where the Buddha's mother was reborn, are said to exist in the realm of form. Given Buddhism's long history and wide geographical spread, it should come as no surprise that these heavens and hells are subject to permutations and multiplications, and that their porous boundaries allow various beings to travel between them. These mythic lands, heavens, and hells are the subject of this chapter.

LANDS OF WOMEN

There are many ancient South Asian tales about a Land of Women,[3] including the story that Śiva and Parvartī created a forest where all males were transformed into females: men, horses, even trees![4] There are tales of male yogis, such as Matsyendra, trapped in a land of sexually predatory women,[5] and the yogi Gopi Chand, who is similarly ensnared by dangerous, highly sexed women in the much mythologized state of Bengal.[6] Two separate Lands of Women are said to have existed on the borders of Tibet, one in the east (Kham), and the other in the west (near Hunza).[7] They were often conflated, but their main characteristics were as follows: they were ruled by a queen whose husband had nothing to do with the government, sons took their mothers' family name, the women did not hold men in high regard, and they possessed rich gold deposits.[8] Perhaps having the same place in mind, the *Mārkaṇḍeya Purāṇa* (LVIII:39) and *Mahābhārata* (XII:4) mention a matriarchal state in the Himalayan northwest, while the *Kama Sūtra*[9] gives a less geographically specific reference. An important point about these stories is that they always take place somewhere else, out there, on the margins of the known world. They are stories about the Other that end up revealing the underside of the author's culture.[10] Being specifically about women, they reveal the underside of male cultural dominance through their fantastic characterizations of women who transgress the norms of patriarchal society. These stories are told from the perspective of the male protagonists; they are men's stories that objectify women and deny the reader/hearer access to the thoughts and feelings of any of the female characters.[11]

This genre of tale seems to have been quite popular in Buddhist circles as variants of one tale are told in several different texts and it has been widely depicted in iconography.[12] One Pali version is the *Valāhassa Jātaka* (No. 196), "The Cloud Horse," a story the Buddha told to a monk whose passion had been aroused by seeing a finely dressed woman.[13] Consequently, it is a tale expressly meant to emphasize women as fatal temptresses, mistresses of womanly wiles (Pali: *itthikuttavilāsehi*) and illusion, who entice men only to destroy them. It is also used to explain why all women are referred to as demonesses (Pali: *yakkinī*, Skt: *yakṣinī*, in other versions *rākṣasī*). Thus some versions of this tale are examples of negative textual representations of *yakṣī*s discussed in chapter 2, tales that capitalize on their beauty, sexuality, and ambivalent power to do good or ill. At the same time stories such as this reveal a male fear of women with power, and in this they are similar to tales about evil queens. It seems that the men who authored and preserved these tales imagined that if women had power they would abuse it as much as some men did.

In the *Valāhassa Jātaka* five hundred merchants were shipwrecked on Sri Lanka,[14] a land of *yakṣī*s, who in this text are cannibals. The *yakṣī*s lured the merchants to their capital city through their beauty, magic powers, and sexuality, saying they want them for husbands. They fed and then slept with the men. Later they feasted on men they had captured earlier. One merchant figured this out, and he fled with most of his companions. In this version the Buddha was a beautiful white flying horse who rescued them.[15] In a Sanskrit version he is the leader of the merchants who is able to locate the magical horse and thus save himself and all his companions.[16]

As many *jātaka*s do, the story features merchants, a dominant group among early converts to Buddhism, who by virtue of their trade routes and their generosity as donors were important to the spread of Buddhism and the establishment of Buddhist communities in major trading centers and along the routes they traveled. This tale, in particular, addresses various anxieties of traders, such as the dangers and uncertainty of foreign travel, the fear of shipwreck and the dangers posed by foreign women. Todd Lewis has analyzed these aspects in a later version of the story,[17] as well as documenting its popularity and relevance to the lives of Nepalese traders who made the frequently dangerous journey to Tibet, some of whom remained there for years, often marrying Tibetan women. The direct relevance of this story to their lives is especially shown by the ferries they used to cross the Brahmaputra river, some of which were constructed to resemble the flying horse of the title.[18] A similar ferry seems to be described in the Tibetan folk drama *sNangsa*, when the heroine sings to the ferryman on the other side of a river, asking him to "bring the big boat with the horse head."[19]

In a Sanskrit version of this story from the *MV*, entitled the *Dharmalabdha Jātaka,* the Buddha is the heroic merchant leader. This past life was told when the Buddha was asked why Māra's daughters had tried to tempt him on the night of his enlightenment.[20] The story explains that the women in the story, who are heavily demonized by being called *rākṣasīs*, are now Māra's daughters. Most *jātaka*s are told to explain that people get in the habit of acting in a certain way from past interactions; Māra's daughters tried to seduce him because that is what they did when they all shared a past life in a Land of Women.

The legends about a Land of Women were preserved in texts controlled by men, not women, and they reveal men's imaginings about women's resentment of their oppression. These legends play out an inversion of sexist society, one in which the division into two genders receives its extreme expressions. For example, their cannibalism has women consuming men, when it is men who dictate and then consume women's labor and products. In other words, in these male fantasies women are believed to express their resentment by acting as men: they are aggressive, sexually predatory, and controlling.

As discussed in chapter 10, Lévi-Strauss argued that throughout most of history society was, and in many ways remains, based on establishing and maintaining bonds between men through the exchange of women. Bearing this in mind, one can understand that men would perceive a Land of Women as a perverse social group based on bonds between women completely unmediated by men and indeed, that such a land would be a radical denial of men's rights over women and instead an assertion by women of rights over themselves and men.

Stories about a Land of Women provided men with an opportunity to portray their idea of women's nature in its purest state, completely free of male influence. Left to their own devices, women are shown to be vicious, evil, sexually voracious killers. They consume men. An interesting contrast to this can be seen in the Buddhist heavens that exclude women—lands without women—which portray men's nature as perfect when free of female influence. (These heavens will be discussed shortly.) Legends about Lands of Women make it obvious that women must be controlled by men and that they must be punished no matter how innocent they seem.

Hells for Women

Legends about the dangers men face in lands ruled by women are inverted in the *Blood Bowl Sutra,* which describes the all-women Hell of the Bloody Pond (based on the Avīci hell of Indian texts)[21] and depicts a male demon inflicting gruesome punishments on women. This text was composed in China where it circulated widely from the time of the Ming dynasty (1368–1644),[22] though its roots are in texts going back to fifth-century China[23] and in Indian legends of journeys to various heavens and hells. In this hell women receive karmic payback for having polluted the earth god with the blood of childbirth and for having offended all the gods and holy individuals by polluting the earth's water through washing menstrual cloths. In other words, punishment for the sin of sexuality and reproduction is visited exclusively on women. This is symbolically represented in texts that have women in this hell nailed down on spiked and heated beds.[24]

Momoko Takemi presents a description of this hell from one of the earliest Japanese versions of this *sūtra*:

> This pond was some 84,000 jujana wide, and in the middle women who were wearing handcuffs and ankle chains were undergoing hardships. The demon who was the lord of this Hell came here three times a day and forced the women sinners to drink the polluted blood; if they refused to do so, he would beat them with an iron rod. Their screams of anguish could be heard from great distances away. The sight of this made me very sad, and so I asked the Lord of the Hell why the women were being forced to undergo such hardships. He replied that the blood the women had shed during the birth of their children had polluted the deity of the earth and that, furthermore, when they washed their polluted garments in the river, that water was gathered up by a number of virtuous men and woman and used to make tea to serve to holy men. Because of these acts of uncleanliness, the women were now forced to undergo sufferings.
>
> Thus Mokuren [the Buddha's disciple Maudgalyāyana] used his holy powers to come to the seat of the Buddha and to inform him of what he had seen with his eyes. He asked, then, what he needed to do for the women to be saved from their punishments in the pond of blood.
>
> The Buddha then answered, teaching Mokuren how to save the women. He said it would be necessary for them to respect the three treasures of filial piety, to call on Mokuren, to hold a Blood Pool Liberation service, to hold a Blood Pool feast, to read sutras, to have an esoteric ceremony, then to make a boat and float it off.[25]

The unreasonableness of sending all women to this hell seems to have been apparent at the time the text was composed, since it carried within itself the means for their salvation. Before they die, in order to escape this fate, women must first accept and fully internalize the belief that they are polluters. The *sūtra* then could be utilized in various ways to save them: believing in it could lead to rebirth in the Western Paradise as a man,[26] or the physical text could be used as an amulet to protect women during childbirth and to transform offerings made while menstruating or after childbirth into pure offerings.[27] Once dead and in the Hell of the Bloody Pond, its recitation by others could release women—it formed the basis for ceremonies performed by sons to free their mothers from that hell.

This *sūtra* enabled men to act out their gender anxieties by developing rituals that sharply distinguish two sexes: women are defined by their biological functions, which are deemed polluting, and men are defined by their power to save women. The practices associated with this *sūtra* spread from China throughout East Asia where they mingled with indigenous beliefs about women's pollution. Today these practices are in decline, despite the continuing practice in Taiwan of breaking the blood bowl at the funerals of women and the presence of blood ponds in some Japanese Buddhist temples.[28] However, it remains in use in Zen practice, even in the West, as this *sūtra* is given to women during their initiations to use as an amulet to purify their worship when they are menstruating.[29]

These practices have several sources. First, there are early Buddhist stories about men journeying to other realms to see their dead mothers, such as the Buddha and his disciple Maudgalyāyana visiting their dead mothers in heaven, discussed in chapter 2. Second, there is the equally early practice of making donations to Buddhist monastics and then offering the merit thus acquired to one's parents. In Chinese and Japanese versions of this tale Maudgalyāyana, called Mu-lien in Chinese and Murkuren in Japanese, visits hell rather than heaven to preach to his mother.[30] Here she had become a hungry ghost (*preta; yi dag*)—ghosts who have huge bellies that can never be filled because of their needle-thin necks. Another source for these practices is the widely popular Chinese ghost festival, a festival attributed to the Buddha,[31] within which Mu-lien's story is enacted. The tale begins when Mu-lien arrives in hell and finds his mother, but is unable to ease her sufferings. He returns to the land of the living to seek advice from the Buddha, who tells him his mother's suffering could be relieved if he provided food and cloth offerings to monastics when they emerged from their annual three-month summer retreats. Appropriately, this is the time when the Buddha returned from preaching to his mother in Trāyastriṃśa heaven, the original Buddhist event of a son rescuing a dead mother. The merit acquired by making offerings could then be transferred to one's ancestors. Making such offerings to Buddhist monastics on behalf of one's ancestors was the focus of the Chinese ghost festival.[32]

Actually, the story of Mu-lien and his mother became both an opera and a ritual. As an opera it is ritually enacted over several days before the entire community, and sections of the opera are excerpted for specific ritual functions at the funerals of women.[33] Gary Seaman describes the practice in present-day Taiwan as follows:

> In the ritual, the sons and daughters of a dead woman mime a descent into hell. A set is built representing the fortress in hell where their mother's soul is imprisoned, and a bowl of wine, dyed red, is placed in the fortress to symbolize the pool of blood in which she is drowning. After the actor who plays the part of Mu-lien vanquishes the jailers of hell (who would keep the woman's soul imprisoned), the bowl of red wine is portioned out to the children of the dead woman. Each of them drinks, wipes the bowl clean, then presents it to Mu-lien for a final purification.[34]

I will take up the issue of modern daughters participating in this ritual below. For now, though, it is important to recall that this literature and these rituals are quite gender specific: they do not focus on parents, but on mothers; nor do they focus on children, but on sons. In fact, in an extended version of Mu-lien's story, *The Illustrated Tale of Mu Lian Saving His Mother from the Netherworld*, Mu-lien first went to heaven to find his mother. Instead, he found his father, who explained that while he had practiced the Buddhist virtues Mu-lien's mother had not and therefore she was in hell.[35] The redemption scenario is clearly one of female sinners and male saviors modeled on the Buddha and Mu-lien having saved their mothers. And, historically, this ritual was performed specifically (if not exclusively) by sons.[36]

Part of the motivation for the ritual stems from the son's need to free himself from the negative karma generated by the birth pains he caused his mother,[37] and from the debt he owed her for having breastfed him.[38] He does this by symbolically drinking the blood that polluted the earth at the time of his birth. By internalizing his mother's pollution of the earth during his birth, he evens the score between them; he exchanges her negative karma of pollution for his negative karma of causing her birth pains and of depleting her through breastfeeding, thus freeing her from her punishment in the Hell of the Bloody Pond. As an added bonus he acquires merit that qualifies him for reincarnation as a god, saint, or pure spirit. It is a rite for the resolution of mother-son conflict, one in which the mother is helpless and the son all-powerful, a complete reversal of the child's experience. In fact, it is a complete reversal of the birth process in which the mother literally births the child into this world; now the child symbolically births the mother into a higher state of being.[39]

In this ritualized scenario all women are believed to be tortured in hell until they fully accept their inferior state, while men, most particularly sons with their complicated power relations to their mothers, compassionately help the women out of the very hell they have created for them. Male fears of powerful women—all mothers appear as powerful beings to their children—are displaced onto women's state of ritual pollution. Their fears are then contained by believing women are imprisoned in the Hell of the Bloody Pond, a containment that allows for a rich range of sadistic fantasies about men torturing women—after all, this hell is ruled by the male demon/god Yāma and Chinese versions are explicit in their presentation of an all-male bureaucracy of torturers.[40] Finally, men can conquer their fears of women through their male power that can release women, but only those women who fully accept male ideas about their polluting physicality and their consequent inferior spirituality. These are stories about the male desire to control the all-powerful mother in order to subvert their early dependence on her love as well as their enduring sexual dependence on other women.[41]

In all this it is hard to ignore the fact that it is the child who corrects, admonishes, enlightens, and saves the parent, perhaps one of childhood's most cherished fantasies. These stories, and later rituals, emphasize the female sinner and the male savior, and completely reverse the power relations of mother and child. In the process, as is particularly clear in Chinese Buddhism, the mother is not in any way exalted as she is in Daoism; rather she is made completely prosaic and of interest to no one but her son.[42]

Chinese Buddhists engaged women in this process mainly through the fear of damnation. This fear impelled mothers first to raise good Buddhist children who will see to their salvation and secondly to make sure that even as adults they remained good Buddhists. Additionally, it armed them in their life-long right to control their sons and their daughters-in-law.[43] Daughters are brought in as an interesting aside. Historically, it is highly unlikely that daughters could actually participate in their mother's funeral ceremonies because that would involve taking resources away from their husbands' families and they owed their allegiance to their husbands' ancestors. Alternatively, daughters were promised they could free all mothers by copying and propagating this text. Not unimportantly, such acts of devotion increased women's chances of being saved from this hell when they died.[44] Thus, the involvement of daughters is shown to be a means of incorporating as many women as possible into this ideology of female degradation and salvation. Given the foregoing, the question arises, Where could women go when they were saved?

PURE LANDS

Belief in a divine realm of the gods, or heaven, is an ancient South Asian religious idea absorbed by Buddhism. The *LV* actually begins in Tuṣita Heaven,[45] where the Buddha is said to have been waiting for the right time to incarnate on earth. As he descended into his mother's womb, the future buddha Maitreya took his place, to await his time to incarnate. Tuṣita Heaven is understood to be a purified Buddha Land or a Pure Land (*pariśuddhaṃ buddhaṣetraṃ; dag pa'i zhing*) where the teachings of a Buddha hold sway. This sets up a dichotomy between pure and impure lands; pure lands have been purified by the presence and teachings of a buddha, in contrast to impure lands that lack a buddha and his teachings.[46] We will see that this complements the dichotomy between pure men and impure women. With the rise of Mahāyana Buddhism around the first century B.C.E. Pure Lands begin to proliferate as the special realms of bodhisattvas who, when they become buddhas, will create their own Pure Lands. From that time forward Pure Lands were described in texts, such as the *Sukhāvatīvyūha sūtra*s, and depicted in murals on the walls of temples and caves, and in paintings.[47] *Maṇḍala*s became an important ritual device for entry into these realms, while paintings and sculptures were used to stimulate meditation upon them, and visualization practices enabled adepts to see themselves as present in the Pure Land. Chinese Buddhist art particularly emphasized Buddhist heavens because devotion to Pure Lands became a separate cult of Buddhism in China and later in medieval Japan.

Without Women

An important description of a Pure Land is contained in the opening of the *Sukhāvatīvyūha Sūtra*s, where the Buddha lists the buddhas of the past, focusing on Dharmākara, who after achieving enlightenment became the Buddha Amitābha. This Pure Land, called Sukhāvatī (Tib: *bDe ba can*), the Land of Bliss, also known as the Western Paradise, is the Pure Land encountered most often in literature and art. Its name, *sukha* (bliss), sets up a contrast with *duḥkha* (suffering), the defining characteristic of cyclical existence with its inevitable round of birth, growing old, and death, followed by rebirth. It is depicted as a sweet-smelling and beautiful garden with lotus ponds and trees made of precious jewels, a place where the plants and birds preach the dharma and all the needs of its inhabitants are satisfied. Rebirth here can be achieved by a combination of good deeds and repeating, in some cases just hearing, the name of Amitābha Buddha.[48] The simplicity of its practice, repeating Amitābha's name, made it accessible to vast numbers of people who were illiterate or who could not pursue more time-consuming practices. The recitation of his name could be done while working at other tasks, such as farming or housework, though ritualized recitation with a group of worshippers was also commonly practiced.[49] Rebirth in this paradise is one's final incarnation, as Pure Lands are by definition outside of cyclical existence and it is inevitable that buddhahood will be achieved here. Needless to say, Pure Land Buddhism became an extremely popular and widespread form of worship throughout Asia.

In Sukhāvatī birth occurs by spontaneous generation (*aupapāduka*) in a lotus (Plates 15 and 16).[50] No women are necessary and the whole messy business of the womb and its pollution is neatly avoided. In fact, women are excluded from this paradise, ensuring that this Pure Land is free of menstrual pollution as well. The absence of women and sexual reproduction in Sukhāvatī appears to be a self-fulfilling prophecy given the cultural denigration of women coupled with their exclusion from significant leadership roles in Buddhism, as well as their exclusion from certain sacred sites. During earthly life men achieve spiritual advancement by separating themselves from women through all-male monastic institutions and lineages and by biologically distinguishing themselves as superior to women because they are less polluted. Thus it should come as no surprise that by the time men reach paradise their efforts to exclude women are represented as being completely successful; paradise, a Pure Land, is by definition a land without women, a land of stable masculinity unthreatened by women.[51] Pure Land *sūtra*s make this clear when they advise women that upon hearing Amitābha's name they should learn to despise the female state—then they will be reborn in Sukhāvatī as males and never again be born as a female.[52] Ironically, Pure Land Buddhism, primarily through its emphasis on devotion and the simple practice of reciting Amitābha's name, made Buddhism more accessible to women, especially given the pollution fears that excluded women from many important monasteries. The fact that Buddha is said to have first preached about this Pure Land to a woman, the Indian Queen Vaidehī, certainly opened its practice to women.[53]

Interestingly, Sukhāvatī seems to be based on Indra's heaven, Trāyastriṃśa, where one is also born through lotuses, not wombs. Females are, however, residents of Indra's heaven, though in subordinate positions, as *apśara*s, beautiful and sensual companions for the male gods.[54] As discussed in chapter 5, the *apśara*s were the reason the

Buddha took his half-brother Nanda there, to get him to forget about the earthly beauty of his wife. Although Buddhists could be born into Indra's heaven through their good karma, inevitably it would run out and they would pass to another, presumably lower rebirth, since the motivation for spiritual advancement in this sensual and luxurious heaven is slight. In contrast, birth in Sukhāvatī is permanent and there is no sexual activity. The *Lotus Sūtra* is explicit on these points when it reiterates that women are not born there and declares that "sexual intercourse is absolutely unknown" in this realm.[55]

Iconography and some texts contradict this exclusion of women in that *apśaras* are occasionally depicted in Sukhāvatī, as is Avalokiteśvara/Kuan Yin.[56] Avalokiteśvara and Mahāsthāmaprāpta are male celestial bodhisattvas who act as Amitābha's assistants, respectively representing his mercy and wisdom. The earliest representations of Avalokiteśvara are male, and even though s/he is later feminized, this sex-changing deity cannot really be thought of as "all-female," nor can a celestial bodhisattva or an *apśara* be equated with human women.

As mentioned in chapter 12, a well-known text about a woman's vow to become a buddha and create a Pure Land is the *Lion's Roar of Queen Śrīmālā*. It was composed in south India in the third century C.E.[57] and presents Śrīmālā as a queen who lived at the time of the Buddha. When the Buddha preached to her, he made the prediction that she would become a buddha and he briefly described her Pure Land. Here no one will be born as an animal, a ghost or a hell being. There will be no suffering of old age or sickness; instead all the inhabitants will be virtuous, strong and beautiful, and they will possess longevity and great happiness.[58] The text does not specify whether Śrīmālā will change into a male or not, which Chinese commentaries on the text discussed at length.[59] The *Śrīmālā* is later than and differs from the *Sukhāvatīvyūha Sūtras* in important ways. In the *Sukhāvatīvyūha Sūtras* the Buddha does all the preaching to a queen and it contains the statement that women must despise the female state. In the *Śrīmālā*, the queen gives a very important preaching on buddha nature and it does not contain any explicitly antifemale statements. Further, having been composed in south India places the *Śrīmālā* in a different social setting, one that seems to have been friendlier to women, as we have seen in the discussion of the woman-centered *Manimekhalaï*. Thus it is possible that becoming male was not an original requirement for rebirth in Śrīmālā's Pure Land, but the absence of a specific statement that females could be born there allowed latter commentators to interpret it within the context of the *Sukhāvatīvyūha Sūtras*.

In contrast to Queen Śrīmālā, another example of a female's vow to become a buddha is the story of an eight year old girl, Sumati, from the *Mahāratnakūṭa*. The description of her Pure Land is that there will be no evil, no evil destinies, or even "the name of woman."[61] In other words, there will be no women.[62] As discussed in chapter 12, Sumati emphasized this by performing an act of truth in order to change her female body into a male body.[63] Similarly, the *Sutra of the Buddha Teaching the Seven Daughters*, which is the story of seven sisters who leap into the air and without apparent reason change into boys upon hearing they will become buddhas, also has a short description of their Pure Land. The text does not specify that women will not be allowed, but the transformation of the girls into boys strongly suggests that this will be the case.[64]

With Women

The woman-friendly nature of Śrīmālā's Pure Land is echoed in more specific detail in the *Akṣobhyavyūha*. This is a description of the celestial buddha Akṣobhya's Pure Land called Abhirati, which not only includes women, but also has procreation, albeit by the male gaze that instantly transports the gazer into meditative absorption rather than sexual activity. For women, pregnancy is not uncomfortable and there is no menstruation. Abhirati has all the characteristics of other Pure Lands, all *sukha* and no *duḥkha*. It is very beautiful and clothing, food, and drink appear when they are desired.[60] But both Śrīmālā's and Akṣobhya's Pure Lands were overwhelmed by the proliferation of the all-male Sukhāvatī and other male-only Pure Lands.

Some pure lands, however, are terrestrial, they are hidden lands, invisible to all but the most developed beings. The possible immanence of these lands and their explicit connection to the earth seems to allow for the presence of women. For instance, the Pure Land of Shambhala (Tib: *bDe 'byung*, meaning "source of happiness")[65] includes women. Paintings of Rudrachakrin, the last king of Shambhala, sometimes depict his queen as well as both mild and fierce *ḍākinīs*.

Shambhala is said to be a beautiful land with a righteous king, a land that is both immanent and transcendent. It is envisioned as a fertile land of valleys and mountains hidden deep within several rings of snow-covered mountain ranges lying somewhere to the north of India. Eight regions surround the central capital where the king, a benevolent and fully enlightened being, rules from a palace constructed of precious jewels. Its residents live in perfect harmony and happiness as all their needs are met. Everyone has long, healthy lives but eventually they do die; most go on to enlightenment and others are reborn once again in Shambhala or in similar divine realms. The main activity in this kingdom is the pursuit of spiritual enlightenment, which is easily achieved in its environment and through the teachings of the *Kālacakra Tantra* (the wheel of time), an extremely esoteric teaching said to have been taught by the Buddha and then preserved for centuries in Shambhala.[66] The *Kālacakra Tantra* consists of teachings about the physical world, especially time and astrology; the psychic world of the subtle body; and visualization practices. During the tenth century very advanced Tibetan yogis were said to have journeyed to Shambhala through visions and dreams in order to retrieve this text and its commentaries. Tibetans believe that initiation into the Kālacakra teachings assures rebirth in Shambhala.[67]

Shambhala is also the focus of apocalyptic beliefs. An important prophecy about Shambhala is that during the reign of its twenty-fifth king, around the year 2425, a great war will engulf the whole world. At that time, just when all seems lost, a great army will march forth from Shambhala to conquer the opposing forces. Peace will be restored throughout the world, ushering in a golden age.

Another important terrestrial Pure Land is Padmasambhava's Glorious Copper-Colored Mountain (*zangs mdog dpal ri*), said to be on the island of Chamara, south of India, an island populated with *rākṣasas*.[68] There is a short description of this land in Padmsambhava's biography (cantos 97 and 107), which locates it in Sri Lanka.[69] Paintings show Yeshe Tsogyel and Mandāravā there, along with many *ḍākinīs* (Plate 14). Glorious Copper-Colored Mountain penetrates down into the domain of the *nāgas*, while its middle section touches the Land of *Ḍākinīs*, and its peak is in the sphere of the gods.[70]

The Land of *Ḍākinīs* (Tib: *mKha' 'gro'i gling*), variously called Uḍḍiyāna, Odiyana, Orgyan, Urgyan, and so on, is said to be in the Swat valley of present-day Pakistan, the birthplace of Padmasambhava. So, it is an actual place with a history of tantric practice at the same time that it is a mystical Pure Land. Liz Wilson embellishes on its multiple meanings when she compares this seemingly all-woman realm with that of the island of the cannibalistic *yakṣīs* we met in the *Valāhassa Jātaka*. She says, it "is both a locus of otherness and an idealized potential within the self—the enlightened mind inherent in all sentient beings. Odiyana is, then, not a distant land in which a man finds himself stranded and eaten alive but a region in which the impure mind (that generates such desire- and fear-based fantasies) is transcended."[71]

More detailed descriptions of the Land of *Ḍākinīs* are contradictory. For instance, Milarepa's biography is filled with *ḍākinīs*; it even begins with Milarepa's disciple Rechungpa having a dream that that he is in "the enchanting country called Urgyan." He sees a great city with houses made of precious materials and whose inhabitants possess tremendous beauty and are richly adorned, and where he is warmly welcomed.[72]

Yeshe Tsogyel's biography presents a darker picture of her visionary journey to Orgyan. She sees a land where

> the fruit trees were like razors, the ground was plastered with meat, the mountains were bristling piles of skeletons and the clods of earth and stone were scattered fragments of bone. In the center of this *maṇḍala* was an immeasurable palace built of skulls and wet [still bleeding] and dry heads, and the ceilings and door-blinds were made of human skin. At a radius of a hundred thousand leagues the palace was ringed by a circle of volcanoes, a wall of *vajras*, a perimeter of falling thunderbolts, a ring of eight cemeteries and a wall of beautiful lotuses. Within this boundary were flocks of flesh-eating blood-drinking birds and crowds of demon savages, male and female, and other brutes, all of whom surrounded me glaring at me threateningly, but thereafter they acted with neither hostility nor friendliness.[73]

All this contrasts sharply with Rechungpa's peaceful dream vision. Yeshe Tsogyel's vision also describes many *ḍākinīs* mutilating their bodies, carving off flesh, ripping veins for blood, even cutting out eye-balls and internal organs to give as offerings to the chief *ḍākinī*.[74] Of course, this points to the ambivalence of the *ḍākinī*, who can appear as a beautiful woman or a revolting hag, who can be consoling or who can fill an adept with terror. They are tantric initiatory goddesses and sometimes living women possessed of tremendous spiritual power, and their imagery, as in Yeshe Tsogyel's vision, can be as terrifying as any tantric gathering in a cremation ground.

Ḍākinīs initiate adepts through dreams and visions, and as sexual partners; rarely as direct teachers within their own female lineage.[75] The Sanskrit term *ḍākinī* was translated into Tibetan as *mkha' 'gro ma*, meaning "sky-goer"—they cross over between realms, that of *saṃsāra* and *nirvāṇa* and that of the living and the dead. Consequently, *ḍākinīs* can confer enlightenment, they can take one beyond death. More broadly, they have an important salvational role in that they can bestow *siddhis*, the supernormal powers that lead to enlightenment. They represent a well-known theme in world religion and mythology, that of male dependence on a female guide in order to complete their quests, win their goal, or achieve enlightenment. Wisdom and insight (*prajñā*) are feminine terms in South Asian languages as well as other religious traditions, and they are frequently personified by goddesses or semidivine women whose aid must be won in order to succeed in gaining spiritual knowledge or power.[76] This has never, however, translated in a higher status for women in social reality because Buddhism disempowers actual women while empowering imaginary women. In effect, female imagery is used to conquer a fear of female powers.[77]

In my earlier study of Buddhist dreams I argued that male Buddhists both co-opt women's subjectivity for themselves and deny the subjectivity of real women. I have been influenced in my thinking on this point by Luce Irigaray, one of the most elegant articulators of the male co-optations of women's speech and subjectivity.[78] In a broad Buddhist context, this point is made repeatedly by Wilson and Campbell.[79] In the present context of the Land of *Ḍākinīs*, Campbell makes the point that men as well as women can enter this supposed women-only realm through dreams, meditation, or as a future destination upon dying. This is completely "unlike the strictures of exclusivity which seem to surround issues regarding the male gender."[80] She makes an additional important point that "the male body resists encroachment by that of the female, [and] further strengthens its own subjectivity by depriving the female body of hers."[81] She elaborates on this point:

> Given that there are no mirror-like comparisons between the male and female domains, the symbolic female, whilst carefully not resting in the control of women, is incorporated completely into the patriarchal system. This enables the men of the lineage to speak not only for themselves, the symbolic male buddha, and his descendents in the lineage, but also on behalf of the divine female, in a way which is quite plainly denied to women. The implications of this gender bias are not just that, at a simplistic level, male power is equated with dominance, but that the complex philosophy which appears to offer models of symbolisms to both men and women actually fails to achieved egalitarianism at the everyday level. This failure is encoded again and again in the commentaries concerning the dakini, whose symbolic presence is interpreted from a point of view which consistently defers to the position of the guru *as male* and the female as *complementary*.[82]

Several points can be made about the gender ideology portrayed in these various spiritual and legendary lands. To begin with, as on earth, men can freely enter women's spaces, sacred or secular—they can even enter women's hells—because unlike women, men are not thought of as polluting. Connected with this is the curious fact that men do not seem to be polluted nor to fear pollution or punishment when they enter female spaces. The complete opposite is the case for women: they pollute any restricted male enclave they enter: restricted areas of monasteries and pilgrimage sites, and even heavens. And women will be prevented and/or punished if they try to do so. Underneath this inconsistent rhetoric of pollution lies the male perspective that what women do is not important—women can be interrupted, they are there to assist and serve men, and finally, it is a good idea to keep an eye on what they are doing because left to their own devices, unsupervised by men, women are sure to be doing the wrong thing. The logical outcome is that male-only Pure Lands proliferate, there are some mixed-sex Pure Lands, but there absolutely are not any women-only Pure Lands.

NOTES

1. See, e.g., R. F. Gombrich, "Ancient Indian Cosmology," in *Ancient Cosmologies*, ed. Carmen Blacker and Michael Loewe (London: George Allen and Unwin, 1975), 110–42. See also Akira Hirakawa's succinct discussion of these three realms, A *History of Indian Buddhism: From Śakyamuni to Early Mahāyāna*, trans. and ed. Paul Groner (1990. New Delhi: Motilal Banarsidass, 1993), 170–74, to which Groner has appended a short bibliographic essay, 335–36. Overall, see La Vallée Poussin, "Cosmogony and Cosmology (Buddhist)," vol. 4, 129–38. Steven Collins has a short discussion of these realms in relation to human consciousness, *Selfless Persons: Imagery and Thought in Theravāda Buddhism* (Cambridge: Cambridge University Press, 1982, 1992), 213–18. W. Randolph Kloetzli discusses mahayanic views based on Vasubandhu's *Abhidharmakośa*, "Cosmology: Buddhist Cosmology," in *EOR*, vol. 4, 113–19. Buddhism affirms the existence of all these realms and the various beings in them while stressing that they too are all impermanent.
2. For instance, see Lamotte, *History of Indian Buddhism*, 77, who discusses them as either five or six in number according to the sects of early Buddhism, 629–30. See also Schlingloff, *Studies in Ajanta Paintings*, 167–74. For additional early sources on the five destinies and the asuras see Rhys Davids and Stede, *Pali-English Dictionary*, under definition four of *gati*, 242, col. b. See also Nebesky-Wojkowitz, *Oracles and Demons of Tibet*, 3–5 and passim for the two types of Tibetan deities, those whose karma has enabled them to go beyond the six realms and those who are still within the six realms.
3. For examples from other cultures see Liz Wilson, "Lands, Mythic," in *EOW*, vol. 2, 569–71; and Ei'ichiro Ishida, "Mother-Son Deities," *History of Religions* 4.1 (Summer 1964): 41–43. See also Christine de Pizan's (c. 1365–1430) delightful use of this idea in *The Book of the City of Ladies*, trans. Earl Jeffrey Richards (New York: Persea Books, 1982).
4. Discussed by Doniger, *Splitting the Difference*, 266–73.
5. White, *The Alchemical Body*, 235–40.
6. Ann Grodzins Gold, "Gender and Illusion in a Rajasthani Yogic Tradition," in Arjun Appadurai, et al., *Gender, Genre, and Power in South Asian Expressive Traditions* (Philadelphia, PA: University of Pennsylvania Press, 1991), 102–35.
7. Stein, *Tibetan Civilization*, 29–35. Gyatso briefly discusses some of these stories; "Down with the Demoness;" 34–35.
8. Several scholars have explored the possibility of such a country. W. W. Rockhill quotes what the Tang annals say about them, *The Land of the Lamas: Notes of a Journey Through China, Mongolia and Tibet* (New York: The Century Co.,

1891), 339–41, and writing in 1890 cited the fact that a queen still ruled in this area, 213. F. W. Thomas uncovered a small text attributed to a woman from the land of Eastern Women that had been recorded and hidden with other documents near Dunhuang early in the eleventh century, *Ancient Folk-Literature from North-Eastern Tibet* (Berlin: Akademie-Verlag, 1957), 103–12. In his *Tibetan Literary Texts* he has a work by a queen of the Western Women entitled *The Prophecy of Vimalaprabhā*, vol. I, 139 ff, which is discussed by Giuseppe Tucci, *Preliminary Report on Two Scientific Expeditions in Nepal* (Roma: Instituto Italiano per il Medio ed Estremo Oriente, 1956), 92–105, along with a discussion of the existence of such a country.

9. Danielou, *Kama Sutra*, 155, 383.
10. Since ancient times South Asia has operated as the Other for westerners who brought home fantastic tales, such as Megasthenes, or the writers Polyaenus and Solinus who reported that Herakles had fathered a daughter in India, named Pandia, who he left behind as its ruler, R. C. Majumdar, *The Classical Accounts of India* (Calcutta: Firma KLM Private Limited, 1981), 455–58. Even Marco Polo describes a Female Island in the Arabian Sea, *The Travels of Marco Polo*, trans. Ronald Latham (London: Penguin Books, 1958), 295, which may be the same as one described by the seventh-century Chinese pilgrim-monk, Hiuen Tsiang, *Buddhist Records*, trans. Beal, Part II, 240, 279. The first example is a clear conflation with the *Mahāvaṃsa* story of King Vijaya emigrating to Sri Lanka and being separated from the women in his party who landed at a different island called the Island of Women (Mahilādīpaka, VI.46).
11. See Liz Wilson on this point, "Lands, Mythic," in *EOR*, vol. I, 569–71.
12. For instance, the story was depicted at Nak Pan to the east of Angkor and at Borobudor, Holt, *Buddha in the Crown*. See also, Siegfried Leinhard, "A Nepalese Painted Scroll Illustrating the *Siṃhalāvadāna*," in *Nepalica*, ed. Bernhard Kolver and S. Lienhard (Sankt Augustin: VGH Wissenschaftsverlage, 1987). It is also depicted on the wall of the Dukhang at Alchi Monastery in Ladakh and in elaborate detail in Cave 17 at Ajanta.
13. The story is also told in the in the *Divyāvadāna*, Cowell and Neil, 120 sq.
14. In the Indian imagination Sri Lanka was famously a land of demons, e.g., the *Rāmāyaṇa*, as well as for Sri Lankans themselves, *Mahāvaṃsa* I.20 and VII. This text also refers to the island of women (vI.46).
15. No. 196, *The Jātakas*, vol. 2, 89–90. Liz Wilson has a thoughtful discussion of various versions of this story, *Charming Cadavers*, 71–76.
16. Holt, *Buddha in the Crown*, 49–50. The seventh-century Chinese pilgrim-monk Hieun Tsiang also tells this story, conflating it with the founding of kingship in Sri Lanka, *Buddhist Records*, trans. Beal, part II, 240–46. Padmasambhava seemingly takes on aspects of this story, see Douglas and Bays, *Life*, canto 107, 783–739.
17. The *Guṇakārandavyūha Sūtra*, an earlier version of which was translated into Tibetan and preserved in the *Kanjur*. It is quite similar to the version of this *jātaka* preserved in the *MV*, to be discussed shortly. Lewis briefly discusses other texts that contain this story as well as its iconography in "Newar-Tibetan Trade," 137, nn. 5, 6 & 7.
18. Ibid., 152 and a photo of such a ferry appears on 153. Additionally, there was a *stūpa* in Lhasa named after the hero (*Siṃhala*), who in this version was the Buddha in a past life. In Kathamandu there is a temple named after him, while another temple contained his large image, and there is a yearly festival including a procession around the city. Curiously, the chief *yakṣī/rākṣasī* (called Ajimā) was propitiated in the Jokhang temple at Lhasa and at several

temples and *stūpas* in Kathmandu, ibid., 152, fn. 60, though in the *MV* version she is one of Māra's daughters. The wife is depicted as a child-eater, similar to Hāritī before her conversion.

19. Allione, *Women of Wisdom*, 105.
20. The *Dharmalabdha Jātaka* in *Mahāvastu Avadāna*, ed. Radhagovinda Basak (Calcutta: Sanskrit College, 1968), III.367–86, trans. by *Jones, MV*, III. 274–87.
21. Cole, *Mothers and Sons*, 163.
22. Momoko Takemi, " 'Menstruation Sutra' Belief in Japan," *Japanese Journal of Religious Studies* 10.2–3 (June–September 1983): 229.
23. Cole, *Mothers and Sons*, 80. See also his subtle and detailed analysis of this *sūtra* and related practices in China, ibid., respectively, 197–214 and 80–102. I briefly discuss this hell in chapters 2 and 11 herein.
24. See, e.g., Cole, *Mothers and Sons*, 178.
25. Takemi, " 'Menstruation Sutra,' " 231–32. She also presents a history of this text in Japan.
26. Takemi is ambivalent on this point, but I think it is a matter of translation problems rather than believing women are born there with women's bodies. See the discussion of Pure Lands, below.
27. Takemi discusses various ceremonies involving the text, such as throwing it into a river and in specially constructed Blood Ponds, as amulets, and its continuing use in Zen sects where it is given to women during their initiations mainly as an amulet to purify their worship while menstruating, " 'Menstruation Belief,' " 240–45.
28. Vivian-Lee Nyitray, "Auspcious and Inauspicious," in *EOW*, vol. I, 73–75. Cole briefly discusses some modern practices in Taiwan and Hong Kong, *Mothers and Sons*, 198–99.
29. Takemi, " 'Menstruation Belief,' " 240–45.
30. Stephen F. Teiser gives the conservative estimate for this story being in circulation by the fifth century C.E. in "The Ritual Behind the Opera: A Fragmentary Ethnography of the Ghost Festival A.D. 400–1900," in Johnson, *Ritual Opera, Operatic Ritual*, 19 and 198. An earlier scholar dates one version of the story, the *Avalambana Sūtra*, to before the third century C.E. Waddell quotes this *sūtra*, *Buddhism of Tibet*, 98–99.

    In addition to his other supernatural powers, in the *Suttavibhaṅga* of the *Vinaya* Maudgalyāyana is able to see the suffering of the dead and to understand its cause, thus he is a good choice for this role. Horner, *Book of the Discipline*, vol. I 181–88.
31. Teiser, " The Ritual Behind the Opera," 192.
32. See Teiser's discussion of this festival, *The Ghost Festival in Medieval China*, passim.
33. Johnson, Preface, to *Ritual Opera, Operatic Ritual*, vii.
34. Gary Seaman, "The Sexual Politics of Karmic Retribution," in *The Anthropology of Taiwanese Society*, ed. Emily Martin Ahern and Hill Gates (Stanford, CA: Stanford University Press, 1981), 388.
35. Cole, *Mothers and Sons*, 168.
36. Interestingly enough, there is a female version of Mu-lien's story. It is the story of princess Miao-shan, an incarnation of Kuan Yin, who descends to the Hell of the Bloody Pond to free women. Reed, "The Gender Symbolism of Kuan-yin Bodhisattva," 161, 166. This must be connected to the gender switch of male Avalokiteśvara into female Kuan Yin, because Avalokiteśvara, out of his great compassion, was known to visit hell beings in order to save them, e.g., Holt, *Buddha in the Crown*, 47. See the discussion of this gender switch in chapter 12.

37. Seaman, "Sexual Politics," 389.
38. Cole, *Mothers and Sons*, 85–86.
39. Cole makes a similar point, ibid., 86.
40. Ibid., 203.
41. The parallels to Bennett's study of differences in goddess worship among Nepalese women and men are quite informative. *Dangerous Wives*, chapter 7, 261–308.
42. See Cole on these points, *Mothers and Sons*, especially 227–28.
43. Cole discusses women's responses to these texts and rituals, ibid., 231–34.
44. Ibid., 208–10.
45. Chapters 2 to 5 of the *LV* take place in Tuṣita Heaven, which is described in terms quite similar to Indra's heaven, discussed below, including the presence of *apśaras*, *LV*, II.22, III.11, and IV.22.
46. Fujita Kōtatsu, "Pure and Impure Lands," in *EOR*, vol. 12, 90–91. See also Paul Williams's thoroughgoing discussion of various Pure Lands and their buddhas, *Mahāyāna Buddhism: The Doctrinal Foundations* (London and New York: Routledge: 1989), 215–76.
47. See, for example, the Chinese caves of Dazu, which also depict Buddhist hells, Bai Ziran, *Dazu Grottoes*, no page numbers. There are more than two hundred and fifty paintings of Amitābha's paradise at Dunhuang as well, An-yi Pan, "Paradise with Strings Attached: Pure Land Death Ritual and Matrons' Predestined Male Birth," *Oriental Art* xlvii.4 (2001): 32–37.
48. The *Sukhāvatīvyūha Sūtras* exist in two versions, the smaller and the larger, and differ from each other on the major point of how to achieve rebirth in this heaven. The smaller stresses just having faith in and reciting the name of Amitāba, while the larger requires good works along with faith and recitation. See Cowell, *Buddhist Mahāyāna Texts*, Part II, viii–ix.

    Some Tibetans believed they could be born there through the practice of transference of consciousness (*'pho wa*), Tucci, *TPS*, 350 and 365.
49. See, for example, Daniel B. Stevenson, "Pure Land Buddhist Worship and Meditation in China," in Lopez, *Buddhism in Practice*, 359–79, and Erik Zürcher, "Amitābha," in *EOR*, vol. 1., 235–37.
50. Cowell, *Buddhist Mahāyāna Texts*, Part II, 62.
51. Paul makes a similar point, but in relation to the Oedipus complex, *Tibetan Symbolic World*, 96.
52. For example, Cowell, *Buddhist Mahāyāna Texts*, Part II, 19.
53. Discussed in chapter 2.
54. Waddell, *Lamaism*, 85–89.
55. Kern, *Saddharma-Puṇḍarīka*, XXII, 389, and XXIV.31.
56. Ziran, *Dazu Grottoes*, no page numbers. See also, Tucci, *TPS*, pl. 49, which shows five adoring goddesses beside Amitābha while he resides in this paradise.
57. Alex and Hideko Wayman, *The Lion's Roar of Queen Śrīmālā* (New York: Columbia University Press, 1974), 1–2.
58. Paul, *Women in Buddhism*, 294–95; and Wayman, *Lion's Roar*, 63.
59. Paul, *Women in Buddhism*, 286–87.
60. Williams, *Mahayana Buddhism*, 243–47.
61. Paul, *Women in Buddhism*, 207, 209.
62. Barnes finds the language ambiguous as to whether there will be no women or no ideas of gender differences, "Changing the Female Body," 62, n. 29. See the discussion in chapter 12 herein.
63. Ibid., 178–80.

64. Paul, *Women in Buddhism*, 22–23.
65. Actual guides (*lam yig*) to Shambhala have been written. See Edwin Marshall Bernbaum, *The Way to Shambhala: A Search for the Mythical Kingdom beyond the Himalayas* (Garden City, NY: Anchor Books, 1980); and John Newman, "Itineraries to Sambhala," in Cabezón and Jackson, *Tibetan Literature*, 485–99.
66. The Buddha is said to have preached this at Amarāvatī in South India one year after his enlightenment, *Kālacakra Tantra: Rite of Initiation for the Stage of Generation*, ed. and trans. Jeffrey Hopkins (London: Wisdom, 1985), 58.
67. It is of interest to note that the present Dalai Lama has begun initiating large groups of people into the *Kālacakra Tantra,* thereby putting them on the path to reincarnate in Shambhala. Given the loss of Tibetan independence in the 1950s to the People's Republic of China and the unlikelihood that Tibetan independence will ever be regained, it would seem that the Dalai Lama, a widely respected religious leader and a recipient of the Nobel Peace Prize, is preparing for a future, final confrontation between the forces of good and evil while offering despairing Tibetans the promise of rebirth in a mystical Tibet. See Donald Lopez for more on these points, *Prisoners of Shangri-La: Tibetan Buddhism and the West* (Chicago, IL: The University of Chicago Press, 1998), 181–207.
68. In some ways Padmsambhava's departure to this land is reminiscent of the *Valāhassa Jātaka,* for he too leaves Tibet on a winged horse; Douglas and Bays, *Life*, 738.
69. Ibid., 739.
70. Rhie and Thurman, *Wisdom & Compassion*, 181, 363, and 476–77, plates 50, 149, 232. Tucci, *TPS*, 617, n. 295.
71. Liz Wilson, "Lands, Mythic," 570.
72. *Life of Milarepa*, 9–10.
73. Dowman, *Sky Dancer*, 65–66; Stag-Śam, *Life of Lady Ye-Śes*, f. 116, l.3-f.117, l.2.
74. Dowman, *Sky Dancer*, 66; Stag-Śam, *Life of Lady Ye-Śes*, f.117.
75. Campbell makes this point very well, *Traveller in Space*, 130. But see Diemberger, "Lhakama," on an all-female lineage that appropriates the term *ḍākinī* for themselves, 143.
76. I have argued these points at greater length in *Dreaming in the Lotus*, 147–62. For a brief discussion of some further examples, see "Wisdom as Feminine" in Young, *An Anthology of Sacred Texts*, xxi–xxii, and various entries in the index under "Feminine." Nathan Katz, "Anima and mKha'-'gro-ma: A Critical Comparative Study of Jung and Tibetan Buddhism," *Tibet Journal* 2.3 (1977): 113–43, is an interesting discussion of *ḍākinīs* as guides.
77. Bennett, *Dangerous Wives*, makes this point in relation to male worship and propitiation of fierce female deities in Nepal, 261–308.
78. See, for example, "The Three Genres," in *The Irigaray Reader*, ed. Margaret Whitford (Oxford: Blackwell, 1991), 140–53, and Irigaray, *Sexes and Genealogies*.
79. Wilson, *Charming Cadavers*, 12–13, 154–57, 181–84; and Campbell, *Traveller in Space*, especially 130–31 and 189–91.
80. Campbell, *Traveller in Space*, 130.
81. Ibid., 130.
82. Ibid., 131.

CONCLUSION

Beginning with the biographies of the Buddha, this study has examined Buddhist practices and beliefs about gender, sexuality, and family life primarily as they are revealed in biographical texts, iconography, and rituals. Sexuality was examined both from within family life among wives and husbands and outside of it among courtesans and tantric practitioners. Attitudes toward procreation and the parent/child relationship were also explored in terms of medical theory, rituals, and the ideology of karma. This exploration of what it meant and continues to mean to be Buddhist, gendered, and sexual has revealed anxieties about the stability of masculinity and argued that the symbolic inclusion of femaleness was accompanied by the actual exclusion of real women.

My focus has been on women, but this inevitably led to men, revealing male fears of female sexuality and pollution, and anxieties about the loss of masculinity. We have seen the early celebration of women's auspicious powers of procreation in the iconography of the Buddha's mother, Queen Māyā, its later elaboration in narratives about courtesans and female tantric consorts, and its apotheosis in *ḍākinīs*, goddesses and female celestial bodhisattvas. In tandem with these articulations about women and the feminine we have seen ambivalent expressions of male reproductive power in ideas about fatherhood beginning with the Buddha's father, King Śuddhodana, the Buddha himself as father, and its apotheosis in the notion of the spiritual father, the guru.

Additional gendered themes surfaced in the abundant literature on sex change, lands without men, and heavens without women. These presented negative images of womanhood, and fractured images of masculinity that revealed its fragility. By relegating self-definition to an opposing other, in this case to not being female, monks and laymen made themselves vulnerable to the very women they endowed with unrealistic powers. The restrictions they placed on women only served to increase male anxiety about female sexuality and pollution.

Some of the biographies and certain texts about sex change were shown to be important indications that such views did not go unquestioned, yet these negative ideas about women were the basis for beliefs and practices in the past and continue to be so in the present.

Buddhism was assimilated by astonishingly diverse populations and belief systems. It adjusted to these new cultural environments by accepting local practices and by promulgating its own beliefs and practices. It exerted a cultural influence by directing indigenous beliefs toward Buddhist ends, such as accepting local deities as part of the Buddhist pantheon, and being tolerant of social attitudes. In terms of gender and sexuality, Buddhist monks, who for the most part were the primary shapers of Buddhist ideology, accepted the gender distinctions around them in ways that not only left them intact, but actually served both to maintain them and to blame women for their existence. This can be seen even in the spread of Buddhism to the West. When a western woman converts to Buddhism and wears the *Blood Bowl Sūtra* as an amulet we see how unthinkingly these notions enter practice. It was the same in the past, as was shown by prominent women who were exceptions to the rule, such as great saints and incarnations, but who were not necessarily freed from negative Buddhist views about women. But the West has also influenced Buddhism, as is shown by the fact that some western women have successfully taken on leadership roles in Buddhist centers. Additionally, due to western colonialism and affluence, and now jet-age travel, westerners have influenced Buddhism in Asia, most notably in the discussion of female ordination.

The wisest teachings of Buddhism say that one must move beyond gender, beyond all dualities, but its rhetoric in texts, iconography, and ritual demonstrates an urge to co-opt and control creative female powers that ends up diminishing women and exalting men. It is my hope that this book has pinpointed some of Buddhism's cultural baggage in relation to gender. History has shown us that Buddhism has continually adjusted its ideas about gender and it can adjust again. Changes need to be made that acknowledge past excesses and that create a future in which both women and men can pursue enlightenment free from false views about what it means to be gendered.

BIBLIOGRAPHY

Texts and Translations

Abhayadatta. *Buddha's Lions: The Lives of the Eighty-Four Siddhas,* with the Tibetan text, *Grub thob brgyad cu rtsa bzhi'i lo rgyus.* Trans. James B. Robinson. Berkeley, CA: Dharma Publishing, 1979.

The *Abhiniṣkramaṇasūtra.* Trans. Samuel Beal from the Chinese edition as *The Romantic Legend of Śākya Buddha.* 1875. Delhi: Motilal Banarsidass, 1985.

Adigal, Prince Ilango, *Shilappadikaram (The Ankle Bracelet).* Trans. Alain Daniélou. New York: A New Directions Book, 1965.

Allione, Tsultrim. *Women of Wisdom.* London: Routledge & Kegan Paul, 1984.

Āryaśūra. *The Jātakamālā.* Trans. J. S. Speyer. 1895. Delhi: Motilal Banarsidass, 1971, 1982.

Aśvaghoṣa. *Buddhacarita.* Ed. and trans. E. H. Johnston. Delhi: Motilal Banarsidass, 1984.

———. *Saundarananda Mahākāvya of Ācārya Aśvaghoṣa with Tibetan and Hindi Translations.* Trans. Ācārya Shri L. Jamspal. Sarnath: Central Institute of Higher Tibetan Studies: 1999. Translated by E. H. Johnston as *The Saundarananda or Nanda the Fair.* Oxford: Oxford University Press, 1932.

Avadānaçataka: A Century of Edifying Tales Belonging to the Hīnayāna. Vol. 2 Ed. J. S. Speyer. Delhi: Motilal Banarsidas Publishers, 1906–1909.

Burlingame, Eugene Watson, trans. *Buddhist Legends.* 1921. New Delhi: Munshiram Manoharlal, 1999.

Caraka Saṁhitā. Ed. and trans. Kaviraj Kunjalal Bhishagratna. Varanasi: Chowkhamba Sanskrit Series Office, 1977.

Chonam, Lama, and Khandro, Sangye, trans. *The Lives and Liberation of Princess Mandarava.* Boston: Wisdom Publications, 1998.

Chöpel, Gedün. *Tibetan Arts of Love.* Trans. Jeffrey Hopkins. Ithaca, NY: Snow Lion Publications, 1992.

Chophel, Norbu. *Folk Culture of Tibet.* Dharamsala: Library of Tibetan Works and Archives 1983.

Cleary, Thomas. *The Flower Ornament Scripture: A Translation of the Avatamsaka Sutra.* Boston & London: Shambhala, 1993.

Cowell, E. B., ed. *Buddhist Mahāyāna Texts.* Oxford: Clarendon Press, 1894.

Dge 'dun rgya mtsho, Dalai Lama II. *Selected Works of the Dalai Lama II.* Glenn H. Mullin. Ithaca, NY: Snow Lion, 1985.

The *Dharmalabdha Jātaka* in *Mahāvastu Avadāna*. Ed. Radhagovinda Basak. Calcutta: Sanskrit College, 1968.

Ten Suttas from Dīgha Nikāya. Sarnath: Central Institute of Higher Tibetan Studies: 1987.

Dīpavaṃsa. Trans. Hermann Oldenberg. 1879. New Delhi: Asian Educational Services, 1992.

Divyāvadāna. Ed. E. B. Cowell and R. A. Neil. Cambridge: Cambridge University Press, 1886.

Dowman, Keith. *Masters of Mahāmudrā*. State University of New York Press, 1985.

Duncan, Marion H. *Harvest Festival Dramas of Tibet*. Hong Kong: Orient Publishing Company, 1955.

———. *More Harvest Festival Dramas of Tibet*. London: The Mitre Press, 1967.

Evans-Wentz, W. Y., ed. *The Tibetan Book of the Dead*. London & New York: Oxford University Press, 1927.

———. *Tibetan Yoga and Secret Doctrines*. London & New York: Oxford University Press, 1935, 1967.

Fahien. *A Record of Buddhistic Kingdoms: Being an account by the Chinese Monk Fa-Hien of his travels in India and Ceylon. (A.D. 399–414) in search of the Buddhist Books of Discipline*. Trans. James Legge. 1886. New York: Paragon Book Reprint Corp., 1965.

Gampopa. *The Jewel Ornament of Liberation*. Trans. Herbert V. Guenther. Boston, MA: Shambhala, 1986.

The Superhuman Life of Gesar of Ling. Trans. Alexandra David-Neel and Lama Yongden. Boston, MA: Shambhala, 1987.

The Gilgit Manuscript of the Saṅghabhedavastu, Being the 17th and Last Section of the Vinaya of the Mūlasarvāstivādin. Ed. Raniero Gnoli. Rome: Istituto Italiano per il Medio ed Estremo Oriente, 1977.

'Gos Lo tsa ba Gźon nu dpal, *The Blue Annals*. Trans. George N. Roerich. 1949. Delhi: Motilal Banarsidass, 1976.

Gtsaṅ smyon He ru ka, compiler. *The Hundred Thousand Songs of Milarepa*. Trans. Garma C. C. Chang. Boulder, CO: Shambhala, 1977.

———. *Mi la ras pa'i rnam thar*. Ed. J. W. de Jong. 's-Gravenhage: Mouton, 1959. Translated by Lobsang P. Lhalungpa as *The Life of Milarepa*. Boulder, CO: Shambhala, 1984.

Guenther, Herbert V., trans. *The Life and Teaching of Nāropa*. Oxford: Oxford University Press, 1963.

Gyasa Belsa: Tibetan Folk Opera Story. Trans. Cynthia Josayma. Dharamsala: Library of Tibetan Works and Archives: 1991.

rGyud bZhi, A Reproduction of a set of prints from the 18th century Zuṅ-cu ze Blocks from the Collections of Prof. Raghu Vira, by O-rgyan Namgyal. Leh: S. W. Tashigangpa, 1975.

The Hevajra Tantra. Ed. and trans. D. L. Snellgrove. London: Oxford University Press, 1952.

Hiuen Tsiang. *Si-Yu-Ki: Buddhist Records of the Western World*. Trans. Samuel Beal. Reprint. New York, NY: Paragon Book Reprint Corp., 1968.

I-Tsing. *A Record of the Buddhist Religion as Practised in India and the Malay Archipelago: AD 671–695*. Trans. J. Takakusu. 1896. Delhi: Munshiram Manoharlal Publishers Pvt. Ltd., 1998.

The Jātaka Together with Its Commentary. Ed. V. Fausbøll. London: Trübner, 1887. Translated as *The Jātaka*. Ed. E. B. Cowell. 1895. London: Pali Text Society, 1973.

Kālacakra Tantra: Rite of Initiation for the Stage of Generation. Ed. and trans. Jeffrey Hopkins. London: Wisdom, 1985.

The Complete Kāma Sūtra. Alain Daniélou. Rochester, VT: Inner Traditions India Home Office: 1994.

mKhas grub rje, *Introduction to the Buddhist Tantric Systems*. Trans. F. D. Lessing and A. Wayman. 1968. New York, NY: Samuel Weiser, Inc., 1980.

Lalitavistara. Ed. P.L. Vaidya. Darbhanga: Mithila Institute, 1958. Translated by Bays, Gwendolyn as *The Voice of the Buddha: The Beauty of Compassion*. Oakland, CA: Dharma Press, 1983.

The Laws of Manu. Trans. Wendy Doniger and Brian K. Smith. London: Penguin Books, 1991.

The Life of the Mahasiddha Tilopa. Trans. Fabrizio Torricelli and Sangye T. Naga. Dharamsala: Library of Tibetan Works and Archives, 1995.

The Life of Marpa. Trans. Nālandā Translation Committee. Boston & London: Shambhala, 1995.

The Life Story of Drowa Sangmo. Trans. Cynthia Bridgman Josayma with Losang Norbu Tsonawa. Dharmasala: Library of Tibetan Works and Archives, 1983.

Mahāparinirvāṇa Sūtra, in *Buddhist Suttas*. Trans. T. W. Rhys Davids. Sacred Books of the East Series, vol. 11. 1881. Delhi: Motilal Banarsidass, 1965.

The Mahāvaṃsa or the Great Chronicle of Ceylon. Trans. Wilhelm Geiger. 1912. London: The Pali Text Society, 1964.

Le Mahāvastu. Ed. É. Senart. 3 vols. Paris: À L'imprimerie Nationale, 1890. English translation, J. J. Jones. *Mahāvastu*. 3 vols. London: Pali Text Society, 1949–56.

Mahendravarma I, King. *Bhagavadajjuka Prahasanam*. Ed. and trans. by Michael Lockwood and A. Vishnu Bhat. Madras: Diocesan Press, 1991.

Milindapañha. Ed. V. Trenckner. London: Williams and Norgate, 1880. Translated by T. W. Rhys Davids as *The Questions of King Milinda*. 1894. Delhi: Motilal Banarsidass, 1965.

Nāgārjuna, *Dharmasaṁgrahaḥ. Excellent Collection of Doctrine of Ācārya Nāgārjuna*. Trans. Tashi Zangmo and Dechen Chime. Sarnath, Varanasi: Central Institute of Higher Tibetan Studies: 1993.

Nidānakathā. In *The Jātaka Together with Its Commentary*. Ed. V. Fausboll. London: Trübner, 1877. Translated by T. W. Rhys Davids as *Buddhist Birth Stories*. 1880. New Delhi: Asian Educational Services, 1999.

Padma bka' thang shel brag ma. Leh, India, 1968. Translated by Kenneth Douglas and Gwendolyn Bays as *The Life and Liberation of Padmasambhava*. Berkeley, CA: Dharma Publishing, 1978.

Phung po gzan skyur gyi rnam bsad. In *Gcod kyi chos skor*. New Delhi: Tibet House, 1974.

Ralston, W. R. S. *Tibetan Tales: Derived from Indian Sources*. 1882. 2d ed., Delhi: Sri Satguru Publications, 1988.

Rhys Davids, T. W., and Rhys Davids, C. A. F. *Dialogues of the Buddha*. Sacred Books of the Buddhists Series, Part 3. London: Oxford University Press, 1921.

Rigs bzang gi mkha' 'gro ma snang sa 'od 'bum gyi rnam thar. From the collection of the American Museum of Natural History, No. 70.2/2502.

Saddharma-puṇḍarīka or the Lotus of the True Law. Trans. H. Kern. 1884. New York: Dover Publications, Inc.: 1963.

Sangs rgyas rgya mtsho, *Vaiḍūrya snon po*. Ed. T. Y. Tashiganpa. Leh: 1973.

Shattan, Merchant-Prince, *Manimekhalaï. The Dancer with The Magic Bowl*. Trans. Alain Daniélou. New York: New Directions Books, 1989.

Simhāsana Dvātriṃśikā: Thirty-Two Tales of the Throne of Vikramaditya. Trans. A. N. D. Haksar. New Delhi: Penquin Books India, 1998.

Śrudraka. *The Padmaprābhṛtakam*. Ed. Johannes R. A. Loman. Amsterdam: Uitgeverij de Driehoek, 1956.

———. *The Toy Cart*. In *Great Sanskrit Plays*. Trans. P. Lal. New York: New Directions Books, 1957, 1964.

Stag-śam Nus-ldan-rdo-rje. *The Life of Lady Ye-Śes-mtsho-rgyal Rediscovered by Stag-śam Nus-ldan-rdo-rje with two hagiographies of Padmasambhava from the terma finds and visions of Ñan-ral Ñi-ma-'od-ze and A-'dzom 'Brug-pa Gro-'dul-dpa'-bo-rdo-rje*. Tashijong: The Sungrab Nyamso Gyunphel Parkhang, 1972. Translated by Keith Dowman as *Sky Dancer: The Secret Life and Songs of the Lady Yeshe Tsogyel*. London: Routledge & Kegan Paul, 1984.

Strong, John. *The Legend of King Aśoka*. Princeton, NJ: Princeton University Press, 1983, 1989.

Suśruta Saṁhitā. Ed. and trans. Ram Karan Sharma and Viadya Bhagwan Dash. Varanasi: Chowkhamba Sanskrit Series Office, 1998.

Swearer, Donald K., and Prenchit, Sommai, *The Legend of Queen Cāma: Bodhiraṃsi's Cāmadevīvaṃsa, A Translation and Commentary* (Albany, NY: State University of New York Press, 1988).

Tāranātha, Jo Nang. *The Origin of the Tārā Tantra*. Trans. and ed. David Templeman. Dharamsala: Library of Tibetan Works and Archives, 1983.

———. *The Seven Instruction Lineages*. Trans. David Templeman. Dharamsala: Library of Tibetan Works and Archives, 1983.

Therīgathā and *Theragāthā*. Trans. by Mrs. Rhys Davids as *Psalms of the Early Buddhists*. London: Pali Text Society, 1909, 1980.

Therīgāthā, The Elders' Verses. Vol. 2. Trans. K. R. Norman. London: Pali Text Society, 1971.

Thurman, Robert A. F., trans. *The Holy Teaching of Vimalakīrti: A Mahāyāna Scripture*. University Park, PA: The Pennsylvania State University Press, 1976.

van Buitenen, J. A. B., trans. and ed. *Tales of Ancient India*. Chicago: The University of Chicago Press, 1959.

Vinaya Piṭaka. Ed. Hermann Oldenberg. 1879. London: Pali Text Society, 1969. Translated by I. B. Horner as *The Book of the Discipline*. 6 vols. London: Pali Text Society, 1951, 1982.

Warren, Henry Clarke. *Buddhism in Translation*. 1896. New York: Atheneum, 1974.

Willis, Janice D. *Enlightened Beings: Life Stories from the Ganden Oral Tradition*. Boston, MA: Wisdom Publications, 1995.

Secondary Sources

Amore, Roy C., and Shinn, Larry D. *Lustful Maidens and Ascetic Kings: Buddhists and Hindu Stories of Life*. New York: Oxford University Press, 1981.

Anderson, Carol S. "Purity and Pollution." In *EOW*, vol. 2.819–821.

Aris, Michael. *Hidden Treasures and Secret Lives: A Study of Pemalingpa (1450–1521) and the Sixth Dalai Lama (1683–1706)*. Shimla: Indian Institute of Advanced Study, 1988.

Aris, Anthony, ed. *Tibetan Medical Paintings*. 2 vols. New York: Harry N. Abrams, 1992.

Atkinson, Clarissa W. " 'Your Servant, My Mother': The Figure of Saint Monica in the Ideology of Christian Motherhood." In *Immaculate and Powerful: The Female in Sacred Image and Social Reality*, ed. Clarisssa W. Atkinson, Constance H. Buchanan, and Margaret R. Miles. Boston, MA: Beacon Press, 1985, 139–172.

Aziz, Barbara. "Moving Toward a Sociology of Tibet." In Willis, *Feminine Ground*, pp. 76–95.

———. "Reincarnation Reconsidered: Or the Reincarnate Lama as Shaman." In *Spirit Possession in the Nepal Himalayas*, ed. John T. Hitchcock and Rex L. Jones. 1976. New Delhi: Vikas Publishing House Pvt Ltd, 1996, 343–60.

———. *Tibetan Frontier Families: Reflections of Three Generations from D'ing-ri.* New Delhi: Vikas Publishing House Pvt. Ltd., 1978.

———. "Women in Tibetan Society and Tibetology." In *Tibetan Studies: Proceedings of the 4th seminar of the International Association for Tibetan Studies*, ed. Helga Uebach and Jampa L. Panglung. Munchen: Kommission für Zentralasiatische Studien, 1988.

Aziz, Barbara, and Matthew Kapstein, eds. *Soundings in Tibetan Civilization.* New Delhi: Manohar, 1985.

Babu, D. Sridhara. "Reflections on Andra Buddhist Sculptures and Buddha Biography." In *Buddhist Iconography.* Delhi: Tibet House, 1989, 97–101.

Bai Ziran, ed. *Dazu Grottoes.* Beijing Foreign Languages Press, 1984.

Bal, Mieke, "The Rape of Narrative and the Narrative of Rape." In Scarry, *Literature and the Body*, 1–32.

Banerjea, Jitendra Nath. *The Development of Hindu Iconography.* 4th ed. Delhi: Munshiram Manoharlal Publishers Pvt. Ltd., 1985.

Bareau, André. "Un personnage bien mysterieux: l'épouse du Buddha." In *Indological and Buddhist Studies, Volume in Honour of Professor J. W. de Jong on His Sixtieth Birthday*, ed. L. A. Hercus et al. Canberra: Australian National University, 1982, 31–59.

Bartholomeusz, Tessa. *Women Under the Bo Tree.* New York: Cambridge University Press, 1994.

Basham, A. L. *The Wonder That Was India: A Survey of the Culture of the Indian Subcontinent Before the Coming of the Muslims.* New York: Grove, 1959.

Bennett, Lynn. *Dangerous Wives and Sacred Sisters: Social and Symbolic Roles of High-Caste Women in Nepal.* Columbia University Press, 1983.

Bernbaum, Edwin Marshall. *The Way to Shambhala: A Search for the Mythical Kingdom beyond the Himalayas.* Garden City, NY: Anchor Books, 1980.

Bertsch, Wolfgang. *A Study of Tibetan Paper Money.* Dharamsala: Library of Tibetan Works and Archives, 1997.

Beyer, Stephan. *The Buddhist Experience: Sources and Interpretations.* Belmont, CA: Wadsworth Publishing Company, 1974.

Bhattacharya, Benoytosh. *The Indian Buddhist Iconography.* Calcutta: Firma K. L. Mukhopadhyay, 1958.

Birnbaum, Raoul. *The Healing Buddha.* Boulder, CO: Shambhala, 1979.

Bivar, A. D. H. "Hāritī and the Chronology of the Kuṣāṇas." *Bulletin of the School of Oriental and African Studies* 33 (1970): 10–21.

Blondeau, A. M. "Analysis of the Biographies of Padmasambhava." In *Tibetan Studies in Honour of Hugh Richardson*, ed. Michael Aris and Aung San Suu Kyi. Warminister, UK: Aris and Phillips, 1979, 45–52.

Bloss, Lowell W. "The Buddha and the Nāga." *History of Religions* 13.1 (August 1973).

Boddy, Janice. *Wombs and Alien Spirits: Women, Men and the Zār Cult in Northern Sudan.* Madison, WI: University of Wisconsin Press, 1989.

Bode, Mable. "Women Leaders of the Buddhist Reformation." *The Journal of the Royal Asiatic Society of Great Britain and Ireland.* (1893): 517–66, 763–98.

Bynum, Caroline Walker. *Fragmentation and Redemption: Essays on Gender and the Human Body in Medieval Religion.* New York: Zone Books, 1992.

———. Introduction to *Gender and Religion: On the Complexity of Symbols.* Ed. Caroline Walker Bynum, et al. Boston, MA: Beacon Press, 1986.

Cabezón, José Ignacio. "Mother Wisdom, Father Love: Gender-based Imagery in Mahŷāna Buddhist Thought." In *Buddhism, Sexuality, and Gender*, ed. Cabezón. Albany, NY: State University Press of New York, 1992, 181–99.

Cadden, Joan. *Meanings of Sex Difference in the Middle Ages: Medicine, science and culture.* Cambridge: Cambridge University Press, 1993.

Campbell, Joseph. *The Hero With a Thousand Faces*. 1949. Cleveland and New York: The World Publishing Company, 1956, 1968.

Campbell, June. *Traveller in Space: In Search of Female Identity in Tibetan Buddhism*. New York: George Braziller, 1996.

Carman, John B., and Frédérique Apffel Marglin, ed. *Purity and Auspiciousness in Indian Society*. Leiden: E. J. Brill, 1985.

Chandra, Lokesh. *Buddhist Iconography: Compact Edition*. New Delhi: International Academy of Indian Culture & Aditya Prakashan, 1991, 1999.

Chandra, Moti. *The World of Courtesans*. Delhi: Vikas, 1973.

Chodorow, Nancy. *The Reproduction of Mothering: Psychoanalysis and the Sociology of Gender*. Berkeley, CA: University of California Press, 1978.

Chow, Rey. "Male Narcissism and National Culture: Subjectivity in Chen Kaige's *King of the Children*." In *Male Trouble*, eds. Penley and Willis, 87–118.

Christ, Carol. "Why Women Need the Goddess." In *Womanspirit Rising: A Feminist Reader in Religion*, ed. Carol P. Christ and Judith Plaskow. San Francisco: Harper and Row, Publishers, 1979.

Clark, Barry, trans. *The Quintessence Tantras of Tibetan Medicine*. Ithaca, NY: Snow Lion, 1995.

Clark, Tom. *The Great Naropa Poetry Wars*. Santa Barbara, CA: Cadmus Editions, 1980.

Cohen, Richard S. "Kinsmen of the Son: Śākyabhikṣus and the Institutionalization of the Bodhisattva Ideal." *History of Religions* 40.1 (August 2000): 1–31.

Cole, Alan. *Mothers and Sons in Chinese Buddhism*. Stanford, CA: Stanford University Press, 1998.

Collins, Steven. *Selfless Persons: Imagery and Thought in Theravāda Buddhism*. Cambridge: Cambridge University Press, 1982, 1992.

Coomaraswamy, Ananda K. *Yakṣas: Essays in the Water Cosmology*. Delhi: Munshiram Manoharlal Publishers, Ltd., 2001, 1993.

Cone, Margaret, and Richard Gombrich. *The Perfect Generosity of Prince Vessantara: A Buddhist Epic*. Oxford: Oxford University Press, 1977.

Corwell, Andrea, and Nancy Lindisfarne. *Dislocating Masculinity: Comparative Ethnographies*. London and New York: Routledge, 1994.

Cozort, Daniel. *Highest Yoga Tantra*. Ithaca, NY: Snow Lion Publications, 1986.

Crooke, William. *The Popular Religion and Folklore of Northern India*. 2 vols. 1896. Delhi: Munshiram Manoharlal, 1968.

Da Cunha, J. Gerson. *Memoir on the History of the Tooth-Relic of Ceylon*. 1875. New Delhi: Asian Educational Services, 2001.

Dallapiccola, Anna Libera, et al., ed. *The Stūpa: Its Religious Historical and Architectural Significance*. Wiesbaden: Franz Steiner Verlag, 1980.

Dargyay, Eva M. *The Rise of Esoteric Buddhism in Tibet*. Delhi: Motilal Banarsidass, 1977.

Dasgupta, Shashibhushan. *Obscure Religious Cults*. 2d ed. 1946. Calcutta: Firma K. L. Mukhopadhyay, 1962.

Davidson, James. *Courtesans and Fishcakes: The Consuming Passions of Classical Athens*. 1997. New York: HarperCollins, 1999.

Davidson, Ronald M. "Political Metaphors in Indian Esoteric Buddhism." Lecture given at the Columbia University Seminar on Buddhist Studies, New York, February 12, 2002.

Dayal, Har. *The Bodhisattva Doctrine in Buddhist Sanskrit Literature*. 1932. Delhi: Motilal Banarsidass, 1970, 1975.

Dehejia, Vidya. "The Collective and Popular Basis of Early Buddhist Patronage: Sacred Monuments, 100 BC–AD 250." In *The Powers of Art Patronage in Indian Culture*, ed. Barbara Stoler Miller. Delhi: Oxford University Press, 1992, 35–45.

———, ed. *Devi: The Great Goddess*. Washington, D. C.: Arthur M. Sackler Gallery, 1999.

———. *Discourse in Early Buddhist Art: Visual Narratives of India*. New Delhi: Munshiram Manoharlal Publishers Pvt. Ltd., 1997.

———, ed. *Representing the Body: Gender Issues in Indian Art*. New Delhi: Kali for Women, 1997.

———. *Yoginī Cult and Temples: A Tantric Tradition*. New Delhi: National Museum, 1986.

de Pizan, Christine. *The Book of the City of Ladies*. Trans. Earl Jeffrey Richards. New York: Persea Books, 1982.

Desai, Vishakha N. "Reflections on the History and Historiography of Male Sexuality in Early Indian Art." In Dehejia, *Representing the Body*, 42–55.

Diemberger, Hildegard. "Lhakama [*lha-bka'-ma*] and Khandroma [*mkha'-'gro-ma*]: The Sacred Ladies of Beyul Khenbalung [*sbas-yul mKhan-pa-lung*]." In *Tibetan History and Language: Studies Dedicated to Uray Gézas on his Seventieth Birthday*, ed. Ernst Steinkellner. Wien: Arbeitskreis für Tibetische und Buddhistische Studien Universistät Wien, 1991, 137–53.

Dimmitt, Cornelia, and J. A. B. van Buitenen. *Classical Hindu Mythology: A Reader in the Sanskrit Purāṇas*. Philadlephia, PA: Temple University Press, 1978.

Doniger, Wendy. *The Bedtrick: Tales of Sex and Masquerade*. Chicago, IL: The University of Chicago Press, 2000.

———. *Splitting the Difference: Gender and Myth in Ancient Greece and India*. Chicago, IL: The University of Chicago Press, 1999.

Douglas, Mary. *Purity and Danger: An analysis of the concepts of pollution and taboo*. London: Routledge and Kegan Paul, 1966.

Douglas, Nik, and Meryl White. *Karmapa: The Black Hat Lama of Tibet*. London: Luzac & Company, 1976.

Edou, Jérôme. *Machig Labdrön and the Foundations of Chöd*. Ithaca, NY: Snow Lion Publications: 1996.

Eichenbaum, Patricia D. *The Development of a Narrative Cycle Based on the Life of the Buddha in India, Central Asia, and the Far East: Literary and Pictorial Evidence*. Ann Arbor, MI: University Microfilm International, 1980.

Eilberg-Schwartz, Howard, and Wendy Doniger, eds. *Off With Her Head! The Denial of Women's Identity in Myth, Religion, and Culture*. Berkeley, CA: University of California: 1995.

Eliade, Mircea. *The Encyclopedia of Religion*. 16 vols. New York: Macmillan, 1987.

Ellwin, Verrier. *Myths of Middle India*. 1949. Delhi: Oxford University Press, 1991.

Falk, Nancy Auer. "The Case of the Vanishing Nuns: The Fruits of Ambivalence in Ancient Indian Buddhism." In *Unspoken Worlds: Women's Religious Lives*, ed. Nancy Auer Falk and Rita M. Gross. San Francisco, CA: Harper & Row, Publishers, 1980, 207–24.

———. "Karma." In *EOW*, vol. I, 560–61.

Falk, Nancy E. "An Image of Woman in Old Buddhist Literature: The Daughters of Māra." In *Women and Religion*, ed. Judith Plaskow Goldenberg. Missoula, MT: American Academy of Religion, 1973.

Faure, Bernard. *The Red Thread: Buddhist Approaches to Sexuality*. Princeton, NJ: Princeton University Press, 1998.

Fenner, Todd. "The Origin of the *rGyud bzhi*: A Tibetan Medical Tantra." In *Tibetan Literature: Studies in Genre*, José Ignacio Cabezón and Roger R. Jackson, eds. Ithaca, NY: Snow Lion, 1996, 458–69.

Fields, Rick. *How the Swans Came to the Lake: A Narrative History of Buddhism in America*. 3rd ed. Boston & London: Shambhala, 1981, 1992.

Fisher, Robert E. *Art of Tibet*. New York: Thames & Hudson: 1997.

Foucault, Michel. *The Birth of the Clinic: An Archaeology of Medical Perception*. Trans. A. M. Sheridan. 1973. New York: Random House, 1973, 1994, 271–91.

Foucher, A. "The Buddhist Madonna." In A. Foucher, *The Beginnings of Buddhist Art*. Trans. L. A. Thomas and F. W. Thomas. 1917. New Delhi: Asian Educational Services, 1994.

———. *On the Iconography of the Buddha's Nativity, Memoirs of the Archaeological Survey of India*. No. 46. Trans. H. Hargreaves. 1934. New Delhi: Archaeological Survey of India, 1999.

———. "The Tutelary Pair in Gaul and India." In A. Foucher, *The Beginnings of Buddhist Art*, 139–46.

Frauwallner, E. *The Earliest Vinaya and the Beginnings of Buddhist Literature*. Roma: Is. M.E. O., 1956.

Freed, Ruth S., and Freed, Stanley A. *Rites of Passage in Shanti Nagar, Anthropological Papers of the American Museum of Natural History*, New York, 1980, vol. 56, Part 3.

Fruzzetti, Lina M. *The Gift of a Virgin: Women, Marriage, and Ritual in a Bengali Society*. 1982. Delhi: Oxford University Press, 1990.

Fujita, Kōtatsu. "Pure and Impure Lands." In *EOR*, vol. 12, 90–91.

Furth, Charlotte. *A Flourishing Yin: Gender in China's Medical History, 960–1665*. Berkeley, CA: University of California Press, 1999.

Garimella, Annapurna. "Apsaras." In *EOW*, vol. I, 48–50.

Geertz, Clifford. "Religion as a Cultural System." *The Interpretation of Cultures*. New York: Basic Books, 1973.

Gellner, David N. *Monk, Householder and Tantric Priest: Newar Buddhism and Its Hierarchy of Ritual*. Cambridge: Cambridge University Press, 1992, 1993.

Germano, David. "Re-membering the Dismembered Body of Tibet: Contemporary Tibetan Visionary Movements in the People's s Republic of China." In *Buddhism in Contemporary Tibet: Religious Revival and Cultural Identity*, ed. Melvyn C. Goldstein and Matthew T. Kapstein. Berkeley, CA: University of California Press, 1998, 53–94.

Getty, Alice. *Gods of Northern Buddhism*. Oxford: Clarendon Press, 1914.

Gohkale, Balkrishna Govind. *Buddhism in Maharashtra: A History*. Bombay: Popular Prakashan: 1976.

Gold, Ann Grodzins. "Gender and Illusion in a Rajasthani Yogic Tradition." In Arjun Appadurai, et al., *Gender, Genre, and Power in South Asian Expressive Traditions*. Philadelphia, PA: University of Pennsylvania Press, 1991, 102–35.

Gombrich, R. F. "Ancient Indian Cosmology." In *Ancient Cosmologies*, ed. Carmen Blacker and Michael Loewe. London: George Allen and Unwin, 1975.

Gombrich, Richard, and Gananath Obeyesekere. *Buddhism Transformed: Religious Change in Sri Lanka*. Princeton, NJ: Princeton University Press, 1988.

Gonda, J. "Ascetics and Courtesans." In J. Gonda, *Selected Studies*. Vol. iv, *History of Ancient Indian Religion*. Leiden: E. J. Brill, 1975.

———. "Karman and Retributive Justice in Ancient Java." In J. Gonda, *Selected Studies*. Vol. iv, 223–47.

Gordon, Antoinette. *The Iconography of Tibetan Lamaism*. 2d rev. ed. Rutland, VT: Charles E. Tuttle, 1959.

Grant, Beata. "The Spiritual Saga of Woman Huang: From Pollution to Purification." In Johnson, *Ritual Opera*.

Grey, Leslie. *A Concordance of Buddhist Birth Stories*. Oxford: The Pali Text Society, 1994.

Gross, Rita M. *Buddhism after Patriarchy: A Feminist History, Analysis, and Reconstruction of Buddhism*. Albany, NY; State University of New York Press, 1993.

Gutschow, Kim. "The Women Who Refuse to Be Exchanged: Nuns in Zangskar, Northwest India." In *Celibacy, Culture, and Society: The Anthropology of Sexual Abstinence*, ed. Elisa Sobo and Sandra Bell. Madison, WI: University of Wisconsin Press: 2001, 47–64. Online at http://www.gadenrelief.org/chu-celibacy.html

Gyatso, Janet. *Apparitions of the Self: The Secret Autobiographies of a Tibetan Visionary*. Princeton, NJ: Princeton University Press, 1998.

———. "The Development of the Gcod Tradition." In Aziz and Kapstein, *Soundings in Tibetan Civilization*, 320–41.

———. "Down with the Demoness." In Willis, *Feminine Ground*, 33–51.

———. "Machig Labdron." In *EOW*, vol. II.

Gyatso, Kelsang. *Guide to Dakini Land*. London: Tharpa, 1992.

Hardy, R. Spence. *A Manual of Buddhism in its modern development*. London: Williams & Norgate, 1960.

Herdt, Gilbert, ed. *Third Sex, Third Gender: Beyond Sexual Dimorphism in Culture and History*. New York: Zone Books, 1994.

Herrmann-Pfandt, Adelheid. *Ḍākiṇīs: Zur Stellung und Symbolik des Weiblichen im Tantrischen Buddhismus*. Bonn, Indicaa et Tibetica Verlag, 1992.

———. "Yab Yum Iconography and the Role of Women in Tibetan Tantric Buddhism." *Tibet Journal* xxii.1 (spring 1997): 12–34.

Hiltebeitel, Alf. "Śiva, the Goddess, and the Disguises of the Pāṇḍavas and Draupadī," *History of Religions* 20.1–2 (August and November 1980): 147–74.

Hirakawa, Akira. *A History of Indian Buddhism: From Śakyamuni to Early Mahāyāna*. Trans. and ed. Paul Groner. 1990. New Delhi: Motilal Banarsidass, 1993.

Hodgson, Marshall G. S. *The Venture of Islam: Conscience and History in a World Civilization*. Vol. II. Chicago, IL: The University of Chicago Press, 1974.

Holt, John Clifford. *Buddha in the Crown: Avalokiteśvara in the Buddhist Traditions of Sri Lanka*. New York: Oxford University Press, 1991.

Horner, I. B. *Women Under Primitive Buddhism*. 1930. Delhi: Motilal Banarsidass, 1975.

Huber, Toni. *The Cult of Pure Crystal Mountain: Popular Pilgrimage and Visionary Landscape in Southeast Tibet*. New York: Oxford University Press, 1999.

Huntington, John C. "The Origin of the Buddha's Image, Early Image Traditions and the Concept of Buddhadarsanapunya." In A. K. Narain, *Studies in Buddhist Art of South Asia*. New Delhi: Kanak Publications, 1985, 23–58.

———. "Pilgrimage as Image: The Cult of the Aṣṭamahāprātihārya." Part I. *Orientations* 18.4 (April 1987): 55–63; Part II. 18.8 (August 1987): 56–68.

———. "Sowing the Seeds of the Lotus: A Journey to the Great Pilgrimage Sites of Buddhism." Part I. *Orientations* 16.11 (November 1985): 46–61; Part II. 17.2 (February 1986): 28–43; Part III. 17.3 (March 1986): 32–46; Part IV. 17.7 (July 1986): 28–40; and Part V. 17.9 (September 1986): 46–58.

Huntington, Susan. *The Art of Ancient India*. New York: Weatherhill, 1985.

Irigaray, Luce. *Sexes and Genealogies*. New York: Columbia University Press, 1993.

Ishida, Ei'ichiro. "Mother-Son Deities." *History of Religions* 4.1 (summer 1964): 30–52.

Jaini, Padmanabh S. *Gender and Salvation: Jaina Debates on the Spiritual Liberation of Women*. Berkeley, CA: University of California Press, 1991.

Jaynes, Gregory. "A Spiritual Leader's Farewell." *Time*, June 22, 1987. Available online at http://www.ramsjb.com/talamasca/avatar/trungpa.html

Jenish, D'Arcy. "A Troubled Church: A Buddhist group recovers from controversy." *Maclean's*, October 29, 1990. Online at http://www.ramsjb.com/talamasca/avatar/vajradhatu.html

Johnson, David, ed. Preface to *Ritual Opera, Operatic Ritual: "Mu-lien Rescues his Mother" in Chinese Popular Culture*. Berkeley, CA: Publications of the Chinese Popular Culture Project, 1989.

Johnson, Elizabeth A. *She Who Is: The Mystery of God in Feminist Theological Discourse.* New York, Crossroad, 1992.
Jones, Ernest. *On the Nightmare.* New York: Liveright, 1951.
Joshi, Lal Mani. "The Monastic Contribution to Buddhist Art and Architecture." In *The World of Buddhism,* ed. Heinz Bechert and Richard Gombrich. 1984. New York: Thames and Hudson Inc., 1991, 1995, 94–98.
Kakar, Sudhir. *Intimate Relations: Exploring Indian Sexuality.* New Delhi: Penguin Books, 1989.
Kandaswamy, S. N. *Buddhism as Expounded in Manimeklalai.* Tamil Nadu: Annamalai University, 1978.
Kapstein, Matthew. "The Illusion of Spiritual Progress: Remarks on Indo-Tibetan Buddhist Soteriology." In *Paths to Liberation: The Mārga and Its Transformation in Buddhist Thought,* ed. Robert E. Buswell, Jr., and Robert M. Gimello. Honolulu, HI: University of Hawai'i Press, 1992, 193–224.
Karetzky, Patricia Eichenbaum. *The Life of the Buddha: Ancient Scriptural and Pictorial Traditions.* Lanham, MD: University Press of America, 1992.
Katz, Nathan. "Anima and mKha'-'gro-ma: A Critical Comparative Study of Jung and Tibetan Buddhism." *Tibet Journal* 2.3 (1977): 113–43.
———. *Buddhist Images of Human Perfection.* Delhi: Motilal Banarsidass, 1982.
Kendall, Laurel. *Shamans, Housewives, and Other Restless Spirits: Women in Korean Ritual Life.* Honolulu, HI: University of Hawai'i Press, 1985.
Kersenboom, Saskia C. "The Traditional Repertoire of the Tiruttaṅi Temple Dancers." In Leslie, *Roles and Rituals,* 131–47.
Khandalavala, Karl. "Heralds in Stone: Early Buddhist Iconography in the Aśokan Pillars and Related Problems." In *Buddhist Iconography.* Delhi: Tibet House, 1989, 19–41.
King, Helen. *Hippocrates' Woman: Reading the Female Body in Ancient Greece.* Routledge: London and New York, 1998.
Kinnard, Jacob N. *Imaging Wisdom: Seeing and Knowing in the Art of Indian Buddhism.* 1999. Delhi: Motilal Banarsidass: 2001.
———. "The Polyvalent *Pādas* of Viṣṇu and the Buddha." *History of Religions* 40.1 (August 2000): 32–57.
Klein, Anne Carolyn. *Meeting the Great Bliss Queen: Buddhists, Feminists and the Art of the Self.* Boston, MA, Beacon Press, 1995.
———. "Primordial Purity and Everyday Life: Exalted Female Symbols and the Women of Tibet." In *Immaculate & Powerful: The Female in Sacred Image and Social Reality,* ed. Clarissa W. Atkinson, et al. Boston, MA: Beacon Press, 1985, 111–38.
Kloetzli, W. Randolph. "Cosmology: Buddhist Cosmology." In *EOR,* vol. 4, 113–19.
Kōgen, Mizuno. "Karman: Buddhist Concepts." In *EOR,* vol. 8, 226–68.
Kōtatsu, Fujita. "Pure and Impure Lands." In *EOR,* vol. 12, 90–91.
Kraemer, Ross S., ed. *Maenads, Martyrs, Matrons, Monastics: A Sourcebook on Women's Religions in the Greco-Roman World.* Philadelphia: Fortress Press, 1988.
Kvaerne, Per. *An Anthology of Buddhist Tantric Songs.* Bangkok: White Orchid Press, 1977, 1986.
Lamotte, Étienne. *History of Indian Buddhism: From the Origins to the Śaka Era.* Trans. Sara Webb-Boin. Louvain-La-Neuve, Institute Orientaliste, 1988.
Laquer, Thomas. *Making Sex: Body and Gender from the Greeks to Freud.* Cambridge, MA: Harvard University Press, 1990.
La Vallée Poussin, L. de. "Cosmogony and Cosmology Buddhist." In vol. 4 of *Encyclopaedia of Religion and Ethics,* ed. James Hastings. New York: Charles Scribner's Sons, 1914, 129–38.

Law, B. C. *The Buddhist Conception of Spirits*. 1923. 2d ed. 1936. Delhi: Pilgrims Book Pvt. Ltd: 1997.

Leinhard, Siegfried. "A Nepalese Painted Scroll Illustrating the *Siṃhalāvadāna*." In *Nepalica*, ed. Bernhard Kolver and S. Lienhard. Sankt Augustin: VGH Wissenschaftsverlage, 1987.

Leslie, Julia, ed. *Roles and Rituals for Hindu Women*. Delhi: Motilal Banarsidass Publishers Pvt. Ltd., 1992.

Levering, Miriam. "Lin-chi. Rinzai Ch'an and Gender: The Rhetoric of Equality and the Rhetoric of Heroism." In Cabezón, *Buddhism, Sexuality, and Gender*, 137–56.

Levine, Nancy E. *The Dynamics of Polyandry: Kinship, Domesticity, and Population on the Tibetan Border*. Chicago, IL: University of Chicago Press, 1988.

Lévi-Strauss, Claude. *The Elementary Structures of Kinship*. Boston, MA: Beacon Press, 1969.

Lewis, I. M. *Ecstatic Religion: An Anthropological Study of Spirit Possession and Shamanism*. Middlesex, U.K.: Penguin, 1971.

Lewis, Todd T. "Newar-Tibetan Trade and the Domestication of *Siṃhalasārthabāhu Avadāna*." *History of Religions* 33.21, (November 1993): 135–60.

Lha-mo, Rin-chen. *We Tibetans*. London: Seeley Service & Co., 1926.

Lincoln, Bruce. *Authority: Construction and Corrosion*. Chicago: University of Chicago Press, 1994.

———. *Death, War, and Sacrifice: Studies in Ideology and Practice*. Chicago, IL: The University of Chicago Press, 1991.

———. "Myths and Symbolism." In *EOR*, vol. 6, 499–505.

Linn, Priscilla Rachun. "Gender Roles." In *EOR*, vol. 5, 495–502.

Lipsey, Roger. "The Human Figure as a Religious Sign." In *EOR*, vol. 6, 505–11.

Lopez, Jr., Donald S., ed. *Buddhism in Practice*. Princeton, NJ: Princeton University Press, 1995.

———. *Prisoners of Shangri-La: Tibetan Buddhism and the West*. Chicago, IL: The University of Chicago Press, 1998.

———, ed. *Religions of Tibet in Practice*. Princeton, NJ: Princeton University Press, 1977.

Lorenzen, David N. *The Kāpālikas and Kālāmukhas: Two Lost Saivite Sects*. 2d ed. Delhi: Motilal Banarsidass, 1991.

Majumdar, R. C. *The Classical Accounts of India*. Calcutta: Firma KLM Private Limited 1981.

Makley, Charlene E. "Gendered Practices and the Inner Sanctum: The Reconstruction of Tibetan Sacred Space in 'China's Tibet'." *The Tibet Journal* xix.2 (summer 1994): 61–94.

Marglin, Frédérique Apffel. "Types of Sexual Union and their Implicit Meanings." In John Stratton Hawley and Donna Marie Wulff, eds., *The Divine Consort: Rādhaā and the Goddesses of India*. 1982. Boston, MA: Beacon Press, 1986, 298–315.

———. *Wives of the God-King*. Delhi: Oxford University Press, 1985.

McDermott, Rachel Fell. "Goddesses and Healing." Lecture, Columbia University, May 1, 1996.

Michael, Franz. *Rule by Incarnation: Tibetan Buddhism and Its Role in Society and State*. Boulder, CO: Westview Press, 1982.

Miller, Allan L. "Spiritual Accomplishment by Misdirection: Some *Upāya* Folktales from East Asia." *History of Religions* 40.1 (August 2000): 82–108.

Mills, Margaret. "Sex Role Reversals, Sex Changes, and Transvestite Disguise in the Oral Tradition of a Conservative Muslim Community in Afghanistan."

In *Women's Folklore, Women's Culture,* ed. Rosan A. Jordan and Susan J. Kalčik. Philadelphia, PA: University of Pennsylvania Press, 1985, 187–213.

Misra, Ram Nath. *Yaksha Cult and Iconography*. Delhi: Munshiram Manoharlal Publishers Pvt. Ltd, 1981.

Monier-Williams, Monier, *A Sanskrit-English Dictionary.* Oxford: The Clarendon Press, 1899, 1976.

Nanda, Serena. *Neither Man nor Woman: The Hijras of India.* Belmont, CA: Wadsworth Publishing Company, 1990.

Nebesky-Wojkowitz, René de. *Oracles and Demons of Tibet: The Cult and Iconography of the Tibetan Protective Deities.* 1956. Graz: Akademische Druck-u. Verlagsanstalt, 1975.

Newman, John. "Itineraries to Sambhala." In José Ignacio Cabezón and Roger R. Jackson, eds. *Tibetan Literature: Studies in Genre.* Ithaca, NY: Snow Lion, 1996, 485–99.

Nyitray, Vivian-Lee. "Auspicious and Inauspicious." In *EOW*, vol. 1, 73–75.

O'Flaherty, Wendy Doniger. *Asceticism and Eroticism in the Mythology of Śiva*. 1973. Delhi: Oxford University Press, 1975.

———. *The Origins of Evil in Hindu Mythology*. Berkeley, CA: University of California Press, 1976.

———. *Women, Androgynes, and Other Mythical Beasts*. Chicago, IL: The University of Chicago Press, 1980.

Ortner, Sherry B. *Making Gender: The Politics and Erotics of Culture*. Boston, MA: Beacon Press, 1996.

———. "Sherpa Purity." *Journal of the American Anthropological Association* 75.1 (February 1973): 49–63.

———. *Sherpas Through Their Rituals*. Cambridge: Cambridge University Press, 1978.

———, and Whitehead, Harriet, eds. Introduction to *Sexual Meanings: The Cultural Construction of Gender and Sexuality*. Cambridge: Cambridge University Press, 1981.

Overmyer, Daniel. L. "Values in Chinese Sectarian Literature: Ming and Ch'ing *Pao-chüan*." In *Popular Culture in Late Imperial China*, ed. David Johnson, et al. Berkeley, CA: University of California Press, 1985, 219–54.

Pan, An-yi. "Paradise with Strings Attached: Pure Land Death Ritual and Matrons' Predestined Male Birth." *Oriental Art* xlvii.4, (2001): 32–37.

Paul, Diana. *Women and Buddhism: Images of the Feminine in the Mahāyāna Tradition*. 2d. ed. Berkeley, CA: University of California Press, 1985.

Paul, Robert A. *The Tibetan Symbolic World: Psychoanalytic Explorations*. Chicago, IL: University of Chicago Press, 1982.

Penley, Constance & Willis, Sharon, eds. *Male Trouble.* Minneapolis: University of Minnesota Press, 1993.

Penrose, Walter. "Hidden in History: Female Homoeroticism and Women of a 'Third Nature' in the South Asian Past." *Journal of the History of Sexuality* 10.1 (2001): 3–39.

Polo, Marco. *The Travels of Marco Polo*. Trans. Ronald Latham. London: Penguin Books, 1958.

Pommaret, Françoise. "Returning from Hell." In Donald S. Lopez, ed. *Religions of Tibet in Practice.* Princeton, NJ: University Press, 1997, 499–510.

Raglan, Lord. *The Hero: A Study in Tradition, Myth, and Drama, Part II.* Reprinted *In Quest of the Hero,* ed. Robert A. Segal. Princeton, NJ: Princeton University Press, 1990.

Ramanujan, A. K. "On Women Saints." In *The Divine Consort: Rādhā and the Goddesses of India,* ed. John Stratton Hawley and Donna Marie Wulff. Boston, MA: Beacon Press, 1982, 316–24.

Rani, Mrs. Sharada, ed. *Buddhist Tales of Kashmir in Tibetan Woodcuts*. Narthang series of Ksemenda's *Avadāna-kalpalata*, in Śata-Pitaka Series, vol. 232. New Delhi: Mrs. Sharada Rani, 1977.

Ray, Reginald. "Mahāsiddhas." In *EOR*, vol. 9, 122–26.

Rechung Rinpoche. *Tibetan Medicine*. 1973. Berkeley: University of California Press, 1976.

Reed, Barbara E. "The Gender Symbolism of Kuan-yin Bodhisattva." In Cabezón, *Buddhism, Sexuality, and Gender*, 159–80.

Reynolds, Frank. "The Many Lives of Buddha: A Study of Sacred Biography and Theravāda Buddhology." In *The Biographical Process: Studies in the History and Psychology of Religion*, ed. Frank Reynolds and Donald Capps, The Hague: Mouton, 1976, 37–61.

Rhie, Marylin M., and Robert A. F. Thurman. *Wisdom and Compassion: The Sacred Art of Tibet*. Expanded ed. New York, NY: Harry N. Abrams, Inc., 2000.

Ricca, Franco, and Erberto Lo Bue. *The Great Stupa of Gyantse: A Complete Tibetan Pantheon of the Fifteenth Century*. London: Serindia, 1993.

Rich, Adrienne. "Compulsory Heterosexuality and Lesbian Existence." *Signs* 5 (1980): 631–60.

Richman, Paula. "The Portrayal of a Female Renouncer in a Tamil Buddhist Text." In *Gender and Religion: On the Complexity of Symbols*, ed. Caroline Walker Bynum, Stevan Harrell, and Paula Richman. Boston: Beacon Press, 1986.

Robinson, Richard H., and Johnson, Williard L. *The Buddhist Religion: A Historical Introduction*. 4th ed. Belmont, CA: Wadsworth Publishing Company, 1997.

Rockhill, W. W. *The Land of the Lamas: Notes of a Journey Through China, Mongolia and Tibet*. New York: The Century Co., 1891.

Roscoe, Will. "Priests of the Goddess: Gender Transgression in Ancient Religion." *History of Religions* 35.3 (February 1996): 195–230.

Rosenfield, John M. *The Dynastic Arts of the Kushans*. 1967. New Delhi: Munshiram Manoharlal Publishers, 1993.

Rubin, Gayle. "The Traffic in Women: Notes on the 'Political Economy' of Sex." In *Toward an Anthropology of Women*, ed. Rayna R. Reiter. New York: Monthly Review Press, 1975, 157–210.

Ruswa, Mirza Mohammad. *The Courtesan of Lucknow*. Trans. Khushwant Singh and M. A. Husaini. 1961. Islamabad: Alhamra Publishing, 2000.

Samuel, Geoffrey. *Civilized Shamans: Buddhism in Tibetan Societies*. Washington, D.C.: Smithsonian Institution Press, 1993.

Sax, William. *Mountain Goddess: Gender and Politics in a Himalayan Pilgrimage*. New York: Oxford University Press, 1991.

Scarry, Elaine, ed. *Literature and the Body: Essays on Populations and Persons*. Baltimore and London: The Johns Hopkins University Press, 1988.

Schimmel, Annemarie. "Numbers: An Overview." In *EOR*, vol. 11. 13–19.

Schlingloff, Dieter. *Studies in Ajanta Paintings: Identifications and Interpretations*. Delhi: Ajanta Publications [India], 1987.

Schober, Juliane, ed. *Sacred Biography in the Buddhist Traditions of South and Southeast Asia*. Honolulu: University of Hawai'i Press, 1997.

Schopen, Gregory. "Burial *Ad Sanctos* and the Physical Presence of the Buddha in Early Indian Buddhism: A Study in the Archaeology of Religions." In Schopen, *Bones, Stones, and Buddhist Monks: Collected Papers on the Archaeology, Epigraphy, and Texts of Monastic Buddhism in India*. Honolulu, HI: University of Hawai'i Press, 1997, 114–47.

———. "Filial Piety and the Monk in the Practice of Indian Buddhism: A Question of 'Sinicization' Viewed from the Other Side." In Schopen, *Bones, Stones*. 56–71.

———. "Monks and the Relic Cult in the *Mahāparinibbāna-sutta*: An Old Misunderstanding in Regard to Monastic Buddhism." In Schopen, *Bones, Stones,* 99–113.
———. "On Monks, Nuns, and 'Vulgar' Practices: The Introduction of the Image Cult into Indian Buddhism." In Schopen, *Bones, Stones,* 238–57.
———. "Two Problems in the History of Indian Buddhism: The Layman/Monk Distinction and the Doctrines of the Transference of Merit." In Schopen, *Bones, Stones,* 23–55.
Schuster, Nancy. "Changing the Female Body: Wise Women and the Bodhisattva Career in Some *Mahāratnakūṭasūtras,*" *JIABS* 4.1 (1981): 24–69.
Seaman, Gary. "The Sexual Politics of Karmic Retribution." In *The Anthropology of Taiwanese Society,* ed. Emily Martin Ahern and Hill Gates. Stanford, CA: Stanford University Press, 1981.
Seth, Vikram. *A Suitable Boy*. 1993. New York; HarperCollins, 1994.
Shastri, Biswanarayan. "The Philosophical Concepts and the Buddhist Pantheon." In *Buddhist Iconography*. Delhi: Tibet House, 1989.
Shaw, Miranda. *Passionate Enlightenment: Women in Tantric Buddhism*. Princeton, NJ: Princeton University Press, 1994.
Sivaramamurti, C. *Amaravati Sculptures in the Chennai Government Museum, Bulletin of the Chennai Government Museum*. 1942. Chennai: 1998.
Smith, Frederick M. "Indra's Curse, Varuṇa's Noose, and the Suppression of the Woman in the Vedic *Śrauta* Ritual." In Leslie, *Roles and Rituals for Hindu Women*.
Snellgrove, D. L. *Buddhist Himalaya: Travels and Studies in quest of the origins and nature of Tibetan Religion*. New York: Philosophical Library, 1957.
———. *Indo-Tibetan Buddhism: Indian Buddhists and Their Tibetan Successors*. London: Serinida, 1987.
Snellgrove, D. L., and Hugh E. Richardson. *A Cultural History of Tibet*. Boston, MA: Shambhala, 1986.
Snodgrass, Adrian. *The Symbolism of the Stupa*. 1985. Delhi, Motilal Banarsidass Publishers, 1992.
Stablein, William. "Medical Soteriology of Karma in the Buddhist Tantric Traditions." In *Karma and Rebirth in Classical Indian Traditions,* ed. Wendy Doniger O'Flaherty. Berkeley, CA: University of California Press, 1980.
Stein, R. A. *Tibetan Civilization*. Trans. J. E. Stapleton Driver. Stanford, CA: Stanford University Press, 1972.
Stevenson, Daniel B. "Pure Land Buddhist Worship and Meditation in China." In Lopez, *Buddhism in Practice*.
Stoddard, Heather. Lecture, Tibet House, New York City, April 2, 2001.
Storm, Mary. "Death," In *EOW*, vol. 1, 243–45.
———. "Hāritī." In *EOW*, vol. 1, 391–92.
Strenski, Ivan. "On Generalized Exchange and the Domestication of the Sangha." *Man* 18.3 (September 1983): 463–77.
Strong, John. *The Experience of Buddhism: Sources and Interpretations*. Belmont, CA: Wadsworth Publishing Company, 1994.
———. *The Legend and Cult of Upagupta*. 1992. Delhi: Motilal Banarsidass Publishers, 1994.
Sutherland, Gail Hinich. *Yakṣa in Hinduism and Buddhism*. 1991. New Delhi: Manohar, 1992.
Takemi, Momoko. " 'Menstruation Sutra' Belief in Japan." *Japanese Journal of Religious Studies* 10.2–3 (June–September 1983): 229–46.
Tarthang Tulku. *Ancient Tibet*. Berkeley, CA: Dharma Publishing, 1986.
Tatelman, Joel. *The Glorious Deeds of Pūrṇa: A Translation and Study of the Pūrṇāvadāna*. 2000. New Delhi: Motilal Banarsidass, 2001.

Teiser, Stephen F. *The Ghost Festival in Medieval China*. Princeton, NJ: Princeton University Press, 1988.

———. "The Ritual Behind the Opera: A Fragmentary Ethnography of the Ghost Festival A.D. 400–1900." In Johnson, ed., *Ritual Opera*.

Tharu, Susie, and K. Lalita. *Women Writing in India: 600 B.C. to the Present*. 1991. Delhi: Oxford University Press, 1995.

Thinley, Karma. *The History of the Sixteen Karmapas of Tibet*. Boulder, CO: Prajñā, 1980.

Thomas, F. W. *Ancient Folk-Literature from North-Eastern Tibet*. Berlin: Akademie-Verlag, 1957.

Tsomo, Karma Lekshe, ed. *Sakyadhītā: Daughters of the Buddha*. Ithaca, NY: Snow Lion Publications, 1988.

———. "Tibetan Nuns and Nunneries." In Willis, *Feminine Ground*, 118–34.

Tucci, Giuseppe. *Preliminary Report on Two Scientific Expeditions in Nepal*. Roma: Instituto Italiano per il Medio ed Estremo Oriente, 1956.

———. *Tibetan Pained Scrolls*. Roma: Liberia dello Stato, 1949.

Tull, Herman W. "The Tale of 'The Bride and the Monkey': Female Insatiability, Male Impotence, and Simian Virility in Indian Literature." *Journal of the History of Sexuality* 3.4 (April 1993): 574–89.

Waddell, L. Austine. *The Buddhism of Tibet or Lamaism*. 2d ed. Cambridge: W. Heffer & Sons, Ltd., 1934, 1967.

Warner, Marina. *Alone of All Her Sex*. New York: Alfred A. Knopf, 1976.

———. *Monuments and Maidens: The Allegory of the Female Form*. Berkeley, CA: University of California Press, 1985.

Wayman, Alex, and Hideko. *The Lion's Roar of Queen Śrīmālā*. New York, NY: Columbia University Press, 1974.

Weiss, Mitchell G. "*Caraka Saṃhitā* on the Doctirne of Karma." In *Karma and Rebirth in Classical Indian Traditions*, ed. Wendy Doniger O'Flaherty. Berkeley, CA: University of California Press, 1980.

White, David Gordon. *The Alchemical Body: Siddha Traditions in Medieval India*. Chicago, IL: University of Chicago Press, 1996.

———, ed. *Tantra in Practice*. Princeton, NJ: Princeton University Press, 2000.

Whitford, Margaret, ed. *The Irigaray Reader*. Oxford: Blackwell, 1991.

Williams, Paul. *Mahāyāna Buddhism: The Doctrinal Foundations*. London and New York: Routledge: 1989.

Willis, Janice D., ed. *Feminine Ground: Essays on Women and Tibet*. Ithaca, NY: Snow Lion Publications, 1987, 1989.

———. "Nuns and Benefactresses: The Role of Women in the Development of Buddhism." In *Women, Religion and Social Change*, ed. Yvonne Yazbeck Haddad and Ellison Banks Findly. Albany, NY: State University of New York Press, 1985.

Wilson, Liz. *Charming Cadavers: Horrific Figurations of the Feminine in Indian Buddhist Hagiographic Literature*. Chicago: University of Chicago Press, 1996.

———. "Henpecked Husbands and Renouncers Home on the Range: Celibacy As Social Disengagement in South Asian Buddhism." *Union Seminary Quarterly Review*, 48.3–4 (1994): 7–28.

———. "Lands, Mythic." In *EOW*, vol. I, 569–71.

Winternitz, Maurice. *A History of Indian Literature*. 3 vols. 1927. Delhi: Oriental Books Reprint Corporation, 1977.

Wohl, Victoria. *Intimate Commerce: Exchange, Gender, and Subjectivity in Greek Tragedy*. Austin, TX: University of Texas Press, 1998.

Yalman, Nur. "On the Purity of Women in the Castes of Ceylon and Malabar." *Journal of the Royal Anthropological Institute of Great Britain and Ireland* 93.1 (1963): 25–58.

Yocum, Glenn E. "Comments: The Divine Consort in South India." In *The Divine Consort: Rādhā and the Goddesses of India*, ed. John Stratton Hawley and Donna Marie Wulff. 1982. Boston, MA: Beacon Press, 1986, 278–81.

Young, Serinity. *An Anthology of Sacred Texts by and About Women*. New York: Crossroad, 1993.

———. *Dreaming in the Lotus: Buddhist Dream Narrative, Imagery, and Practice*. Boston, MA: Wisdom Publications, 1999.

———, ed. *The Encyclopedia of Women and World Religion*. New York: Macmillan, 1998.

———. "Gendered Politics in Ancient Indian Asceticism," *Union Seminary Quarterly Review* 48.3–4 (1994): 73–92.

———. "Tantra." In *EOW*, vol. 2, 956–59.

———. "Women Changing Tibet, Activism Changing Women." In *Women's Buddhism, Buddhism's Women: Tradition, Revision, Renewal*, ed. Ellison Banks Findly. Boston, MA: Wisdom Publications, 2000, 229–42.

Yuichi, Kajiyama. "Women in Buddhism." *The Eastern Buddhist* xv.2 (autumn 1982): 53–70.

Zelliot, Eleanor. "Buddhist Women of the Contemporary Maharashtrian Conversion Movement." In Cabezón, *Buddhism, Sexuality, and Gender*, 91–107.

Zürcher, Erik. "Amitābha." In *EOR*, vol. 1.

Zwilling, Leonard, and Michael J. Sweet. " 'Like a City Ablaze': The Third Sex and the Creation of Sexuality in Jain Religious Literature." *Journal of the History of Sexuality* 6.3 (1996): 359–84.

Zysk, Kenneth. *Asceticism and Healing in Ancient India: Medicine in the Buddhist Monastery*. New York: Oxford University Press, 1991.

INDEX

descent, biological, 76
See also patrilineal descent; matrilineal descent
desire, 92, 101, 107, 121, 123, 125, 153, 162, 211
Devadasi Act, 109
devadāsī/s, 107–12, 125, 141, 174, 176
Dhammapada, 42
Dhammapada-Aṭṭhakathā, 42
dharma, 5, 45, 89–90, 106, 200, 203, 219
D'ing-ri, 175
Dipaṃkara, 52, 91–92, 102
disciple/s, 74, 76
Divyāvadāna, 42, 54
Dōgen, 192
dogs, 142
dohada, 27–30
donations, donors, 11, 34, 37–38, 43, 50, 52, 100, 124, 126, 204, 213
Doniger (O'Flaherty), Wendy, 117, 141, 145, 152
Douglas, Mary, 180
drama
Buddhist, 117
Indian, 106–07
Tibetan, 94, 169–70, 206, 213
dreams, 16, 50, 51, 59, 72, 74, 78–79, 88, 92–95, 102, 142, 152, 158–59, 171, 185, 199, 223–25
Queen Māyā's, 3, 27, 67–68,
duality, 136, 165, 168, 232

earth, 12, 97, 107, 180, 211–12, 215, 217, 222, 224–25
earth goddess, 12, 15, 114
Edou, Jérôme, 152, 160, 201
ejaculate, 113, 138–39, 145
embryo, 59–62, 64
embryonic mixture, 59, 92
emptiness, 133, 136, 140, 157–58, 168, 191, 196–97
enlightenment, 9–16, 35, 41, 57, 69–70, 72, 92, 105, 114, 125, 133, 135, 137–38, 142, 144, 152–53, 165, 168, 206, 211, 214, 219, 222–23, 232
and women, 5–6, 11–16, 61, 83, 90–91, 95, 123, 126, 129, 157–58, 162, 166, 192–201, 203, 224
See also bodhicitta
eunuch, 205
exchange, 5, 122
See also commodity-exchange; gift-exchange; traffic in women

Fahien, 55, 192–94
Fa Hsien, 42
family, 70, 74–75, 83, 85–86, 90, 97, 100, 112, 125, 166–68, 171–72, 175, 231
fantasy/ies, 191, 214, 218
fathers, 3, 13, 42–44, 47, 49, 59, 61, 63, 67–75, 77, 86, 90, 98, 122, 125, 137, 166–67, 171, 173–74, 176, 185, 217, 231
Faure, Bernard, 183
fecundity, 8, 9, 23, 34, 41, 72, 100, 105, 110, 114, 121, 181
fellatio, 84
female and male
as binary opposites, xxv, 62, 136
forms, 9, 30–31
as a human continuum, xxv, 61–62
feminine, the, 12–14
feminine characteristics, 77
feminism, 5
feminization, 31, 77
fertile, fertility, 15, 23, 30–31, 34, 38–39, 41, 47–48, 54, 70–71, 78, 91–92, 99, 105, 107, 111–14, 123–25, 128, 135–36, 167, 173, 175
fetus, 58, 63, 75
See also embryo
fidelity, 85
filial piety, 43–47, 55, 69, 215
five m's, 135, 141, 144
folk beliefs, 30, 183, 185
folk tales, xxv, 23, 182, 198
food, 9–11, 39, 44, 54, 83, 86, 99, 100, 123–26, 180, 194, 216
Foucher, A., 50
four, 4, 7
visions of Buddha, 3–5, 7
Four Tantras (rGyud bZhi), 57–58
Frauwallner, E., 71
Freed, Stanley, 56
funeral rites, 46–47, 206–07, 216–18
Furth, Charlotte, 63

Gampopa, 48, 62, 163
gender, 57–59, 77, 126, 136, 140, 167–68, 170, 176, 183, 191–92, 195–96, 200, 202–03, 208, 214, 216, 225, 231, 232
genitals, xxv, 112, 185
Gesar, 72–73, 79, 182
gestation, 59, 62
gift-exchange, 12, 89, 108–09, 112, 122, 156, 166–67, 176
goddess/es, 195–97, 200, 202, 224, 231